FIGURES OF TRANSITION

THE MACMILLAN COMPANY
NEW YORK · BOSTON · CHICAGO · DALLAS
ATLANTA · SAN FRANCISCO

MACMILLAN & CO., LIMITED
LONDON · BOMBAY · CALCUTTA
MELBOURNE

THE MACMILLAN CO. OF CANADA, LTD.
TORONTO

FIGURES OF
TRANSITION

A Study of
BRITISH
LITERATURE
at the End of the
NINETEENTH CENTURY

BY

GRANVILLE HICKS

NEW YORK
THE MACMILLAN COMPANY
1939

PRINTED IN THE UNITED STATES OF AMERICA
BY THE VAIL-BALLOU PRESS, INC., BINGHAMTON, N. Y.

For

Dorothy

ACKNOWLEDGMENTS

THE author wishes to record his gratitude to the authors and publishers of all works quoted in this book. In particular he thanks the following:

THE BOBBS-MERRILL COMPANY
  for permission to quote from
    Dramatis Personae, by Arthur Symons.
DODD, MEAD AND COMPANY
  for permission to quote from
    Charles Dickens, by George Gissing.
DOUBLEDAY, DORAN AND COMPANY
  for permission to quote from
    Rudyard Kipling's Verse, by Rudyard Kipling. Inclusive Edition, 1885–1932. Copyright, 1891–1932.
    Plain Tales from the Hills, by Rudyard Kipling. Copyright, 1899, 1927.
    Poems 1886–1929, by Rudyard Kipling.
    Something of Myself, by Rudyard Kipling. Copyright, 1937.
    Life's Handicap, by Rudyard Kipling. Copyright, 1899, 1927.
    Sea to Sea, by Rudyard Kipling. Copyright, 1899, 1907.
    Many Inventions, by Rudyard Kipling. Copyright, 1893, 1921.
    Workers in the Dawn, by George Gissing.
    George Gissing, by Frank Swinnerton.
    The Exquisite Tragedy, by Amabel Williams-Ellis.
E. P. DUTTON AND COMPANY
  for permission to quote from
    The Shrewsbury Edition of the works of Samuel Butler.
    Samuel Butler and His Family Relations, by Mrs. R. S. Garnett.
    Demos, The Nether World, The New Grub Street, The Private Papers of Henry Ryecroft, and *Thyrza,* by George Gissing.

HARCOURT, BRACE AND COMPANY
  for permission to quote from
    A History of the English People, 1830–1841, by Élie Halévy.
    The Rise of Modern Industry, by J. L. and Barbara Hammond.
HARPER AND BROTHERS
  for permission to quote from
    *Desperate Remedies, Far from the Madding Crowd, The Hand
    of Ethelberta, Jude the Obscure, A Pair of Blue Eyes, The
    Return of the Native, Tess of the D'Urbervilles,* and *The
    Woodlanders,* by Thomas Hardy.
    The Rise of Liberalism, by Harold Laski.
INTERNATIONAL PUBLISHERS
  for permission to quote from
    The Selected Correspondence of Marx and Engels.
    This Final Crisis, by Allen Hutt.
LITTLE, BROWN AND COMPANY
  for permission to quote from
    Robert Louis Stevenson, by John A. Steuart.
LONGMANS, GREEN AND COMPANY
  for permission to quote from
    The Life of William Morris, by J. W. Mackail.
THE MACMILLAN COMPANY
  for permission to quote from
    The Cambridge History of English Literature.
    Collected Poems and *The Dynasts,* by Thomas Hardy.
    The Early Life of Thomas Hardy and *The Later Years of
    Thomas Hardy,* by Florence Emily Hardy.
    Carlyle, by Louis Cazamian.
    The Life of George Moore, by Joseph Hone.
    Experiment in Autobiography, by H. G. Wells.
    Autobiography, by William Butler Yeats.
    The Life of Algernon Charles Swinburne, by Edmund Gosse.
    Recollections, by John Morley.
    Ruskin, by Frederic Harrison.
    Thackeray, by Anthony Trollope.
    The Eighteen-Seventies, edited by H. Granville-Barker.
G. P. PUTNAM'S SONS
  for permission to quote from
    Shelburne Essays, Volume V, by Paul Elmer More.
    De Profundis, by Oscar Wilde.

CHARLES SCRIBNER'S SONS
  for permission to quote from
    The Letters of George Meredith, edited by his son.
    The Letters of Henry James, edited by Percy Lubbock.
    Notes on Novelists, by Henry James.
    The Letters of Robert Louis Stevenson, edited by Sidney Colvin.
    The works of Robert Louis Stevenson.

INTRODUCTION

This book grew out of a plan for a study of modern British literature, which, as I originally conceived it, would have surveyed the past forty years. Since, however, the literary movements in which I was interested all had their roots in the closing decades of the nineteenth century, I found myself paying more and more attention to an earlier generation of writers. These writers, who link Victorian and modern literature, proved interesting enough, and seemed important enough, to deserve a volume of their own. The book about the literature of the past forty years, if it is written, will rest upon this preliminary study.

My "figures of transition"—the phrase is William Butler Yeats's—are William Morris, Thomas Hardy, Samuel Butler, George Gissing, Oscar Wilde, and Rudyard Kipling. Concentration on six men permits detailed treatment of each, and at the same time it is possible, in writing about the six, to say most of the things that ought to be said about the literature of the period.

I have not, however, wanted to isolate these men from their contemporaries. Thus, in writing about Morris as a Socialist, I discuss briefly other Socialist men of letters, and, in talking about Gissing, I refer to the growth of naturalism and particularly to the early work of George Moore. Wilde cannot be separated from the writers for the *Yellow Book* and *Savoy,* and I have given almost as much space to them as to him. Stevenson was too influential in his own day to be ignored, and, moreover, his code of morals, his theory of romance, and his success, all help us to understand Kipling.

The book does not try to discuss every writer of the eighties and nineties. Some I omit because I have nothing to say about them. Others are excluded by the narrow time limits of the book: I do not discuss authors who did the major part of their work after 1900, even though they began their writing in the preceding decade.

Since I am concerned with a process of transition, it is necessary for me to say something about Victorian literature and life as the point of departure. Because the survey is necessarily brief, the method of the first chapter differs from that of the other six. After describing the broad economic movements of the nineteenth century and the philosophical systems, religious beliefs, and popular dogmas of the first part of Victoria's reign, I try to define the relationship of literature to the prevailing attitudes. Since criticism of Victorianism was the theme of the eighties and nineties, I am interested in earlier criticisms. In the first twenty or twenty-five years after Victoria came to the throne, criticism was often directed against economic theories and industrial practices. After 1850, on the other hand, for reasons that are discussed, it was more frequently concerned with questions of taste and conduct. Changes in the economic structure, coupled with the growth of dissatisfaction, at last led to the breakdown of Victorianism.

In so brief a survey rigorous selection has been inevitable. No Victorian author is treated adequately, and some—the Brontës and the Brownings, for example—are not treated at all. This would be inexcusable were it not that I am concerned with the traditions that must be understood if one is to understand the changes that took place at the end of the century. Other traditions, equally important perhaps from other points of view, are therefore disregarded.

In writing about the eighties and nineties I try to use history as an aid to the understanding of literature and literature as an aid to the understanding of history, and I am interested in both parts of the process. It would not occur to me to deny that there are many valid ways of writing about literature. I only maintain that this is one of them.

Discussing an author from this point of view, I naturally want to know what he thought and felt about his own times, and so, I think, do most readers. The contemporary sense of crisis may have made us unduly attentive to the more obvious manifestations of political sympathies, but at least we have learned that no author can be wholly untouched, even if he thinks he can, by the problems with which his contemporaries are concerned. It is, to be sure, by going beyond superficial responses, and examining complex, subtle, and often unconscious reactions, that we learn most about literary processes—and perhaps about historical processes as well. In other words, we must reject any identification of literary and political values, but doing so only makes clearer the real relationship between literature and the changing organization of society.

So far as possible I have let authors speak for themselves, and there are many quotations and paraphrases. To have given a reference for each of these would have meant cluttering the pages with footnotes. The general source of quotations is usually indicated in the text, and the bibliography lists the various books about the period and about individual authors that I have used. If anyone needs exact references, I shall be glad to supply them.

On the other hand, I have used footnotes, especially in the first chapter, for the purpose of furnishing additional information. In general these notes consist of quotations that amplify or confirm statements made in the text.

I am grateful to the John Simon Guggenheim Memorial Foundation for making possible a year of uninterrupted research. I also wish to thank Robert G. Davis, Daniel J. Boorstin, Richard M. Bennett, Zoe Christman, Lee Levenson, and my wife.

G. H.

Grafton, New York
August 1, 1939

CONTENTS

FIGURES OF TRANSITION

Chapter I

VICTORIAN FLOOD AND EBB

Now, nearly forty years after the death of Victoria, "Victorian" has ceased to be a term of abuse. No longer occupied with urgent resistance to outworn moral and literary standards, we can look calmly enough upon their merits and weaknesses and examine their origins and decay. Knowing that it is impossible to return to Victorianism, and with no desire to do so, we can do the Victorians justice. We can even recognize that, if much was gained by the destruction of the Victorian way of life, something was lost.

No literary period has definite dates, and neither the life nor the literature of any period is all of one piece. The Victorian era is more easily defined and more homogeneous than most. Victorianism can be found before 1832. (The first reform bill rather than Victoria's accession provides the usual and more nearly accurate date for the beginning of the period.) It can also be found after 1901. But Victorianism was certainly not triumphant during most of the Regency or under Edward VII. Victorian morals, Victorian piety, Victorian taste, Victorian economics, and Victorian politics made a speedy conquest after 1832. They were in full sway by 1848, and for thirty years thereafter, though not unchallenged, were not seriously threatened. The opposition steadily gained force in the late seventies and eighties, and Victoria survived her era.

Victorianism, we now realize, was not an aberration of the nineteenth century mind. It can be interpreted in terms of the rise of the middle class, which in turn is explained by the progress of industrial capitalism. The examination of that process helps us to understand what Victorianism was, and it enables us to see why the great Victorians stood in a curiously complicated relationship to the dominant ideas and attitudes of their period.

1. The Middle Class in Power.

The flying shuttle, the spinning jenny, the spinning frame, the mule jenny, Cartwright's power loom, the steam engine, improvements in iron smelting, changes in the manufacture of pottery—they came one after the other from 1733 on. The inventions brought about the industrial revolution, but the inventions were used—and more frequently than not were made—because capitalism was ready for them. Great fortunes —solid blocks of capital waiting for investment—had been accumulated during two centuries. The manufacturing that went on in homes was more and more under the control of large capitalists. Even agriculture was adopting capitalist methods,[1] and as a result the landowners, many of whom already had close ties with commerce, became capitalistic in spirit. More important, a mass of "free" laborers was created: the small farmers, driven from their land by a legal system completely controlled by the large landowners, had to sell themselves in the agricultural or industrial labor market. Capitalism had created internal security, a system of transpor-

[1] "What accounts for the change in rural conditions, for the enclosures, the division of the common lands and the engrossing of farms, is the introduction of a business spirit into the management of agriculture, landowners thereafter considering their land as capital, from which a better income could be drawn by improved methods of exploitation." Mantoux, *The Industrial Revolution in the Eighteenth Century,* 190. See Hammond, *The Village Laborer,* chs. 3 and 4, for an account of the enclosures.

tation, and a prosperous foreign trade; it had financial reserves, raw materials, markets, and a proletariat. It was ready for the machines and they came.

For many years it had been possible, under favorable circumstances, for the rare individual to become rich as a merchant or, in the textile industry, as a merchant-manufacturer. If the lucky man became very rich, he usually bought an estate, and in due season he might be given a title and his family reckoned among the aristocracy. That was, in fact, the way the British aristocracy had come into existence. When the Wars of the Roses bankrupted the Norman feudal lords, the men of the middle class bought their estates. When Henry VIII dissolved the monasteries, he bestowed much land on business men who could supply him with funds. More and more land fell into the hands of traders during the sixteenth and seventeenth centuries. The aristocracy of the eighteenth century had its roots in trade.[1]

It insisted, nevertheless, on making the ownership of land the mark of social distinction, and it was determined to preserve its traditions and its privileges. It controlled both houses of Parliament and the major offices of government, church, and military services, and though it was quite willing to act in the interests of commerce and industry when its own interests could thus be served, it held on to its power. It was prepared to adopt as its own particular men of business, but only on condition that they accepted its standards and manner

---

[1] "The upper class had become predominantly Middle Class in substance; and its surrender to the increasing scale of expenditure made it in effect dependent upon trade and speculation." Gretton, *The English Middle Class,* 158. "Several authorities have proved that we have practically no titles older than the early Tudor period. In other words, the highest class of the eighteenth century was made up principally of the families which had risen in the first land speculation of the Middle Class." *Ibid.,* 171. "The real old families of this country are to be found among the peasantry; the gentry, too, may lay some claim to old blood. . . . But a peer with an ancient lineage is to me quite a novelty. . . . I take it after the Battle of Tewkesbury, a Norman baron was almost as rare a being in England as a wolf is now." Disraeli, *Coningsby,* 141.

of living—as they were usually glad to do. Robert Peel's grandfather combined farming and domestic manufacturing in the old-fashioned way; the next generation acquired wealth and a title; the third produced a Tory spokesman and prime minister.

By Sir Robert Peel's time, however, as a result of the industrial revolution, rich men were emerging too rapidly to be assimilated. The aristocracy had lost none of its glamor for men of the middle class, but they saw that they had to act as a class, and demand for themselves some of the social and political rights that had been reserved for the landowners. The Whig aristocrats—a relatively small group of landed proprietors with important commercial connections—had strengthened their power throughout the eighteenth century, and authority was more concentrated in 1789 than it had been in 1698. One hundred and fifty-four individuals controlled three hundred and seven seats in the House of Commons, choosing whomever they pleased to fill them. The attack on this domination began boldly at the end of the century, but was quickly checked by the fears that the French Revolution roused in British men of substance. For a time in the early nineteenth century the landowning families seemed stronger than ever. With the post-Waterloo depression, however, the demand for reform was again made. The business men, their pride injured and their pocketbooks hurt by antiquated laws, led a campaign in which great masses of Englishmen participated. The Whig aristocrats thereupon adopted the cause as their own, some of them because they saw an opportunity of maintaining the power of their party through the support of new elements, others—with greater foresight —because they saw that the ruling class needed the strength of the men of affairs in order to resist the demands of the populace.

The reform bill was the official recognition of a change of

vast dimensions and incalculable consequences,[1] but it did not involve a fundamental transfer of power. The struggle was not between capitalism and feudalism; it was between the newer capitalism and the older, between talent and privilege, between the recognition of changed conditions and the refusal to recognize them. The landowners, having destroyed whatever remained of feudalism and the old independent peasant economy, offered no real alternative to capitalism. The Whigs might be slow in accepting change and the Tories remain irreconcilable; both might be sincere in their contempt for business; but Tories and Whigs alike had too many ties with business enterprise to want to see it destroyed.[2]

What 1832 brought was a working compromise, and both sides were content to let it work. The bondholders, manufacturers, and shopkeepers had won a great victory, but they did not, as one would expect, use the franchise they had so arduously secured to send themselves and their like to the House of Commons. There were no more business men in Parliament in 1833 than there were in 1831, and in every cabinet from 1833 to 1884 the aristocrats were in the majority. Hav-

---

[1] Engels wrote in the forties: "Sixty, eighty years ago, England was a country like every other, with small towns, few and simple industries, and a thin but proportionally large agricultural population. Today it is a country like no other, with a capital of two and a half million inhabitants; with vast manufacturing cities; with an industry that supplies the world, and produces almost everything by means of the most complex machinery; with an industrious, intelligent, dense population, of which two-thirds are employed in trade and commerce, and composed of classes wholly different; forming, in fact, with other customs and other needs, a different nation from the England of those days." *Condition of the Working Class,* 15.

[2] "Neither Conservative nor Radical offered any distracting or competing motive, for while they disagreed about political and administrative reform, they did not disagree about the advantages of a system under which acquisition and profit-making were unimpeded. If it was the manufacturers who promoted the new system in industry, the landowners were equally active in promoting it on their estates. The most important force in making the English an industrial people was the destruction of the village . . . and it was the landowner, often of course the new landowner, who had come from the world of finance and industry, who pushed the English peasant out." Hammond, *The Rise of Modern Industry,* 213.

ing indicated in what direction it wanted the government to move, the middle class was apparently content to leave administration in the hands of those who were accustomed to it.

Although the differences between the landowners and the business men were not fundamental, or else they would not have been so readily compromised, the struggle would surely have been more bitter if both groups had not been made conscious of their common interests by the existence of a common enemy. The industrial revolution, together with the enclosures, had created a proletariat with a grievance. Austere as the life of the small farmer, the cottager, the rural laborer, or the domestic textile worker of the early eighteenth century may have been, it at least had elements of both security and independence. The factory worker of the thirties, on the other hand, was exploited with a ruthlessness that perhaps has never been paralleled. The gruesome story, no matter how many times re-told, never loses its horror. Official reports describe children of from six to eight working ten or twelve hours a day as stocking weavers, often fainting at their work, and slowly losing their eyesight. They describe needle-women who received 1½ pence for a shirt, and others who were paid 4½ pence a week for working sixteen hours a day on neckties. They speak of child labor in the mines, arsenic poisoning in the potteries, men fined for talking at their work, women in the last stages of pregnancy fined for sitting down. They record that one-fifth of the population of Liverpool lived in cellars, that 12,000 persons lived in 1400 houses in a London block four hundred yards square, that twenty persons could be found lying huddled on the floor of a single Glasgow room. This was the fruit of the industrial revolution.[1]

[1] Friedrich Engels summarizes many of these reports in his *Condition of the Working Class in England in 1844*. On one of them he comments: "When one

Of course the workers were not quietly suffering this ruthlessness. There were trade unions early in the eighteenth century, as soon as workers no longer owned their means of production. Tailors, textile workers, miners organized. The pitmen of Northumberland and Durham won a strike in 1765. The famous Spitalfields silkweavers secured by their belligerence the act of 1773 that protected their rights for the next fifty years. Cotton spinners struck in 1818, 1829, 1830. In Nottingham, where the Luddite movement began in 1811, the smashing of machinery was a direct attack on employers that carried on an ancient tradition and had a shadow of legal sanction in old regulations of apprenticeship. In Lancashire and Yorkshire, it was simply a demonstration against what was to be known as technological unemployment.

Rebellious workers had no easy time of it. Despite what later sentimentalists might say, the landowners showed themselves no more merciful than the business men. It was a gentlemen's government that in 1799 passed the Combination Acts, which for twenty-five years made the formation of a union illegal. The laws were enforced by magistrates who were often industrialists and always men of property, and they fought the workers with spies, troops, and barbaric sentences. Lancashire magistrates, after the suppression of the Luddites, hanged eight men and transported seventeen. In Yorkshire fourteen were hanged for breaking frames and three for the murder of William Horsfall, a manufacturer. When a Luddite attack on William Cartwright's mills was re-

reads all this and a hundred other villainies and infamies in this one report, all testified to on oath, confirmed by several witnesses, deposed by men whom the commissioners themselves declare trustworthy; when one reflects that this is a Liberal report, a bourgeois report, made for the purpose of reversing the previous Tory report, and rehabilitating the pureness of heart of the manufacturers, that the commissioners themselves are on the side of the bourgeoisie, and report all these things against their own will, how can one be otherwise than filled with wrath and resentment against a class which boasts of philanthropy and self-sacrifice, while its one object is to fill its purse *à tout prix?"* P. 167.

pulsed, two wounded workers were left untended all night because they would not give the names of their associates, and a soldier who had refused to fire on the workers was sentenced to receive three hundred lashes.

The "Six Acts" came in 1819, suppressing almost all public meetings, enabling the magistrates to search for arms, subjecting working-class papers to the stamp duty, and strengthening the law on seditious libels. In spite of these measures protest continued, and in 1824 the Combination Laws were repealed.[1] The rapid growth of labor organizations followed, culminating in 1834 with the formation of the Grand National Consolidated Trade Unions, soon numbering half a million members. That year, when the Tory Lord Robert Peel surrendered the government to the Whig Lord Melbourne, he warned him that the unions were "the most formidable difficulty and danger with which we had to contend." The Whigs desired more stringent measures,[2] but dared not adopt them, and Melbourne, forced to rely on existing laws, urged

[1] In the struggle for repeal, the workers' demands were given effective parliamentary expression by Francis Place, who conducted the campaign with great skill. Place was a sincere Radical, who believed that the doctrine of laissez-faire ought to be consistently applied. "Combinations," he wrote to Sir Francis Burdett in 1825, "will soon cease to exist. Men have been kept together for long periods only by the oppressions of the laws; these being repealed, combinations will lose the matter which cements them into masses, and they will fall to pieces." Webb, *History of Trade Unionism,* 97.

[2] Nassau Senior, requested by Melbourne to make a report on the situation, convinced him that "if the innocent and laborious workman and his family are to be left without protection against the cowardly ferocity by which he is now assailed; if the manufacturer is to employ his capital and the mechanist or chemist his ingenuity, only under the dictation of his short-sighted and rapacious workmen, or his equally ignorant and avaricious rivals; if a few agitators are to be allowed to command a strike which first paralyzes the industry of the peculiar class of workmen over whom they tyrannize, and then extends itself in an increasing circle over the many thousands and tens of thousands to whose labor the assistance of that peculiar class of workpeople is essential;—that if all this is to be unpunished, and to be almost sanctioned by the repeal of the laws by which it was formerly punishable;—it is in vain to hope that we shall long retain the industry, the skill, or the capital on which our manufacturing superiority, and with that superiority our power and almost our existence as a nation depends." Webb, *History of Trade Unionism,* 124.

magistrates to act "with the promptitude, decision, and firmness which are so imperatively required." The Tolpuddle martyrs, transported for having taken an oath of membership in a friendly society of agricultural laborers, were victims of the Melbourne hysteria.

The workers were rapidly learning to stand together as a class. The Factory Law of 1833 had remedied the conditions of but a small minority, whereas the New Poor Law of 1834, the first fruits of middle-class victory, had subjected the unemployed to outrageous indignities and given the factory owners yet another advantage. Robert Owen was teaching the workers that they alone were the creators of wealth, and their organizational experiments, though individually failures, had hinted at their strength. They felt, moreover, that they had been in large measure responsible for the victory of 1832, and yet had not shared in its benefits.[1] Those who, under the leadership of such reformers as Cobbett, Bright, and Place, had formed the National Union of the Working Classes, and aided the middle class to win the reform bill, were forced to see that they must act with and for their own class.

Chartism rose in three waves—1839, 1842, 1848—each following a severe crisis. The Charter was written by William Lovett, a follower of Owen and a believer in peaceful methods, who formed the London Working Men's Association in 1836. His associates, Feargus O'Connor, the movement's most powerful orator, and James Bronterre O'Brien, its theoretician,

---

[1] Macaulay said that the reform act was intended to enfranchise "the middle class of England, with the flower of the aristocracy at its head, and the flower of the working class bringing up the rear." He went on: "If I would refuse to the working people that larger share of power which some of them have demanded, I would refuse it because I am convinced that, by giving it, I should only increase their distress. I admit that the end of government is their happiness. But that they may be governed for their happiness, they must not be governed according to the doctrines they have learned from their illiterate, incapable, low-minded flatterers." "Speech on Reform," Dec. 16, 1832; quoted in Blease, *A Short History of English Liberalism*, 168–9.

favored violence as a last resort. To the left of them were George Julian Harney and Ernest Jones, who advocated immediate insurrection. After Parliament had rejected the Charter in 1839, the militants gained influence. In Wales John Frost, a draper and former mayor of Newport, led a march to release an imprisoned Chartist. Ten men were killed, fifty wounded, and hundreds arrested.

There were three years of divided leadership and dissipated energy, but, amid the widespread distress of 1842, the Charter was again circulated, and this time was presented to Parliament with more than three million signatures. It was rejected, but in 1845 the Corn Laws were repealed, a concession on the part of Tory landowning politicians to business men and workers. Three years later the Chartists, stimulated by the revolutions in Europe, made their last attempt. The response was poor, and the government, quickly realizing the weakness of the movement, used a show of force to prevent a procession from taking the petition to Parliament. O'Connor and other leaders, who had made extravagant threats and claims, were discredited.

Though Chartism's six points called merely for parliamentary reform, it was the social rebellion of a class.[1] "Political power our means, social happiness our end," was the Chartist slogan. J. R. Stephens told a Manchester demonstration: "Chartism, my friends, is no political movement where the main point is your getting the ballot. Chartism is a knife and fork question: the Charter means a good home, good food and drink, prosperity, and short working hours." As early as 1833 the *Poor Man's Guardian* declared: "An entire change in society—a change amounting to a complete subversion of the existing 'order of the world'—is contemplated by the work-

---

[1] "The Chartists, although their programme was strictly political, counted on universal suffrage to ensure the advent of a social republic and to suppress the privileges enjoyed by the capitalists." Halévy, *The Growth of Philosophic Radicalism*, 513.

ing classes. They aspire to be at the top instead of at the bottom of society—or rather that there should be no bottom or top at all."

Not every Chartist held such revolutionary aims, but they were common enough. Where the sharpest disagreement came was in the discussion of means. Some Chartists, like O'Connor, called for a return to the land, the creation of a peasant Paradise. Others, under the influence of Owen, argued that the establishment of co-operatives, without benefit of parliamentary reform, would end exploitation. Still others put their hope in religion or education or the temperance movement. With such confusion it was natural for the average worker to feel, after the fiasco of 1848, that the years of struggle had been wasted and that he had better do as well for himself as he could.

The conditions of the workers were improving. Acts had been passed regulating hours for women and children and remedying some other of the grosser evils. Employers had learned that they could afford to make such concessions, for, after the repeal of the Corn Laws in 1845, their great age of prosperity had begun. Exports and imports nearly doubled between 1840 and 1850, and expansion continued without serious check for twenty-five years. With England the highly profitable workshop of the world, it was only good business to raise wages a little and shorten hours slightly, rather than risk the interruption of production, to say nothing of social upheaval.

To be sure, no millennium dawned for the working class. The Parliamentary commissions of the sixties could still find women and children in brass foundries, salt mines, and tile fields, working long hours at heavy labor. Girls sorting rags caught and carried deadly diseases. The number of consumptive lace-makers increased from one in forty-five in 1852 to one in eight in 1861. Children of five worked twelve hours a day in domestic industries. Housing, as the cities filled up, grew steadily worse. In Bradford eighteen persons lived in a single room; sixteen in another and thirteen in another. A Bradford doctor found in one district 223 houses having 1450 inhabitants, 435 beds, and 36 privies.

All that had happened was that the better organized sections of the working class had been given just enough to dull their militancy. Unions in the skilled trades began to limit their numbers, organize elaborate schemes of sick and death benefits, rely more and more on negotiation and less and less on strikes. The Amalgamated Society of Engineers was the "new model" for an aristocracy of labor. It was true that most of the workers were very badly off indeed, and that even skilled workers suffered in times of depression. It was true that the ruling class, through judicial decisions, tried to rob the unions of their legal status, and that the workers had to fight stubbornly for the right of collective bargaining. But, just as, by and large, England prospered from the end of the forties to the end of the seventies, so, by and large, labor was given enough to keep it quiet.

After 1848 the working class did not try to exercise independently its political power. Usually it supported the Liberals, and the Tories, seeing this, made a bid for its support with the reform bill of 1867. A few reactionaries continued, on general principles, to lament the acceptance of democratic formulas, but the vote, like the industrial concessions, was little enough to pay for peace in such a time for harvesting profits.

The workers of the North, whom three years before the London bourgeoisie had been preparing to meet with guns, streamed into the city in 1851 for the Prince Consort's Great Exhibition. The era of good will, the mid-Victorian period, had begun, and would last almost to the Golden Jubilee of 1887. The bitterness of the thirties and forties had vanished. Labor was happy, or at least docile. The landowners were for the most part on pleasant terms with the business men. England was a unified nation, unified, that is, for all practical purposes, which meant the purposes of business enterprise.

2. *The Mind of the Middle Class.*

So far as the middle class had a mind, it seems to have been both shaped and expressed by utilitarianism and evangelicalism, two sets of ideas and attitudes that make up a good deal of what we know as Victorianism. It was Jeremy Bentham, of course, who gave utilitarianism its most logical statement. He did not invent individualism; there he was quite in the tradition of Locke. Beccaria, Helvétius, Hutcheson, and Priestley were all talking about "the greatest good of the greatest number," and the test of utility had been applied by Samuel Johnson in morals, Paley in religion, and Burke in government. In economics he was indebted to Adam Smith and in psychology to Hartley. He was not, in short, an original thinker.[1] But if he borrowed widely, he organized his borrowings into what his disciples regarded as a water-tight system. Legislation, he taught, was a science. It was possible to devise measures that would secure the greatest possible amount of happiness. And the measures he recommended included that elimination of governmental interference that business men desired above all else.[2]

---

[1] Marx called Bentham "the insipid, pedantic, leather-tongued oracle of the commonplace bourgeois intelligence." "Bentham," he continued, "is among philosophers what Martin Tupper is among poets. Neither of them could have been made anywhere else than in England." Not satisfied, he added in a footnote, "I declare that at no time and in no country has the most trivial commonplace ever before strutted with such appalling self-satisfaction. The principle of utility was not discovered by Bentham. He merely reproduced in a dull and spiritless fashion what Helvétius and other French writers of the eighteenth century had said before him so brilliantly." *Capital,* 671.

[2] "He wished to sweep away precisely those things that stood in the way of the English industrialist—feudal law, primogeniture, the tariff, apprenticeship, the old poor law, sinecures and extravagant government generally, nepotism in Church and State, the lack of enterprise characteristic of a landed aristocracy. . . . Above

Utilitarianism in the broad sense cannot be reduced to the teachings of Jeremy Bentham. It was greatly strengthened by Robert Malthus' *Essay on the Principle of Population,* which was written as a reply to William Godwin's *Social Justice* and as a criticism of the Speenhamland system of poor relief. Godwin's theory of human perfectibility had seemed utter nonsense to the average man of the middle class, and the French Revolution had promptly proved that it was nonsense of the dangerous kind. Malthus gave an apparently scientific basis for this opposition to Godwinian ideas, and his book was welcomed by the Whig *Edinburgh Review* and similar journals. If one applied utilitarian principles to Malthus' conclusions about the dangers of pampering the poor, it became quite clear that ruthlessness was compatible with the kindliest intentions and a clear conscience.

The economists were seldom professed Benthamites, but they too argued from utilitarian assumptions. If the economic laws they set forth were valid, then utilitarianism sanctioned the course of action they recommended to the manufacturers. It was the economists, as a matter of fact, who most widely disseminated the popular version of utilitarianism, and it was they who most clearly betrayed the influence of practical middle-class interests. Smith and Ricardo may have tried to be logical, but they were followed by flagrant apologists for capitalism. McCulloch, for example, swept aside the doubts Malthus and Ricardo had raised, promising the people of England an earthly paradise if they would adopt the principle of laissez-faire. Ure, in his *Philosophy of Manufacturers,* wrote of a spinning mill: "In these spacious halls the benignant power of steam summons around him his myriads of willing menials." Of child laborers he wrote, "The work of

all, by his insistence that the new order was in accordance with so English a thing as usefulness rather than with foreign and dangerous notions of right, he converted many a man frightened by the excesses of the French revolution." Brinton, *English Political Thought in the Nineteenth Century,* 26.

these lively elves seemed to resemble a sport, in which habit gave them a pleasing dexterity." He attributed illness among certain mill operatives to "their high wages which enabled them . . . to pamper themselves into nervous ailments, by a diet too rich and exciting for their indoor employments." And, unfair as it is to judge classical economics by the writing of such men, we must remember that it was their version that gained popularity and influence.

In politics as in economics Bentham was seldom acknowledged, but his principles were nonetheless followed. Lord Brougham, for example, criticized Bentham in the *Edinburgh Review,* but in his writings, his speeches, and the work of his Society for the Diffusion of Useful Knowledge, he was as good a utilitarian as Bentham could ask for. Brougham did not hesitate to flatter the middle class that he sought to serve. "I speak now," he said on one occasion, "of the middle classes—of those hundreds of thousands of respectable persons —the most numerous, and by far the most wealthy order in the community. . . . They are solid, right-judging men, and, above all, not given to change. If they have a fault, it is that error on the right side, a suspicion of state quacks—a dogged love of existing institutions—a perfect contempt of all political nostrums." He moved slowly on the question of reform, seldom, as John Stuart Mill pointed out, much in advance of the average member of the middle class. He took an orthodox stand on the question of poor relief, was an ardent follower of Malthus, believed implicitly in laissez-faire. Yet his sternness could be tempered by mercy: he wanted the lot of the workingman improved, and devoted himself to education as the means to this end. "When there is too much labor in the market and wages are too low, do not combine to raise the wages," he advised; "do not combine with the vain hope of compelling the employer to pay more for labor than there are funds for the maintenance of labor; but go out of the market. Leave the relations between wages and labor to equalize themselves."

Brougham exemplifies what Dicey calls "the Benthamism of common sense." He appears in a poor enough light, but it would be a mistake to think there is a vast difference between him and the more orthodox followers of Jeremy Bentham. Since he held that the individual was the best judge of his own good, Bentham's theories seemed to point to the most complete democracy, and some of his followers accepted this conclusion. Others, however, remembered his contention that the interests of a broad and varied class might correspond with the interests of the people as a whole. Confident that the middle class satisfied this condition, they could see no reason for going beyond 1832. Thus it happened that such rigid Benthamites as John Austin and Robert Lowe were among the die-hards of 1867.

Utilitarianism in the stricter sense was a theory of morals and of government, in the broader sense an attitude towards life and a practical encouragement to the man of enterprise. The business man seized upon the idea that the greatest good of the greatest number would be served if he was let alone, and that was what utilitarianism meant to him. The little group of philosophical radicals, the more speculative Benthamites, might look beyond the immediate needs of the middle class, but their speculations were laughed at by the men of affairs.

In its broader sense utilitarianism, in fact if not in name, was accepted by the largest and most important sections of the middle class. So was evangelicalism. From the early seventeenth century class lines had been drawn in religion: the strength of the Church of England was in the nobility and landed gentry; the strength of the Dissenters in the middle class. Especially after the rise of Methodism in the eight-

eenth century, the traders, shopkeepers, artisans, and manufacturers were likely to be outside the established church.
Almost immediately a movement developed within the
church that resembled Methodism at many points. Evangelicalism grew steadily in the late seventeen-hundreds, and
by 1832 it was at its height.[1] Two or three thousand clergymen
had given their adherence to evangelical doctrines, and their
influence permeated the church.

Anyone can understand why evangelicalism would please
the middle class. Its cardinal doctrine was personal piety, the
individual relationship between the soul and God, and thus
it both appealed to and strengthened the individualism that
the middle class practiced in its economic and political affairs. Its moral standards were adapted to the needs of frugal,
hard-working, single-minded business men, as those of the
Church of England had been to the habits of the gentry. It
permitted, if it did not actually preach, the assumption that
worldly success is the evidence of God's favor and hence of
personal righteousness. Finally, it was a religion that the
middle class could not object to having disseminated among
the working class. When we remember Hannah More distrib-

---

[1] Evangelicalism, like utilitarianism, was ubiquitous and indefinable: "Starting
early in the eighteenth century as far back as William Law, author of the *Serious
Call*, coming down through the Wesleys and Whitefield, Johnson and Cowper,
Clarkson and Wilberforce and the Clapham 'Sect,' great schoolmasters like Thomas
Arnold and Charles Wordsworth, great nobles like the Greys on the Whig side
and the philanthropic Lord Shaftesbury on the Tory, not to mention many
nineteenth-century preachers and divines, it became after Queen Victoria's marriage practically the religion of the court, and gripped all ranks and conditions of
society. After Melbourne's departure, it inspired nearly every front-rank public
man, save Palmerston, for four decades. That does not mean that they were all
evangelicals in the sense of being bigots for the low church, as Shaftesbury and
Cairns were—Bright was a quaker; Gladstone and Selborne and Salisbury were
pronounced high churchmen; Livingstone, like many another, was reared in
Scottish presbyterianism. But nothing is more remarkable than the way in which
evangelicalism in the broader sense overleaped sectarian barriers and pervaded men
of all creeds." Ensor, *England, 1870–1914*, 137.

uting tracts to the poor and telling them to forget their earthly troubles in thoughts of heaven, we realize how powerfully, if unconsciously, the doctrine must have appealed to every employer of labor.

So much is clear; the remarkable thing is the spread of evangelicalism among the upper classes. They were frightened, to be sure, by the French Revolution, but beyond that there must have been a partly unconscious recognition of the need for preparation for a new role. The figure of the fox-hunting parson—so familiar in eighteenth century fiction —disappeared. Clergymen were no longer mere appendages of country life; their responsibility was increasingly to sober-minded men of affairs. Under the guidance of this new kind of clergyman the nobility and gentry reformed. The public schools, which had not discouraged drinking, gambling, wenching, and other relaxations of an extravagant, largely irresponsible class, fell into the hands of the Thomas Arnolds. The duel was abolished, temperance societies were formed, the observance of the Sabbath was insisted upon. If, after 1832, the middle class was content to leave the administration of government to the aristocracy, that was in large measure because the aristocracy had been brought by evangelicalism to a satisfactory degree of conformity with middle-class standards.

Evangelicalism and utilitarianism are related in more than the fact that they rose at exactly the same time. At their extremes, it is true, they have slight resemblance. Many of the close followers of Bentham were freethinkers, and nothing could be less agreeable to them than the anti-intellectual piety of the disciples of Bishop Wilberforce. On the other hand, a certain number of leading evangelicals were staunch Tories, and some of these—especially Oastler, Sadler, and Lord Shaftesbury—challenged the assumptions of laissez-faire economics in the course of their fight against child labor. There was in evangelicalism a strong humanitarian tendency, and this, though it often expressed itself in concern for the hereafter rather than the present, and was more frequently concerned with slavery abroad than with industrial evils at home, ran counter to the Malthusian ruthlessness of the advocates of laissez-faire. But there was a large central area in which utilitarianism and evangelicalism re-enforced each other, and the ordinary representative of the middle class was concerned only with that area in each.

Religion, which had been taken lightly by many of the better educated in the eighteenth century, became almost obligatory. There is nothing formal or casual about the piety of Lord Shaftesbury or W. E. Gladstone. The latter wrote in his diary on his first birthday after becoming prime minister, "The Almighty seems to sustain and spare me for some purpose of His own, deeply unworthy as I know myself to be. Glory be to His name." Skepticism became dangerous. Macaulay once said that not two hundred men in London believed in the Bible, and John Stuart Mill wrote, "The world would be astonished if it knew how great a proportion of its brightest ornaments are complete skeptics in religion." But this body of doubters was for the most part discreet.

Even more remarkable was the rule of evangelicalism in the realm of morality.[1] The middle class had always regarded the division of the human race into sexes as one of God's devices for testing the faithful. Now it insisted on imposing this view upon the aristocracy, which just a few years earlier, during the Regency, had hilariously followed a dif-

---

[1] "During the nineteenth century evangelical religion was the moral cement of English society. It was the influence of the evangelicals which invested the British aristocracy with an almost Stoic dignity, restrained the plutocrats who had newly risen from the masses from vulgar ostentation and debauchery, and placed over the proletariat a select body of workmen enamoured of virtue and capable of self-restraint. Evangelicalism was thus the conservative force which restored in England the balance momentarily destroyed by the explosion of the revolutionary forces." Halévy, *A History of the English People, 1830–1841,* 166.

ferent code, and upon the working class, which had seldom bothered to practice what the middle class preached. Even open skeptics in religion did not venture to challenge middle-class morality. Spencer wrote, "Further evolution along lines thus far followed may be expected to extend the monogamic relation by extinguishing promiscuity, and by suppressing such crimes as bigamy and adultery." John Stuart Mill, in his reasonable and enlightened essay, *The Subjection of Women,* implied that the sexual act, if not necessarily distasteful to women, was at best a matter of toleration. And Thackeray, though he gibed at hypocrisy and wanted more freedom for writers, never seriously questioned the Victorian concept of morality.[1]

If men of this caliber accepted so uncritically the current views of chastity, monogamy, and the sex life in general, it is not hard to imagine how pertinaciously those views were held by the majority of the people. What the average middle-class Victorian really believed—or thought he ought to believe—can be judged, not from such writers as Thackeray and George Eliot, but from Charlotte Yonge and Dinah Mulock Craik. Something can be said for the Victorian emphasis on the home and on responsibility in personal relationships, but modern taste is inevitably offended by the lack of candor and intellectual objectivity. Victorian delicacy [2] dictated silence not merely on sexual matters but on all subjects connected with the body. The London *Times* rebuked a Parliamentary

---

[1] It was Thackeray, after all, who wrote, "We have a love for all the little boys at school; for many scores of thousands of them read and love *Punch:*—may he never write a word that shall not be honest and fit for them to read!" (*Book of Snobs,* ch. XIII.) Nor should we forget the opening scene of *The Newcomes,* in which Colonel Newcome rebukes Captain Costigan for singing a vulgar song.

[2] Robert Palfrey Utter and Gwendolyn Bridges Needham in *Pamela's Daughters* show that the "Victorian" conception of indelicacy made its appearance in fiction early in the eighteenth century. They are quite right. As soon as the middle class—with such writers as Richardson—begins to contribute to literature, prudery appears, but it does not become dominant until the middle class is dominant.

committee for asking a woman if she had ever miscarried, and the *Economist* refused to go into the details of the public health bill of 1847.

It is not to be assumed that everybody in England in the mid-nineteenth century was a heartless believer in laissez-faire and a pious prude, but on the surface the triumph of utilitarianism and evangelicalism was complete. The widespread popularity of Martin Tupper's platitudes,[1] the millions of copies of Samuel Smiles' *Self-Help* and its successors, the gift annuals such as *Friendship's Offering,* the *Keepsake,* Heath's *Book of Beauty,* the novels that described the triumph of piety and enterprise, and the sermons that preached the same lesson—these are what we mean by Victorianism.

Again and again the middle class sought to impress upon the world that the virtues by which it had risen were the only virtues that mattered. And it enforced its tastes as well as its principles. Any reader of Victorian fiction recalls the descriptions of rooms: the mantelpieces, console tables, pier glasses, chairs of rosewood, album tables, glass chandeliers, ottomans, chiffoniers, whatnots, pianos, music boxes, and papier-mâché chairs that filled every corner of a well-equipped drawing-room. In lower-middle-class parlors souvenirs, bottles, pictures, and knickknacks covered the mantelpieces; the chairs and tables were elaborately adorned; the walls were crowded with mottoes, landscapes, still lifes, and family portraits. One remembers also in Victorian novels the solemn, heavy meals, the obligatorily stupid social occa-

[1] Martin Tupper's *Proverbial Philosophy* was not only a popular success, with a sale of millions of copies, but was praised by sober critics. The *Church of England Journal* called it "poetry exquisite, almost beyond the bounds of fancy to conceive, brimmed with noble thoughts and studded with heavenward aspirations." The *Saturday Review* predicted that it would be hailed in the twentieth century as it was in the nineteenth. And the *Spectator* ranked Tupper with Wordsworth, Tennyson, and Browning. John Drinkwater, "Martin Tupper," in *The Eighteen-Eighties,* edited by Walter de la Mare, 199–200.

sions, the funerals—black horses with black plumes, hearses painted with gilded skulls, mutes and mourners hired from an undertaker.

"I have never," wrote Engels in 1844, "seen a class so deeply demoralized, so incurably debased by selfishness, so corroded within, so incapable of progress as the English bourgeoisie. . . . For it nothing exists in this world, except for the sake of money, itself not excluded. It knows no bliss save that of rapid gain, no pain save that of losing gold." A few years later Engels might have added another count to his indictment: the English bourgeoisie was as stupid in spending its money as it was greedy in making it.

3. *The Critics of Laissez-Faire.*

So widespread was the acceptance of utilitarianism and evangelicalism, at least in their broader forms, that one would expect to find contemporary literature full of them. But actually Macaulay is the only representative Victorian man of letters who speaks for the commercial middle class. Most of the Victorian writers vigorously criticized utilitarianism, and, though they usually accepted evangelicalism in principle, and permitted it to dictate their choice of subjects and the moral tone of their work, they objected to much that most evangelicals stood for, and their revolt grew stronger as Victoria grew older.

The opposition to utilitarianism stems from the romantic movement. Samuel Taylor Coleridge, like Wordsworth and Southey, lost his faith in revolutionary principles during the reign of terror in France, and "alighted on the firm ground of common sense from the gradually exhausted balloon of youthful enthusiasm." He became a reactionary, but of a special kind. Since he was sensitive to human suffering, he could not endure the callous calculations with which laissez-faire economists justified long hours, low wages, and unemployment, and Bentham's mathematical hedonism was impossible to one who believed so ardently in intuition. On the other hand, though he turned to the Tory Party, he saw the stupidity of many of the landowners, their hysteria during the French Revolution and their consequent cruelty, and their willingness to compromise with the commercial spirit. He had to find his own means of political salvation. So successful was he that John Stuart Mill could say, "Every Englishman of the present day is by implication either a Benthamite or a Coleridgean; holds views of human affairs which can only be proved true on the principles either of Bentham or of Coleridge."

Coleridge opposed Bentham on every possible front. In philosophy he was an idealist, and his system of morality derived from his transcendentalism. In politics he argued against both Hobbes and Rousseau, basing his conception of the state on a quasi-mystical theory of corporate unity. He not only upheld the Church of England, to the extent of opposing Catholic emancipation, but desired the church to assume a role in English life comparable to that of the state. An ardent nationalist, he repudiated both the theoretical cosmopolitanism of the Jacobins and the utilitarians' practical subordination of national to commercial interests. At a time when the Benthamites, following their theories of free trade, were willing to emancipate all colonies, he advocated further colonization, saying, "God seems to hold out his finger to us over the sea." Like Edmund Burke, his master in political thinking, he was predisposed in favor of tradition, and was loyal to the Crown and the House of Lords. He never referred to Bentham's views except with some such phrase as "canting foppery," and he described Malthusianism as "this abominable tenet."

Coleridge attacked classical economics as "solemn humbug." "Things find their level," the economists said. "But persons are not things," Coleridge cried; "but man does not find his level." The poor-rates he shrewdly called "the consideration paid by, or on behalf of, capitalists, for having labor at demand." He opposed the reform bill, not, he maintained, because he objected to enlargement of the franchise, but because this particular measure was intended to "throw the balance of political power into the hands of that class (the shopkeepers), which, in all countries and in all ages, has been, is now, and ever will be, the least patriotic and the least conservative of any." The result, he predicted, would be "a practical disfranchisement of all above, and a discontenting of all below, a favored class," and he lived long enough to hold that his prophecy had been fulfilled.

All his beliefs were summed up in his doctrine of the state. "The negative ends of government," he wrote in *The Friend,* "are the protection of life, of personal freedom, of property, of reputation, and of religion, from foreign and from domestic attacks." So far any Benthamite would have gone. But Coleridge added: "The positive ends are:—First, to make the means of subsistence more easy to each individual:—Secondly, that in addition to the necessaries of life, he should derive from the union and division of labor a share of the comforts and conveniences which humanize and ennoble his nature; and at the same time the power of perfecting himself in his own branch of industry by having those things which he needs provided for him by others among his fellow-citizens. . . . Thirdly, the hope of bettering his own condition and that of his children."

It was not in democracy that Coleridge trusted for a government that would perform such functions. He believed that "property must be the grand basis of the government, and that the government was the best in which the power or the political influence of the individual was in proportion to his property." It was by the spiritual regeneration of the nation's rulers that reform of government was to come. This regeneration, largely to be accomplished by the restoration of the church to its true ideals, was to affect men of power not only in their political activities but in their private concerns as well. In particular he pleaded with the landed gentleman to make "the marketable produce of his estates . . . a subordinate consideration to the living and moral growth that is to remain on the land—I mean a healthful, callous-handed but high-and-warm-hearted tenantry, twice the number of the present landless, parish-paid laborers, and ready to march off at the first call of their country with a Son of the House at their head."

Such were the ideas that were to be repeated, with changes of emphasis and modifications of detail, by an impressive majority of the novelists, poets, and essayists of the early Victorian period. This Coleridgean tradition was opposed to the practice of the landowners, to the theory and practice of the business men, and to the beginnings of class-consciousness among the workers. In large part it was reactionary and sentimental. When it did not actually aspire to the restoration of something like feudalism, it advocated forms of church and state that were possible only under conditions that had irrevocably passed. Its criticisms of industrialism were inspired, not by an understanding of capitalism, but by nostalgia, uneasiness in a changing world, and a certain sympathy for the sufferings of the workers. It was a tradition likely to appeal to men on the margins of the social order, to those not immediately drawn into either the struggle for wealth and power or the struggle for mere survival. It would appeal to some of the landowners, who cared more for their past glories than for their present opportunities, and to some of the lower middle class, especially those troubled by rapid change. But it was particularly a tradition for men of sensibility. The romantic revolution was from the outset an assertion of the value of certain elements in experience that the eighteenth century synthesis had disregarded: love of natural beauty, sympathy for man and beast, spontaneity, enthusiasm, appreciation of the past. Utilitarianism, as John Stuart Mill was to discover, offered nothing on which the emotions could feed, and, as the mood of utilitarianism triumphed, even where its dogmas were rejected, the only vital alternative seemed to be that which the poets had created in the realm of faith.

That there must be some alternative to laissez-faire more and more persons were eager to believe. Coleridge had predicted doom, but Thomas Carlyle could show its agents assembling by the millions. The first thrust of Chartism convinced him that laissez-faire had "reached the suicidal point." The second led him, in *Past and Present,* to prescribe a remedy. Aware that the productive system of the Middle Ages could not be restored, he called for a revival of the medieval spirit. An heroic industrial class, freed from the mammonistic nonsense of laissez-faire, could yet save England from the horrors of revolution.

Past and Present owed its effect less to the remedies it proposed than to the vividness with which it portrayed evils and their possible outcome. The fear of revolution was strong, and Carlyle knew how to play upon it. By 1850, however, when he wrote *Latter-day Pamphlets,* England was beginning to recover from its terror. He attacked the pig philosophy with his usual savageness, and in other ways he repeated his old formulas, but, so far as government was concerned, his aim seemed to be efficiency rather than justice. His attack on prison reform, his imperialism, and his increasing bitterness against democracy made him sound like a die-hard Tory. Thereafter, as the pressure of the working class was reduced, he became more and more unmistakably reactionary.

But he had made himself Coleridge's successor in the fight against laissez-faire, and he had his disciples. The English novel, which often enough had been didactic, very naturally turned, in the turmoil of the mid-century, to social problems. Two of the novelists who were roused by Chartism, and who came to regard it, as Carlyle did, as a challenge to leadership, believed they could meet the challenge. One was a politician, the other a parson, and they deliberately used their novels to set forth doctrines they were also advancing in other ways. There were differences enough, certainly, between Benjamin Disraeli and Charles Kingsley: the former was precocious, unpredictable, and ambitious; the latter was as solid a Briton as ever occupied a country pulpit. But their literary aims were very much alike and their political aims by no means wholly dissimilar.

Disraeli, who was elected to Parliament in 1837 after being thrice defeated, chose the novel as the method which "in the temper of the times offered the best chance of influencing opinion." He planned a trilogy: *Coningsby,* to show the failure of the old political parties; *Sybil,* to reveal the predicament of the working class; and *Tancred,* to call for a religious revival. *Coningsby* appeared in 1844, *Sybil* [1] the next year. Disraeli had given evidence of his good faith by speaking in Parliament on behalf of the Chartist petition,

---

[1] The subtitle of *Sybil* is *The Two Nations,* a phrase derived from a speech of one of the characters: "Two nations; between whom there is no intercourse and no sympathy; who are as ignorant of each other's habits, thought, and feelings as if they were dwellers in different zones, or inhabitants of different planets; who are formed by a different breeding, are fed by a different food, are ordered by different manners, and are not governed by the same laws." *Sybil, 76.* At almost exactly the same time Engels was writing: "In view of all this, it is not surprising that the working-class has gradually become a race wholly apart from the English bourgeoisie. The bourgeoisie has more in common with every other nation of the earth than with the workers in whose midst it lives. The workers speak other dialects, have other thoughts and ideals, other customs and moral principles, a different religion and other politics than those of the bourgeoisie. Thus they are two radically dissimilar nations, as unlike as difference of race could make them." *Condition of the Working Class,* 124.

and he had prepared himself to write about the Chartists' grievances by making a trip to Manchester and its vicinity and by studying the Blue Books produced by Lord Shaftesbury's committees on factories and mines. The picture of working-class life, however, is but roughly sketched: some conversation in a drinking place, the lamentations of a sweated worker, a vivid account of a tommy shop, and allusions to a benevolent manufacturer. The description of a trade union initiation might have been written by Lord Brougham, and most of the references to Chartism emphasize the selfishness and incompetence of its leaders. The theme of the book is stated in the plea of Charles Egremont, an enlightened aristocrat, to Sybil Gerard, daughter of a Chartist: "The People are not strong," he tells her; "the People can never be strong. Their attempts at self-vindication will end only in their suffering and confusion." Hope lies in the awakening of the nobility, presumably as a result of Disraeli's Young England movement: "They are the natural leaders of the People, Sybil; believe me, they are the only ones."

Disraeli saw in Chartism an opportunity for his party, Kingsley an opportunity for his church. After his first, chaotic, high-pitched novel, *Yeast,* he wrote, "The real battle of the time is . . . the Church, the gentleman and the workman against the shopkeepers and the Manchester School." By the time he began *Alton Locke,* he was already in the fight. He and his friends—Frederick Denison Maurice, J. M. Ludlow, and others—had founded Christian Socialism, and in "Cheap Clothes and Nasty," Kingsley had muckraked the sweat shops of the clothing industry. In another tract, "My Political Creed," he had attacked the Benthamites and at the same time warned the workers against "the mistake of fancying that legislative reform is social reform, or that men's hearts can be changed by legislation." He had also said, "I believe that the Crown has now too little and not too much power."

It was from these ingredients—an awareness of the misery of certain sections of the working class and a political outlook closely akin to Carlyle's and not much removed from Disraeli's—that he created *Alton Locke*. More detailed and more moving than *Sybil* in its depiction of workers' lives, it is scarcely more just in its account of Chartism. There is real bitterness in Alton's story of his becoming a Chartist, but the entire book is written from the point of view Alton finally adopts, which is as scornful as Carlyle's of "Morison's-Pill-remedies" and "the possession of one ten-thousandth part of a talker in the national palaver." The theme of the book is the futility of all political reform and the immorality of violence.

Alton Locke looked two ways: it threatened the upper class with revolution, and it held before the workers the spectacle of Chartist collapse. Christian Socialism, which was founded on the ruins of Chartism, lost its reason for existence as Chartism failed to revive. Its working-class following deserted it, and it became chiefly a refuge for conscience-smitten clergymen, who made some slight contribution to popular education. Kingsley himself defended it on the ground that it made workers "more respectful to those institutions of which they have never been taught the value." Instead of attempting other novels like *Alton Locke,* he wrote much that fostered the imperialistic spirit, which, having found its politician in one adherent of the Coleridge-Carlyle tradition, found its novelist in another. The preface he wrote for the edition of *Alton Locke* that appeared in the sixties gives the measure of his progress towards complacency.

Elizabeth Gaskell had neither political nor ecclesiastical ambitions, but she did have some knowledge of industrial conditions. Coming to Manchester in 1832 as the wife of its Unitarian minister, she had learned how much there was in the city to fear and regret. Although she did not question laissez-faire theories, she could not ignore the consequences of their application, and the Chartist riots of 1842 convinced her that the evils she had long known could not forever be endured. When, almost accidentally, she began to write her first novel, she put into it all she knew of the life of the poor, their unhealthy food in good times and their starvation in bad, their crowded, unsanitary rooms, their illnesses and dreary deaths, their sense of slavery when employed and their hopelessness when out of work. Of the mid-century novels of industrial conditions, *Mary Barton* is the truest and most moving.

Yet Mrs. Gaskell was far from approving of Chartism. She could understand its origins, and she thought it might serve a useful purpose by calling the sufferings of the poor to the attention of those whose duty it was to relieve them, but she had no more confidence in political reform than Kingsley or Carlyle. All she maintained was that employers should show something of the spirit of Christian brotherhood. To Mr. Carson, father of the belligerent manufacturer murdered by John Barton, Job Legh says, "I have lived long enough to see that it is part of His plan to send suffering to bring out a higher good; but surely it's also part of His plan that as much of the burden of suffering as can be should be lightened by those whom it is His pleasure to make happy and content in their own circumstances. . . . What we all feel sharpest is the want of inclination to try and help the evils which come like blights at times over the manufacturing places, while we see the masters can stop work and not suffer."

This was surely a modest enough proposal, and yet *Mary Barton* was harshly criticized by the orthodox economists.

W. R. Greg tried to show in the *Edinburgh Review* that the workmen were themselves responsible for their sufferings, and the *Manchester Guardian* denounced "this morbid sensibility to the condition of factory operatives." The trouble was, perhaps, that even an economist could see how inadequate Mrs. Gaskell's remedies were for the evils she portrayed. No economist could object to a plea for better understanding between masters and men, but any economist might wonder if such an understanding would be served by the indictment of capitalism implicit in *Mary Barton.*

Mrs. Gaskell herself came to feel that she may have been unjust to the manufacturers, and seven years later, after *Ruth* and *Cranford* had added much to her reputation, she came back to the theme of Manchester industry. The hero of *North and South,* John Thornton, is a loyal adherent of the Manchester School and a determined enemy of the trade unions, but he is an honorable and by no means cruel employer. All that is necessary, from Mrs. Gaskell's point of view, is for him to learn to co-operate with his hands, to explain to them his difficulties and to demonstrate his interest in them, and his learning of this lesson is the theme of the book. *North and South* won the approval of the *Edinburgh Review's* Mr. Greg, but *Mary Barton* could not be wiped off the record.

North and South was serialized in Charles Dickens' magazine, *Household Words,* closely following his own novel of Manchester, *Hard Times.* It was a bold choice, for the comparison of the two novels makes clear the limitations of Dickens' knowledge. What he had seen were the indirect consequences of the industrial revolution, the deposits its great tides had left in the slums of London. No one could describe so well as he the criminal or semi-criminal or merely miserable dregs of the working class. No one knew so closely the men and women who had no class, the people who had lost their original status and found no other. Such people he portrayed in *Oliver Twist, Bleak House, David Copperfield,* and other novels, and no one has ever portrayed them so well. But he did not have Mrs. Gaskell's knowledge of industrial populations. London he understood, but he did not understand Manchester or the world-transforming changes that were going on in that and other smoky cities of the North.

His political and economic insight matched his personal experience. The period of his poverty-burdened youth was the period before the reform bill, when the middle class, upper and lower, was allied with the working class in a struggle against the landowners. All his life Dickens called himself a Radical and a democrat, and he earned the names by attacking the aristocracy and trying to improve the conditions of the masses of the people.[1] But in the conflict that developed after the passage of the reform bill, he could not go wholeheartedly with either side. With the laissez-faire Liberals he had no sympathy, and he was too removed from the working class to support Chartism. Thus he was driven to take the position of Carlyle, to whom he dedicated *Hard Times.* With Carlyle's attacks on democracy Dickens could not agree, though he was more willing as time went on to admit there was a measure of truth in them, and he had little patience with attempts to idealize the nobility. What attracted Dickens to Carlyle and the Coleridge-Carlyle tradition was the basis provided for opposition to laissez-faire economics.

It was almost inconceivable that Dickens, the great re-

---

[1] George Saintsbury writes: "His politics and his sociology themselves are hot ashes at which there is no need to burn discreet feet or fingers. Certainly he, perhaps more than anyone else, started that curious topsy-turvyfied snobbishness— that 'cult of the *lower* classes'—which has become a more and more fashionable religion up to the present moment." *Cambridge History of English Literature,* XIII, 375–6. Actually Dickens' interest in reform grew out of exactly the same qualities of mind that made him a great novelist.

former, should not sooner or later write about the factories and the people who worked in them. He had attacked debtors' prisons, the treatment of the poor, educational abuses, the delays of the law, corruption in business and in politics. How could he remain silent on what one Parliamentary report after another proved to be the greatest evil of the day? *Hard Times* was a courageous attempt, but we cannot be surprised if it is, as most critics consider it, the author's poorest novel. The overwhelming richness of his best work grew out of intimate knowledge, and in *Hard Times* he was trying to write about lives with which he was only superficially acquainted. Instead of the sense of omniscience that Dickens usually gives, the novel leaves us with a rather abashed awareness of his ignorance.

Yet *Hard Times* is, for our purposes, a significant novel. What, when he finally came to the subject of industrialism, did Dickens single out for emphasis? The book, as we would expect, shows a deep sympathy with the exploited workers, but their suffering is not its theme. The attack is directed against the spirit of the business men, against the spirit of utilitarianism, and for this spiritual evil Dickens preaches a spiritual remedy. Though he never denied the right of labor to organize, he always qualified his approval of trade unions, and the union organizer in *Hard Times* is only slightly less a villain than the utilitarian Mr. Bounderby. When this organizer, this Slackbridge, low, cunning, and cowardly, forms a union, Stephen refuses to join it, and Stephen is the hero. For Dickens unionism has the same significance as Chartism for Carlyle, and he puts the lesson in Stephen's mouth. Bounderby in his bullying way denounces Slackbridge, and Stephen says: "I'm as sooary as yo', sir, when the people's leaders is bad. They taks such as offers. Haply 'tis no' the sma'est of their misfortuns when they can get no better."

Hard Times, like all Dickens' novels, is a plea for imagination and the emotions. He believes that only a change of heart, such as Gradgrind experiences and Bounderby does not, will alleviate the sufferings of the Stephens and Rachaels, purge the Coketowns of their smoke and grime, and save young whelps from the fate of Tom Gradgrind. The book is a plea for the understanding that Mrs. Gaskell believed to be a sovereign remedy, and the scene between Stephen and Mr. Bounderby closely matches her more realistic conversation between Job Legh and Mr. Carson. It is also, by implication, a plea for the kind of leadership that Carlyle had called for in *Past and Present,* a plea for heroic captains of industry in the place of Mammon-worshiping Bounderbys. It is no wonder that Ruskin thought *Hard Times* in many respects the greatest of Dickens' novels and said it "should be studied with great care by persons interested in social questions." Nor is it surprising that Macaulay wrote of it in his diary, "One excessively touching, heart-breaking passage, and the rest sullen socialism," though "socialism" is as inept a word as "sullen."

The Coleridge tradition not only influenced those who were acutely conscious of contemporary evils and determined to remedy them; it also touched writers whose interests were of other kinds. Newman, for example, though he disagreed with Coleridge's theology and was far from sharing Carlyle's interest in the "Condition-of-England Question," regarded utilitarianism as pure heresy, encouraged reliance on the past, and opposed to individualism the idea of corporate existence and responsibility. Tennyson accepted the middle-class dogma of progress, but he considered himself a disciple of Carlyle, and his increasing distrust of democracy, his devotion to the Crown, and his imperialism were doctrines of which Carlyle could approve. George Eliot, rationalist though she was and adherent of

Positivism, reached much the same social conclusions as the idealist Carlyle: the lesson of *Felix Holt,* explicitly stated in an article called "An Address to Working Men," is that the working class must cultivate patience and purity of heart.

Even John Stuart Mill, who had been carefully educated as the heir apparent to the utilitarian throne, testified in the modification of his theories to the strength of the rival doctrine. Having discovered, as a result of his personal experience, that Bentham, who denounced all generalizations, had himself generalized on the basis of his own rather unrepresentative and limited personality,[1] and had created a dogma that ignored much of man's nature, Mill had sought, both in the romantic poets of England and in the Utopian Socialists of France, for a doctrine to meet his new-found needs. At this time Carlyle believed Mill might become his ally, but he was wrong. Mill still believed that the faults of utilitarianism were not fundamental, and he could not accept Coleridge's idealism. In the same way, though he criticized the view of orthodox political economy on dis-

---

[1] "Bentham's knowledge of human nature . . . is wholly empirical, and the empiricism of one who has had little experience. He had neither internal experience nor external; the quiet, even tenor of his life, and his healthiness of mind, conspired to exclude him from both. He never knew prosperity and adversity, passion nor satiety; he never had even the experiences which sickness gives; he lived from childhood to the age of eighty-five in boyish health. He knew no dejection, no heaviness of heart. He never felt life a sore and a weary burthen. He was a boy to the last. . . . How much of human nature slumbered in him he knew not, neither can we know. . . . Other ages and other nations were a blank to him for purposes of instruction. He measured them but by one standard; their knowledge of facts, and their capability to take correct views of utility, and merge all other objects in it. His own lot was cast in a generation of the leanest and barrenest men whom England had yet produced, and he was an old man when a better race came in with the present century. . . . Knowing so little of human feelings, he knew still less of the influences by which those feelings are formed: all the more subtle workings both of the mind upon itself, and of external things upon the mind, escaped him; and no one, probably, who, in a highly instructed age, ever attempted to give a rule to all human conduct, set out with a more limited conception either of the agencies by which human conduct *is,* or of those by which it *should* be influenced." *Dissertations and Discussions,* I, 354–5.

tribution, he did not despair of making economics a science. When, with *Latter-day Pamphlets,* Carlyle revealed himself as a reactionary, Mill broke with him. He had his own doubts about democracy, but they grew out of his desire to preserve individuality and had little in common with Carlyle's hero-worship. He did not wholly trust the working class, but he was confident that, with education, it would become worthy of power. If he had some objections to independent political action by the workers, he was strongly in favor of action through the co-operative movement. In short, as Carlyle, Kingsley, Disraeli, Tennyson, and to some extent Dickens became more reactionary, Mill moved, slowly and with many qualifications, in the direction of democratic collectivism. But if he moved away from Carlyle, he also moved away from Benthamism, especially the distorted Benthamism of class interest, and he was always quick to acknowledge that he owed to the Coleridge-Carlyle tradition his understanding of the inadequacies of utilitarianism.

Mill's progress shows how, by the fifties, both utilitarianism and the Coleridge-Carlyle tradition had been so modified by class interests, individual needs, and temperamental differences, and by contact with each other, that neither could be defined with complete clarity. All that could be done was to sketch roughly the opposing forces. On the one hand were the great majority of industrialists, many other business men, and most of the professional economists, who embodied the spirit if not the logic of utilitarianism, and who regarded the laissez-faire economics of Smith, Ricardo, and Mill as a body of eternal truths. In all practical issues they had the support of the more successful and ambitious in the middle class, of large sections of the aristocracy, and, after 1848, of many leaders in the trade union movement. On the other hand were the poets, some in-

fluential clergymen, and a few landowners. They had sym-
pathizers, perhaps, in all classes, though very few among
the active business men. Most of their followers belonged
to the lower middle class. The driving force, however, that
put some of their ideas into practice came from the working class, from the Chartists, whom they feared.

When the pressure of the working class diminished, when
there was no longer a threat of revolution, most authors
lost interest in "the Condition-of-England Question." The
Great Exhibition of 1851 was the symbol of the practical
compromise that had been effected. The gentry, having a
share in the industrial prosperity of the nation, and having
discovered that they could still occupy the majority of public offices so long as they did not offend against capitalism,
were not too discontented. The labor movement, having
been defeated on the political field, was engaged in making
and consolidating gains for the favored minority of the
workers. There was an underprivileged majority, but it was
so nearly inarticulate that no strident voices reached the
studies of middle-class writers.

Without working-class pressure behind it, criticism of
capitalist theories and practices, so far as it survived, came
to seem rarefied and futile. It survived chiefly in the angry
words of John Ruskin, who kept up the attack when most
of the other disciples of Coleridge had lapsed into reaction
or indifference. Ruskin was the most popular of art critics
and the accepted arbiter of artistic tastes when, in 1850, he
introduced into *The Stones of Venice* an attack on "our
manufacturing cities." In 1854 he began teaching at the
Working Men's College that Maurice and other Christian
Socialists had founded. In 1860 he shocked a Parliamentary
committee by "casting a slur on the principle of competition." And in the same year he began to publish, in Thackeray's *Cornhill Magazine,* an attack on the doctrine of lais-

sez-faire that, mild as it now seems, was an unpardonable offense to the *Cornhill's* readers.[1]

Ruskin persevered. In *The Crown of Wild Olive* he used the descriptive powers that had delighted the admirers of *Modern Painters* to reveal in full hideousness the destruction wrought by industrialism. In *Munera Pulvis* he returned to economic theory. And in January, 1871, he began publication of his series of letters to workmen, *Fors Clavigera*. "I simply cannot paint," he said, "nor read, nor look at minerals, nor do anything else that I like, and the very light of the morning sky, when there is any—which is seldom, nowadays, near London—has become hateful to me, because of the misery that I know, and see signs of." In the fifth letter he made a specific proposal: "some small piece of English ground, beautiful, peaceful, and fruitful . . . no steam-engines upon it, and no railroads . . . no untended or unthought-of creatures on it . . . no liberty upon it, but instant obedience to known law and appointed persons . . . plenty of flowers and vegetables in our gardens, plenty of corn and grass in our fields . . . some music and poetry." To help make this possible he would give a tenth of all he had and all he should thenceforth earn.

What happened to the Guild of St. George [2] does not

[1] "The scandal, outrage, and tumult which were caused by this essentially mild book were extreme. Reading the newspaper attacks upon him, it seems impossible that Ruskin had not married two wives, stolen money out of the poor-box, or been involved in an Oscar Wilde scandal. . . . The contemporary press outdid itself in abuse of Ruskin, who formerly could do no wrong. His economic essays were called 'intolerable twaddle,' and the author 'a perfect paragon of blubbering.'" Amabel Williams-Ellis, *The Exquisite Tragedy*, 184. Copyright 1928 by Doubleday, Doran and Company.

[2] "It would be an ungracious task to record the pitiful story of the industrial projects which grew out of the central company. How a small group of Secularists, Unitarians, and Quakers induced the Guild to buy a farm for them to start a Communist project for £2287, 16s, 6d; how the Communists discovered they could not farm; how two acres of rock and moor were given at Barmouth, and twenty acres of woodland at Bewdley, and nothing grew on either; how a home-

concern us, for Ruskin's Utopian schemes are important only as evidence of his sincerity. He was a critic of Victorian society, a critic endowed with a fine sensibility, which, under the circumstances, found expression in eloquent, ferocious satire. His training as a student of art, his early exposure to more spacious and dignified cultures, had made him almost pathologically sensitive to Victorian vulgarity. "Simple and innocent vulgarity," he wrote, "is merely an untrained and undeveloped bluntness of body and mind: but in true inbred vulgarity there is a dreadful callousness, which, in extremity, becomes capable of every sort of bestial habit and crime—without fear, without pleasure, without horror, and without pity." Slowly he learned that this vulgarity was a product of the economic system, and he began to attack prevailing economic theory. Never understanding capitalism, he did realize that the only way to meet the economists was to destroy the assumptions on which their concept of value rested. He did not comprehend the terms on which production for use could be established; indeed he was always looking back to a kind of reformed feudalism rather than ahead to anything that might be described as Socialism; but he did question capitalist theories, and he did expose capitalist practice.

The indifference with which Ruskin met in the sixties and seventies was so complete that he himself felt it was

spun woollen industry without steam was started in the Isle of Man; how hand-spinning and hand-loom weaving were carried on at Langdale; how the May Queens at Chelsea were crowned and decorated; how, after seven years, the Master came to see that all interest on realized capital was usury forbidden by Scripture, an abomination in the sight of God and of man; how, finally, he came to act strictly on this strange delusion which, if generally adopted, would destroy the bases of civilization." Harrison, *John Ruskin,* 178. Note, by the way, Mr. Harrison's comment on the last item in this amusing summary: it is not merely capitalism that will be destroyed by the forbidding of interest but civilization itself. Thus this eminent Positivist and Radical carried into the twentieth century the utilitarian dogma that capitalism is identical with civilization.

responsible for the unbalancing of his reason.[1] On some levels, it is true, he found a response. The Pre-Raphaelites, in certain respects his avowed disciples, echoed his attacks on Victorian vulgarity. Matthew Arnold was as bitter as he in denouncing Philistinism. Meredith and Swinburne would have quarreled with his disparagement of democracy but not with his contempt for exploiters. But none of these men cared very much or thought very much about the theory of laissez-faire. They took it for granted that the state would have to exercise some control over business, but this was now being conceded even by some of the industrialists. Though its influence was by no means dead, the Coleridge-Carlyle tradition had lost its old urgency.

When we evaluate that tradition, especially as a literary force, we must grant that, since few writers were likely to give unqualified support to Chartism or any other working-class movement, it provided the only practical basis for comment on the social scene, and thus sustained the novel of social conditions. Moreover, it kept alive the sympathy with the lower classes that was one of the achievements of the romantic movement. The utilitarians regarded workers as "hands" and dealt with them in statistical masses; the interventionists,[2] in the spirit of Cowper, Crabbe, Burns, and Wordsworth, regarded them as individual human beings. Finally, interventionism established a critical tradition. If, throughout the Victorian period, a period usually celebrated for conformity, literature is almost invariably a dis-

---

[1] "The doctors said that I went mad . . . from overwork. . . . I went mad because nothing came of my work. People would have understood my falling crazy if they had heard that the manuscript on which I had spent seven years of my old life had been used to light the fire like Carlyle's first volume of *The French Revolution*. But they could not understand that I should be in the least annoyed, far less fall ill in a frantic manner, because, after I had got them published, nobody believed a word of them." *Fors Clavigera* (Works, XXIX, 386).

[2] This is the term that Louis Cazamian uses, in *Le Roman Social en Angleterre*, to distinguish the followers of Coleridge from the advocates of laissez-faire.

senting voice, the precedent had been established by Coleridge and Carlyle.

The social effects of the tradition are harder to estimate. Such reforms as the factory laws would not have taken place without pressure from the working class, but that is not to say that the literature of protest was valueless. One of the ways that working-class demands found expression was in the writings of the interventionists, not direct or adequate expression, but on certain levels the only expression there was, for the few Chartist poets, such as Capel Lofft and Thomas Cooper, could not command the following of Dickens or even of Disraeli, Kingsley, and Mrs. Gaskell. One might describe the role of Carlyle and his followers as that of preparing middle-class minds for changes that had to be made.

So far, the tradition justifies itself, but there is much more to be said. From the working-class point of view nothing could be more dangerous than the constant insistence that workers must not act for themselves. Carlyle called for heroic dictators, Disraeli and Kingsley for more power for Church and Crown, Dickens and Mrs. Gaskell for charitable employers, Ruskin for "obedience to known laws and appointed persons." All of them preached the futility of both political and economic action, of both Chartism and trade unionism. The workers wanted more democracy and were told by the anti-utilitarians that they ought to have less. They wanted peace and were instructed in the glories of imperialism.

This reminds us that, if the interventionists rejected much of Benthamism and of Ricardian economics for humanitarian reasons, they also had grounds for rejection that can only be called obscurantist. If, as John Stuart Mill recognized, the rationalism of the eighteenth century had been narrow and unrealistic, the alternative was not necessarily mysticism. Bentham, with all his temperamental liabilities, had tried to broaden that rationalism. Ricardo, apologist for a class though he was, had looked for laws of human society, and some of his discoveries were important. What Carlyle wanted to do was to check every effort of the mind to bring human behavior within the scope of science,[1] and on this, as on so many other grounds, it is impossible not to feel that we are at the very source of the Fascist way of looking at life.

The choice is not an easy one: on the one hand, science, belief in progress, and a tendency towards democracy, coupled with the glorification of self-interest and a theoretical defense of a very practical indifference to human suffering; on the other, sympathy for the oppressed and labor on their behalf, as well as emotional warmth and poetic richness, coupled with reactionary politics, paternalism in labor relations, and opposition to the growth of science. Fortunately the choice did not present itself in just those terms to class-conscious workers of the forties and fifties. It was not necessary to be converted to Christian Socialism in order to be moved by the description of sweatshops in *Alton Locke,* nor did one endorse Young England because one shuddered at the portrayal of the mines in *Sybil.* Mr. Greg, as we have seen, rightly felt that the harmlessness of Mrs. Gaskell's remedies did not offset the disturbing effects of reading *Mary Barton.* The many Socialists who attributed their Socialism to their reading of Carlyle were thinking of his attacks on laissez-faire, not of his doctrine

[1] Carlyle, says Louis Cazamian, "denies and destroys the whole effort of the modern mind: in his glorification of the unconscious he seizes at one move upon all the formulae and programmes of reaction, political, religious or purely mystical. . . . All his life . . . he will denounce as a danger and as a disease every conquest that clear thinking and clear consciousness have made over the activities which are instinctive, and as such subject to the blind but infallible orders of life itself." *Carlyle,* 98–9.

of hero-worship. It is an unreal dilemma we create when we assume that the ideas of the interventionists had to be accepted in their totality. The truth in their pictures of industrialism—and it was a truth that the mass of people, who do not read Parliamentary Blue Books, found only in their works—was more important than their theories.

Yet there was a paradox, and it was effectively dramatized in the sixties. In October, 1865, there was a revolt of the distressed Negroes of Jamaica, and the governor of the island suppressed it by killing more than four hundred persons and cruelly flogging six hundred others. He was recalled by the Liberal government, but was in large measure vindicated by a Parliamentary inquiry. Thereupon a committee was formed to bring Governor Eyre to trial for murder. John Stuart Mill became its chairman, and P. A. Taylor, Goldwin Smith, Frederic Harrison, and other Radicals were among the members. John Bright, leader of the Manchester School, supported Mill, and so did Thomas Henry Huxley, Sir Charles Lyell, and other scientists.

The landowners, the Church of England clergy, and other Tories—the groups that had upheld the Confederacy during the American Civil War—formed an Eyre Defense Committee. Carlyle, Ruskin, Tennyson, and Kingsley joined the committee, and Dickens was counted among its supporters. Carlyle, indeed, became one of the principal spokesmen for the group, belaboring "the rabid Nigger-Philanthropists" for trying to conceal the failures of Mammonism by taking up the cause of the Negro in the United States and the colonies. Tennyson paid tribute to Eyre's nobility, and Kingsley held that he was being "hunted to death by fanatics." The *Pall Mall Gazette* wrote: "It would be curious also to know how far Sir Charles Lyell's and Mr. Huxley's peculiar views on the development of species have influenced them in bestowing on the negro that sympathetic recognition which they are willing to extend even to the ape as 'a man and a brother.'"

It seems difficult to believe that justice was not wholly on the side of Mill and his Jamaica Committee. Yet, especially when the Manchester Liberals on that committee are considered, there was some basis for Carlyle's charges, and he could plausibly assert that even Mill himself had done little enough to alleviate the sufferings of the working class in England. Moreover, in the statements of the members of the committee there is far more concern for abstract justice and legal correctness than for the miseries of the inhabitants of Jamaica, and, even if one makes full allowance for the tactical necessity of limiting the issue to considerations of law and propriety, it is impossible to find evidence of a strong and imaginative sympathy with the lot of the oppressed. It was wise, perhaps, to disapprove of the leaders of the revolt, but one feels that the disapproval was all too genuine and that the committee could no more understand than it could approve.

No one can blame the British workingman if he refused to commit himself to either the Benthamite or the Coleridgean tradition. In the thirties and forties, after his disillusionment with the first reform bill, he tried, as we have seen, to establish a position of his own, and in this period he was bitterly opposed to laissez-faire economics and not unwilling to accept support from the interventionists. In the fifties, when free trade was bringing prosperity, he made a practical compromise that brought him into a loose political alliance with the industrial middle class, and if at the same time there was often economic warfare between the workers and the industrialists, there was no suggestion of revolution in the workers' demands. The compromise was, however, purely practical, a truce and not a solution.

Meanwhile, though few workers and even fewer individuals in other classes knew it, the intellectual needs and the material demands of the working class had at last been systematically formulated. Moreover, the paradox involved in the conflict between Benthamites and Coleridgeans had been solved. In 1867, while the Eyre case was still being fought in the courts and the press, and while Disraeli's government was adopting the second reform bill, Karl Marx, who had been living for almost twenty years in London, published the first volume of *Capital*. The basic principles of that study had been enunciated in the *Communist Manifesto* in 1848, and in a variety of articles and books that had appeared thereafter. Though Marx knew personally some of the leaders of the British labor movement, and had won their support for the First International, his theoretical studies were not to be appreciated in England for at least a score of years. Nevertheless, it is worth observing that, while British labor engaged in its practical and purely temporary compromises, Marx was making a definitive statement of the relations between labor and capital.

Marx did not shrink, as the Coleridgeans did, from the scientific methods and the materialist implications of Benthamism; on the contrary, his method was even more rigorously scientific and his materialism avowed. Instead of denouncing Adam Smith and Ricardo as hard-hearted monsters, he pointed out the class basis of their theories, and at the same time seized upon whatever was sound in their studies. He saw, as the Coleridgeans did not, that much in laissez-faire economics was true, but only for capitalism, and capitalism, he knew, was not eternal. His awareness of its transitory nature came from his understanding of history, and this he owed to the German philosophers who had given Coleridge and Carlyle their insight into historical processes. But the idealist dialectic, which had encouraged mysticism in Coleridge and Carlyle, was transformed by Marx into historical materialism. Marx not only reconciled the scientific method of the laissez-faire economists with the humanitarian impulses of the interventionists; he also reconciled what was sound in eighteenth century materialism with what was sound in Hegelianism. By shifting his basis, so to speak, from the upper classes to the working class, he solved the conflicts that divided British thought throughout the greater part of the nineteenth century. It would be some time, however, before there would be English writers willing to follow him.

4. The Decline of Evangelicalism.

The two decades after the passing of the first reform bill were, thanks to Chartism, turbulent ones. The years from 1848 to 1887, on the other hand, may be regarded as a period of calm and integration.[1] Class warfare had almost ceased, even if the causes of class conflict had not been eliminated. The idea of progress had seized many minds, and it was easy to believe that such evils as persisted would be destroyed by the onward march of history. In the fifties there was less questioning, less open questioning at least, of orthodox Christianity than there had been half a century earlier. One code of morality was accepted, and to a considerable extent practiced, by aristocrats, bourgeois, and workers. The two-party system operated smoothly, with no serious setback to industrial progress whether Liberals or Conservatives were in office. The Queen, without threatening Parliamentary supremacy, was an increasingly useful symbol of national solidarity. Despite wars in the Crimea, Persia, India, and

---

[1] "Victorian civilization is something more than a mere struggle. It is a brief, but real, moment of social equilibrium, comparable in a way to the Augustan age of Pope and Walpole." Crane Brinton, *English Political Thought in the Nineteenth Century*, 87.

China, the Liberal conception of a peace good for trade seemed likely enough of general acceptance. If the middle-class spokesmen were unpleasantly complacent, no one could contradict their boast that Britain's material progress was spectacular and unprecedented. And they could boast of other kinds of progress as well. Cambridge and Oxford were made less exclusive by the abolition of religious tests. New universities were founded in Manchester, Birmingham, and other industrial cities. Colleges were founded for women, and the various institutes for working-class adult education grew in size. In 1870, after a long campaign, an elementary education act was passed that led to the founding of tax-supported schools and to compulsory school attendance. British literature flourished; British scientists were leading the world; even British art and architecture were healthier than they had been for decades.

The most representative writer of the period was probably Anthony Trollope. "The object of a novel," he said flatly, "should be to instruct in morals while it amuses." "The bulk of the young people in the upper and middle classes receive their moral teaching chiefly from the novels they read. . . . Shall he, then, to whom this close fellowship is allowed—this inner confidence—shall he not be careful what words he uses, and what thoughts he expresses, when he sits in council with his young friend?" His own aim was to impregnate "the mind of the novel-reader with a feeling that honesty is the best policy; that truth prevails while falsehood fails; that a girl will be loved as she is pure, and sweet, and unselfish; that a man will be honored as he is true, and honest, and brave of heart; that things meanly done are ugly and odious, and things nobly done are beautiful and gracious."

Trollope was close to the middle-class norm in other ways. Thackeray satirized the upper classes; Trollope not only refused to follow his example but in this respect ventured to rebuke his master. The point of *Yellowplush Papers,* he wrote, "seems to be that a gentleman may, in heart and action, be as vulgar as a footman. No doubt he may, but the chances are very much that he won't." Trollope opposed the application of civil service examinations to his own department, the post office, on the ground that "there are places in life which can hardly be well filled except by 'Gentlemen.'" He was the son of an impoverished barrister, it may be recalled, and had suffered at Harrow and Winchester because he was scorned and persecuted by those of better birth and more money. The highest moment in the *Autobiography* is when he says, "I became known there almost as well as though I had been an Essex squire, to the manner born."

Yet Trollope, for all his admiration for the gentry and his concern with class distinctions, did not believe that England had been corrupted by its commercial prosperity. "We do not put very much faith in Mr. Carlyle," he said, "nor in Mr. Ruskin and his other followers. The loudness and extravagance of their lamentations, the wailing and gnashing of teeth which comes from them, over a world which is supposed to have gone altogether shoddy-wards, are so contrary to the convictions of men who cannot but see how comfort has been increased, how health has been improved, and education extended—that the general effect of their teaching is the opposite of what they have intended." All that he objected to in business was the meanness and corruption of some business men, and he wrote a satire, *The Way We Live Now,* to keep the example of successful dishonesty from leading youth astray.

In politics he called himself "an advanced Conservative-Liberal," one who believed there should be "a tendency towards democracy," but not too rapid a tendency. He believed that "to sit in the British Parliament should be the highest object of ambition to every educated Englishman," and he offered himself as a candidate in 1868. He was unsuccessful, and his ambitions thus checked, he used his novels for "the expression of my political or social convictions." But the reader of *Phineas Finn, Phineas Redux, The Prime Minister,* and *The Duke's Children* will look in vain for sharp analyses of contemporary issues. These are political novels only in the sense that they deal with persons who are or would like to be in office. Superb as Trollope was in his own sober-sided way, an understanding of what was really happening to British life was not one of his virtues. As so often happens, his books were better than his theories, but his deepest insights were not likely to diminish Victorian complacency.

Coventry Patmore's *The Angel in the House* was perhaps a more perfect rendering of the evangelical spirit than anything of Trollope's, but Patmore himself, with his subsequent conversion to Catholicism and his ferocious Toryism, was less representative. Other and greater authors, if they were less completely evangelical, by no means escaped from pious moral influences. If, for instance, Carlyle hated the ruthless struggle for success, which evangelicalism as well as utilitarianism encouraged, his gospel of work was purely evangelical and helped to strengthen the tradition. All the novelists were preachers, and their sermons were more often evangelical than not. Tennyson—laureate of the British people in more than name—hid his minor heresies in the language of poetry, just as he concealed his contempt for the masses in a vague lip-service to democracy. Individualism, piety, patriotism, faith in progress, and blindness to disturbing facts—these qualities of the Victorian synthesis were all in Tennyson, and they made him the idol of his age. Contriving to be a disciple of Carlyle without offend-

ing the utilitarians, and to pay his respects to science without distressing the evangelicals, he symbolized the vast but
temporarily satisfying confusion of Victorianism.

In 1851, when the Prince Consort held the Great Exhibition and Tennyson assumed the laureateship, piety, morality,
and prudery—in a word, evangelicalism—seemed terribly
victorious. But only eight years later Darwin published *The
Origin of Species,* and the foundations began to crumble. If
the struggle for success under capitalism had called forth
the evangelical type of character, the rise of capitalism had
also liberated other forces. From the time of the renaissance,
commerce, requiring a science of navigation, had given an
impetus to mathematics and astronomy. The growth of industrialism at the end of the eighteenth century turned attention to chemistry and physics. Developments in agriculture, as well as the progress of medicine and the growth of
the other sciences, stimulated biology. Thus business and
government helped to put the sciences to work. It is symbolic, even if not very significant, that the voyage of the
Beagle was one of many expeditions that the British government undertook in the interests of commerce.

The theory of evolution in itself strengthened the hand
of the advocates of laissez-faire, for it permitted them to
argue, as Spencer did, that "the starvation of the idle" and
"the shoulderings aside of the weak by the strong" are "the
decrees of a large, far-seeing benevolence." Spencer said:
"Blind to the fact that under the natural order of things
society is constantly excreting its unhealthy, imbecile, slow,
vacillating, faithless members, these unthinking, though well-
meaning men advocate an interference which not only stops
the purifying process but even increases the vitiation."

But at the same time Darwinism threatened the religious
views that served to cement the Victorian compromise and
to consolidate the power of the middle class, especially its

power over cultural life. After the furious controversy over Genesis had died down, there were many men of letters, and men of science too, to argue that evolution and religion could be reconciled, and so, on one level or another, no doubt they could, at least to the satisfaction of many believers. But the number of atheists, agnostics, and skeptics had greatly increased, and the unbelievers had become bolder and more articulate. More important, perhaps, orthodoxy was losing its hold on great numbers of those who continued to go to church. The fierce piety of the evangelicals and the Puritan non-conformists did not disappear, but it lost influence as the broad theory of evolution became more and more firmly established. Resistance to scholarly analysis of the Bible and logical analysis of theological dogmas was weakened, and the pious were put in the position of having to defend what it had once been enough for them to assert.

The destruction of the theological bases of evangelicalism contributed to the undermining of the whole Victorian concept of life, but that was a long process, and the attack was made on many fronts. Matthew Arnold, for example, constituted himself the chief critic of the phenomenon Ruskin had already denounced, middle-class vulgarity. He did not clamor, as Carlyle and Ruskin had, for political and social reform, for he belonged to the later Victorian age, when the hope of such change seemed slight. Indeed, he convinced himself that action was wrong. "What," he asked, "if rough and coarse action, ill-calculated action, action without sufficient light, is, and has for a long time been our bane? What if our urgent want now is, not to act at any price, but rather to lay in a stock of light for our difficulties?" Thus armed with his theory of disinterestedness, protected in this way from the reprisals of the men he attacked, Arnold advanced to the battle.

If he was making a virtue of necessity, at least it was a virtue he made, for he managed to say a certain number of shrewd and valuable things about contemporary England. His attack ranged from top to bottom. The aristocracy, he repeatedly said, had sweetness but not light: "One has so often wondered whether upon the whole earth there is anything so unintelligent, so unapt to perceive how the world is really going, as an ordinary young Englishman of our upper class." He knew that "our aristocracy, from the action upon it of the Wars of the Roses, the Tudors, and the political necessities of George the Third, is for the imagination a singularly modern and uninteresting one," and he knew that it was incapable of counteracting the rise of Philistinism.

It was with the middle class that he chiefly concerned himself, for he saw that it was the class with power: "The Barbarians administer, the Philistines govern. . . . One class contributes its want of ideas, the other its want of dignity." An anthology of middle-class complacency could be compiled from Arnold's essays. He quotes the utilitarian leader, John Roebuck, who, speaking of the condition of England, said, "I ask you whether, the world over or in past history, there is anything like it? Nothing. I pray that our unrivalled happiness may last." He quotes another utilitarian, Robert Lowe, who, opposing the extension of the franchise, maintained that perfection had been reached by the middle-class Parliaments following the reform bill of 1832. "With all this continued peace, contentment, happiness, and prosperity,— England in its present state of development and civilization, —the mighty fabric of English prosperity,—what," Mr. Lowe asked, "can we want more?" On the subject of middle-class education he quotes Mr. Bazley, who "did not think that class need excite the sympathy either of the legislature or the public," and Mr. Miall, who protested against the idea that the class "which has astonished the world by its energy, enterprise, and self-reliance, which is continually striking out new paths of industry and subduing the forces of nature, cannot, from some mysterious reason, get their children properly educated," and the *Daily News,* which said, "All the world knows that the great middle class of this country supplies the mind, the will, and the power for all the great and good things that have to be done, and it is not likely that that class should surrender its powers and privileges in the one case of training its own children."

Arnold's words strike one as a trenchant and not too smugly disinterested account of Victorian civilization. If there is something a little waspish in his tone, something rather petty in his distress over such measures as the legalization of marriage with a deceased wife's sister, who can wonder? Even though he was not made to feel so desperately futile as Ruskin, he can scarcely have flattered himself that his words had great effect. He did provoke the Philistines, for they were, contrary to general impression, a thin-skinned lot, and replied with considerable acerbity to his attacks, but he could not change their ways. His talk about culture and the search for perfection and the best that has been thought and said and sweetness and light brought only jeers. He asked for three specific measures: "a reduction of those immense inequalities of condition and property amongst us, of which our land-system is the base; a genuine municipal system; and public schools for the middle classes." They were reasonable measures, too reasonable if anything, and would be adopted in some degree before many years had passed, but Arnold's arguments for them were received with ridicule.

No one can be surprised that, towards the end of his life, Arnold began to despair of the upper and middle classes. He had always been as sharply critical of the working class as of any other. In *Culture and Anarchy,* when he passed all the classes in review, he had not only, as was to be expected, deplored the workers' lack of education, but also attacked their leaders. They were led by agitators like Edmond Beales, or enemies of culture like Frederic Harrison, or bitter fanatics like Charles Bradlaugh, or middle-class Philistines like John Bright. Arnold was particularly conscious of the process of Philistinization that was going on in the upper levels of the working class. Bright, for example, "leads his disciples to believe—what the Englishman is always too ready to believe—that the having a vote, like the having a large family, or a large business, or large muscles, has in itself some edifying and perfecting effect upon human nature." He flattered the workers as Roebuck and Lowe flattered the middle class —"only the middle classes are told they have done it all with their energy, self-reliance, and capital, and the democracy are told they have done it all with their hands and sinews."

Yet at the end of the seventies, speaking to the Ipswich Working Men's College, Arnold turned, as he said, to the Gentiles—to the working class. He urged them to labor for what he called middle-class education, for a national system, that is, of secondary schools. "For twenty years," he said, "I have been vainly urging this upon the middle classes themselves. Now I urge it upon you. Comprehend, that middle-class education is a great democratic reform, of the truest, surest, safest kind." As he proceeded, he compared middle-class education with Christianity. The apostles found the Jewish community "narrow, rigid, sectarian, unintelligent, of impracticable temper," and they turned to the Gentile world, "a world with a thousand faults, no doubt, but with openness and flexibility of mind, new and elastic, full of possibilities." So he turned from "our Judaic and unelastic middle class" to the workers, and asked them to adopt the cause: "Do you, then, carry it forward yourselves, and insist on taking the middle class with you."

No one could be foolish enough to assume that Arnold had gone or ever would go far in the direction of the working class. He had neither any great sympathy with the workers nor any understanding of the economic changes that would give them more and more importance. Unless we can accept whole-heartedly his conception of culture, we are likely to feel that his ideal for them was as narrow as John Bright's, and his notion of their rising immediately above class interests was as romantic as the speeches of George Eliot's Felix Holt. Yet it is interesting to observe that, just as Carlyle and his disciples thought that the working class might be the force by which their particular ends could be accomplished, so Arnold, with his much more abstract and intellectual program, came to hope that even a brutalized working class might do what a vulgarized middle class would not do.

Victorianism had reached a stage at which almost any kind of criticism was likely to prove subversive. In 1859, the year that Darwin published *The Origin of Species,* young George Meredith brought out *The Ordeal of Richard Feverel,* as moral a novel, if one regards the teaching of sexual fidelity as moral, as could be desired. But good Victorians demanded more than that. The passion that spoke in the Ferdinand-Miranda scene, though pure enough, was scarcely docile; there was a power felt in the relations of this boy and girl that Victorians had agreed to ignore. Sir Austen's reflections on the subject of wild oats taught an admirable lesson, but they opened, just a crack, a door that was sacred to the skeleton inside. Mrs. Berry, advocate of monogamy that she was, approached the subject of sex in the spirit of common sense, not in the spirit of breathless concealment.

But objections could not be confined to particular chapters; the tone of the whole book was subversive. Mr. Meredith seemed to be saying that sexual passion was powerful and natural and even, in itself, good. It made no difference that he regarded it as good only under certain conditions and that his conception of those conditions corresponded closely to conventional views on monogamous marriage; anyone could see that he had made a serious admission. If the difference between lust and love was only a matter of degree, of very subtle and debatable intentions and spiritual attitudes, then the way was open to antinomianism. The *Spectator* criticized the book for its "low ethical tone" and "immoral tendency." Meredith was told by correspondents that it was "dangerous and wicked and damnable." Clergymen undertook a campaign against it, so successful that Mudie's library refused to circulate the three hundred copies it had bought.

Swinburne's *Poems and Ballads,* which appeared seven years later, was even more shocking. Readers were particularly disturbed by the poet's anatomical frankness, his references to "quivering flanks," "splendid supple thighs," "white arms and bosom," "scourged white breast," to "ravenous teeth," "blushes of amorous blows," and "bruised lips." But on second thought they were more alarmed by the author's strangely ambiguous attitude towards passion. The Victorians recognized two categories: love and lust. Lust was sinful and was punished in hell, but it was reported to have its pleasant aspects. Swinburne described lust with licentious frankness, but, instead of calling attention to its joys, as surely a son of Belial could be expected to do, he associated it with pain and satiety and death. And, though this might seem to point a useful moral, its actual effect was to make passion so complex that Victorian standards were proved inadequate. Indignation rolled across the British

Isles. One of the more moderate critics, John Morley, called Swinburne "an unclean fiery imp from the pit" and "the libidinous laureate of a pack of satyrs."

Both Meredith and Swinburne felt the power of enraged Victorianism. Meredith resolved to be more careful, when *Modern Love* had met with the same abuse as *Richard Feverel,* and thereafter his attacks were so subtle that the middle class was undisturbed by them. In private he was bitter against all prudishness, but he was resolved that his works would "never again offend young maids." In private he denounced the clergy as "sappers of our strength," but he recognized that, as he wrote Captain Maxse, the parsons were "interwound with the whole of the Middle Class like the poisonous ivy" and had "a terrific power." Politically he leaned towards Radicalism, but he contented himself with oblique gibes at the wealthy in *Harry Richmond* and *Beauchamp's Career,* and in *The Tragic Comedians* he subordinated Lassalle's political career to his passion for Helene von Donniges.

To justify his reticence, he had his idea of comedy, just as Arnold had his disinterestedness. Up to a certain point the idea of comedy enabled him to do his work without too much damage to his conscience, but the result of his concern with "the narrow enclosure of men's intellects" was to drive him in upon himself.[1] His mannerisms became more and more marked, his allusions more and more delicate, his analyses of character more and more refined, his develop-

---

[1] "The notion that such men as Meredith are wilfully, mischievously obscure is an impertinence. They have much to express, and, left with themselves for an audience, the plain thing seems hardly worth saying, for it is known already. But let Meredith the talker start a bright idea, Meredith the listener will start him refining it, and refining again, twisting it this way and that till it is running exhausted in a circle—a vicious circle—and, expressed at last, may drop dead. This is the danger run by all men of teeming minds, driven in on themselves by neglect." H. Granville-Barker, "Tennyson, Meredith, Swinburne," in *The Eighteen-Seventies,* 193–4.

ment of scenes more and more dependent on suggestion. In the early work there is a fertility of thought, a liveliness of interest, and a generosity of feeling no more common in our times than in his. Here, one feels, is a man who has a love of life, a wondering sense of its potentialities, and therefore a relentless opposition to whatever would limit human possibilities on any level. These qualities flash out in the later work; one recognizes them in the midst of the most intricate paragraphs in *The Egoist, Diana of the Crossways,* and *The Tragic Comedians;* but only the patient and sympathetic reader could discover them, and Meredith never had many readers of any kind.

Reticence was not characteristic of Swinburne. When he turned from defiance of the current moral code to defiance of prevailing political opinion, he spoke with the same belligerence. A bellicose republican at the age of twenty, with Mazzini for his god and Napoleon III for his devil, he put his political convictions into "A Song in Time of Order" and "A Song in Time of Revolution." But it was not until 1867, the year after *Poems and Ballads* appeared, that he became the avowed bard and prophet of worldwide republicanism. His adoption of this role was brought about by a conspiracy of friends who, in order to check the dissipation of his energy, sought for him a cause on which his enthusiasm could be concentrated. Introduced to Mazzini by the conspirators, the poet kissed the liberator's hand, read him the thousand lines of "A Song for Italy," and swore eternal loyalty to his cause.

The result was, as Swinburne's friends had hoped, the pouring forth of the poems about Italy, the songs of world revolution, and the hymns to liberty that, together with earlier verses of the same character, were published in 1871 in the volume *Songs Before Sunrise.* The revolutionary intentions of the collection were clear enough, but its message was more difficult to decipher. Even if the reader resolutely set himself to discover what Swinburne was talking about, resisting the hypnotic effect of the meter, the rhymes, and the alliteration, he was likely to be bewildered. It was not merely that, as in the earlier poems, Swinburne so often let himself go where the flow of words led him; the clearest statements were curiously unrelated to anything the informed observer was likely to find in contemporary Europe. It was apparent that Swinburne opposed priests and kings, admired Mazzini, Victor Hugo, and Shelley, hated Napoleon III, thought Milton would disapprove of nineteenth century England, and wanted a republic. But somehow it seemed that more concrete and pertinent hopes, fears, and hatreds were necessary to justify the torrents of emotion.

Some critics had suggested that the love poems, for all their voluptuousness, did not bear any evident relation to experience. The same comment was invited by *Songs Before Sunrise*. Yet it would be wrong to say that the poems are empty and merely derivative. However inadequately Swinburne may have visualized the practical implications of the liberty he believed in, he did believe in it, and liberty as an immediate value for him was something that he could understand and could sing. "Hymn of Man" is moving with its hatred of ecclesiastical tyranny and its faith in human capacities, "Perinde ac Cadaver" with its contempt for the middle class, "Hertha" with its consistent pantheism, "Tenebrae" with its humanitarian feeling, "A Year's Burden" with its sober, responsible facing of difficulties and dangers. Here was a Swinburne who offered more than mere intoxication, a Swinburne to whose brave music the England that looked towards the future might march.

Unfortunately the clearer trumpet tones were often obscured by loud and meaningless tumult, and in a little while they were stilled. At the moment when Swinburne was celebrating human brotherhood, his own idiosyncrasies were isolating him from the already narrow society that he knew. There was only a suggestion of revolutionary spirit in the second series of *Poems and Ballads,* published in 1878, and it was clear that his zeal had cooled. The brevity of love became his theme, and this merged with a more general melancholy. Memorial and elegiac poems give the volume its tone, and the best of these, such as "Ave atque Vale," are in praise of death.

With the thirty years' epilogue to Swinburne's poetic life we are not concerned. Nothing that he wrote during his three decades at Number 2 The Pines with Theodore Watts-Dunton can be regarded as entering into the main literary stream. The collapse of his revolutionary impulses is, however, worth commenting on. In the nineties he wrote several poems, including "The Union," "The Commonweal," and "The Question," against home rule, attacking the Irish with the virulence he had once reserved for oppressors, and at the end of the decade, in "The Transvaal," "Reverse," "The Turning of the Tide," and other poems, he defended England's war against the Boers. This complete repudiation of his past [1] has been regarded as evidence of Watts-Dunton's influence over him, but it is easy to see that the decline had begun before he went to The Pines.

---

[1] Edmund Gosse does not consider it such. Speaking of "the fine sonnet which closes with the words, 'Strike, England, and strike home,' " and of the other Boer War poems, "all inspired by the noblest and purest indignation, and by a burning pride in our country," Mr. Gosse says, "He went far in his attitude of complacency with what might even be called British prejudice, but he did not admit, and we need not perceive, any inconsistency between this 'Jingo' patriotism and the ardors of his youthful republicanism. He would have said that what he desired was liberty for nations that are still captive, and not the disturbance of those that are already free." In defense of this amazing statement, Mr. Gosse goes so far as to misinterpret "Perinde ac Cadaver," quoting as serious lines that Swinburne obviously intended to be ironic. It may be observed that Mr. Gosse's book was published in 1917, and that he tells with pride "how accurately Swinburne predicted the treachery of Germany almost with his latest breath." *Life of Algernon Charles Swinburne,* 291–4.

Pessimism dominated the closing decades of the Victorian era. The official belief in progress continued to hold the majority of the middle class, but not the poets. Tennyson had his moments of gloom; Arnold deplored his life in an age of uncertainties; Arthur Hugh Clough tremulously tried to be brave in a world that did not seem made for the tender-minded. They attributed their gloom to religious doubts, but some at least of its causes were purely secular. Arnold's sense of the irresistibility of middle-class vulgarity we have already seen, and that Clough shared his friend's convictions is suggested by some of the satirical lines in *Dipsychus* and by such verses as "In the Metropolis" and "The Latest Decalogue."

While Tennyson, Arnold, and Clough lamented the passing of Christianity, other authors, such as Swinburne, welcomed the rise of paganism. But they were just as pessimistic. Fitzgerald's immensely popular translation of the *Rubaiyat* offered a subdued version of the new hedonism. Rossetti's paganism was of the most somber kind. Even Robert Louis Stevenson, romanticist that he was and advocate of the strenuous life, could only advise his readers to make the most of the brief time that was given them.

The younger artists and writers began to maintain that only the pleasures of art could provide proper solace for the inadequacies of life. Sometimes the pessimism was emphasized, sometimes the estheticism, but always it was insisted that life was brief and inherently unsatisfactory and nothing but the experience of the moment, as intensified by art or as lived in the artistic spirit, was good. The definitive statement of this philosophy, so far as its adherents were concerned, could be found in the famous passage at the end of Walter Pater's *Studies in the History of the Renaissance,* published in 1873. Life is a constant process of change, and we are all under sentence of death. Only so many pulses of life have been granted us, and the only way to use them fruitfully is to see that each provides us with the most intense, most ecstatic experience that is possible. And it is art that gives the highest quality to our moments as they pass.

Pater's view is pessimistic certainly, and some persons might draw from his premises the bleakest kind of conclusions, but his disciples often used the pessimism to shock the bourgeois and emphasized for themselves the pleasures of burning with a hard, gem-like flame. To James Thomson such an attitude seemed a cowardly ignoring of patent facts. In the middle of the century, when he was in his twenties, Thomson met Charles Bradlaugh, a belligerent atheist, the cause of a major Parliamentary scandal, a devout believer in laissez-faire, and a kind friend. Bradlaugh converted Thomson to atheism. The view of a universe indifferent to man's welfare was confirmed by Thomson's experience, and he found nothing in human society to attenuate his gloom. The despair of "The City of Dreadful Night" was bred by personal misfortune, observation of social evils, and the starkest possible interpretation of materialistic science. In 1874, while Tennyson was still working on *The Idylls of the King,* Thomson wrote:

> As if a Being, God or Fiend, could reign,
> At once so wicked, foolish, and insane,
> As to produce men when He might refrain.
>
> The world rolls round, for ever like a mill;
> It grinds out death and life and good and ill;
> It has no purpose, heart or mind or will.
>
> While air of Space and Time's full river flow,
> The mill must blindly whirl unresting so;
> It may be wearing out, but who can know?

Man might know one thing were his sight less dim;
That it whirls not to suit his petty whim,
That it is quite indifferent to him.

Nay, does it treat him harshly as he saith?
It grinds him some slow years of bitter breath,
Then grinds him back into eternal death.

Here, for the first time, we confront the kind of pessimism of which Thomas Hardy, six years Thomson's junior, was already becoming the most famous spokesman. Evangelicalism had lost its hold on literature. It was still the doctrine of the middle class, but the majority of authors neither accepted its tenets nor submitted without protest to its tabus, and they had their supporters. There were still many battles to be fought, but emancipation, for whatever it might be worth, was now possible.

5. *The Scene Changes.*

There is more to be said about the writers of the nineteenth century than has been said here. We do not read Shelley because he was a radical or Wordsworth and Coleridge because they became reactionaries. *The Friend* is interesting, but not to be compared with *The Ancient Mariner* or *Christabel*. Carlyle, Ruskin, and Arnold were essentially prophets, writers who lived to express their opinions, and yet our judgment of them is in some measure independent of our estimate of the rightness or wrongness of their theories. Tennyson we value for sharp perceptions and technical skill, not for the orthodoxy that delighted his sovereign. Few of their admirers care what Dickens and Thackeray taught, and the stuffy Mr. Trollope gives pleasure in spite of his stuffiness.

The bulk of memorable work written in the Victorian period is astonishing. Once certain critics found it necessary to attack everything Victorian in order to clear the way for change, but today few deny the greatness of Tennyson, Carlyle, Browning, Ruskin, Arnold, Dickens, and Thackeray. And they were public figures as virtually none of their predecessors had been. Scott was probably the first British man of letters to achieve through his writing a prominence in the public mind comparable to the prominence of a prime minister or a victorious general. Carlyle, Tennyson, and Dickens reached the same eminence, for there was a new reading public, a ravenous reading public, and it was generous to its favorites. Zola once contrasted the prestige of Balzac with the limited influence of Malherbe and La Fontaine. One wonders how many Englishmen in the year 1700 had heard of Dryden, and how many in the year 1860 had not heard of Tennyson and Dickens.

Talented young men growing up in the fifties, sixties, and seventies could not escape the influence of such dominating figures, but we cannot assume that they were chiefly concerned with their opinions, any more than we are today. They argued, no doubt, about Dickens' proposals for reform, but they were more impressed by the picture of British life he so magnificently unfolded. They agreed or quarreled, as the case might be, with what the age called Tennyson's sentiments, but they responded to the melody and imagery. They may have deplored the Carlyle of *Latter-day Pamphlets* but been stirred by the Carlyle of *Sartor Resartus,* roused by the Ruskin of *Modern Painters* but bored by the Ruskin of *Fors Clavigera,* guided by Arnold's appreciations though irritated by his scoldings. The Brontës may have meant more to them than Dickens, and Meredith more than Trollope. They may have preferred Clough or Patmore or Christina Rossetti to Browning or Tennyson. In any case they must have felt that the Victorians had broadened the novel, created a forceful kind of social criticism, and given to romantic poetry new forms and a wholly new breadth of appeal.

That the younger writers were interested in more than the ideas of their predecessors would be too obvious to be worth saying if we had not been so exclusively occupied with particular opinions of particular authors. And we must return to those opinions. The social phenomena of the nineteenth century still are part of our lives. As capitalism flowered in the extraordinary growth of industrialism, a new class consolidated the political power it had been slowly gaining and established itself as the ruler of the nation. In the course of its rise it had given birth to or had accepted sets of ideas adapted to the process of its growth—ideas loosely organized in utilitarianism and evangelicalism. Those ideas became part of the intellectual world of the Victorian authors, and how they approached the ideas, whether they accepted or rejected or modified them, is a matter of some importance.

The whole question had a particular relevance in the latter part of the century because the course of capitalism was changing. In 1874 there was a decline in trade, followed by the cutting of wages and a series of strikes, including the first strike of the newly organized agricultural workers. By 1878 industry had revived, but agriculture had not, and there was renewed talk about protective tariffs. This was laughed down by those who pointed out that England was still the workshop of the world, but when 1883 brought another depression, self-confidence was shaken. Although Britain still led the world, and the value of its foreign trade was still mounting, Germany, France, and the United States were increasing their exports more rapidly. Not only did Engels say that England had been "in a chronic state of stagnation" since 1876; the president of the economic section of the British Association admitted that "the days of great trade profits were over," and announced that the country was entering "the non-progressive state." Unemployment grew steadily from 1883 to 1886, and began to be talked of as a problem.[1] In the year of Victoria's jubilee there were unemployment demonstrations and battles for freedom of speech.

A few observers were beginning to say that capitalism was breaking down. To most Victorian Englishmen, who believed that capitalism had been ordained by God and had existed from a period shortly after the expulsion of Adam and Eve from the Garden of Eden, this was unthinkable, but they could not deny that the economic laws revealed by Adam Smith and his disciples were operating less inexorably and certainly less advantageously, so far as England was concerned, than had been promised. No one could understand the seventies and eighties unless he could stand a little distance outside the capitalist system and look at it with a measure of objectivity.

The later Victorian writers naturally formed their views of capitalism out of knowledge of various kinds, but the opinions of their predecessors had an important influence. The Victorian authors, as we know, had not accepted uncritically either the capitalist system or the sets of ideas that developed with it, and the later writers, therefore, were neither misled nor forced into extravagant revolt. But the Victorians had not understood the nature of capitalism. Even their dismay at the sufferings it caused dwindled with the decline of Chartism, and they turned their attention to what was happening in the middle class. It was useful to

---

[1] "It is symptomatic that the word 'unemployed' used as a noun is first recorded by the Oxford English Dictionary from the year 1882; the word 'unemployment' from the year 1888." Ensor, *England, 1870–1914*, 112.

have such constant and shrewd criticism of Victorian vulgarity, but there was a danger in isolating this from other consequences of the rise of capitalist industry, as the vogue of estheticism at the end of the century showed. Sharper insights were necessary to prepare men to understand the changes that were beginning to take place.

What the writers of the eighties and nineties chiefly felt was the absence of certainties. The Victorians had either regarded capitalism as a boon or been sure that they knew what was wrong with it. Their successors saw that capitalism had grown fabulously and yet was periodically reduced to impotence. A few writers found in the depression of the seventies and eighties evidence of the ultimate collapse of the system of private ownership, and some began to think of superseding it. Others pointed to the Empire as a source of permanent prosperity. Most were simply bewildered by the sudden changes from wealth to poverty. Just as they were eloquently preaching the evils of prosperity, prosperity vanished, and they could not be any better pleased with what took its place.

The decline of evangelicalism touched many writers even more closely. Some were overwhelmed by the implications of the scientific view of the universe, while others welcomed the triumph of rationalism over superstition. But every one of them had to go to work and create his own philosophy of life. Furthermore, since he could not automatically accept evangelical morality, he had to devise his own code of ethics. Nothing seemed permanent. There was no assurance that God was in his heaven, and a great deal was wrong with the world. Neither the doctrine of laissez-faire nor Ruskin's criticism of it seemed pertinent. Swinburne's revolt came to as little as Trollope's conventionality. Darwin appeared to be right, but to what conclusions did Darwinism point? Questions were easy, answers hard.

Fortunate is the artist whose age permits him to concentrate. If he must be philosopher, sociologist, economist, and warrior, then he must, but he need not be envied his tasks. The passing of the Victorian certainties was necessary and desirable, but perhaps the generation that saw them slip away deserves our sympathy.

Chapter II

SOCIALISM AND WILLIAM MORRIS

WHEN, in 1874 and again in 1883, depression paralyzed British industry, criticism of laissez-faire began to take on a new character. Though Karl Marx had been living in England for many years, he was personally known only to a handful of Englishmen, and his writings were scarcely familiar to that handful. In 1873, however, *Das Kapital* was translated into French, and thus became available to a certain number of British intellectuals. Henry Mayers Hyndman was one of its readers, and in 1881, in a book called *England for All,* he produced a kind of summary of Marx's work, though the "great thinker and original writer" to whom he expressed his gratitude remained anonymous. In the same year Engels wrote a series of articles for the *Labour Standard,* and both the *Contemporary Review* and *Modern Thought* published essays on Marx.

There was, then, a good chance that Marxism might come to have an influence on British men of letters, but it would have seemed rash to predict that it would capture as disciple a highly esteemed poet who had written a series of verse romances on ancient and medieval themes. In retrospect William Morris' progress towards Socialism is not too difficult to trace, but it still seems remarkable that he followed Marx. Other literary men, whose training might have prepared them for the understanding of *Capital,* enlisted under the Fabian banner. Only Morris, of well-known men of letters in the eighties, became a Marxian Socialist.

The new turn that his life took when he was more than forty entitles us to separate him from his contemporaries and to consider him, at least in the later phases of his career, with his juniors. Since Socialism was to become more and more important in what we call modern literature, the first author to adopt it as his political creed becomes in some sense a modern. No label could, on the surface of things, seem less applicable to William Morris, and that is what gives us our problem.

1. The Busy Singer.

In 1853 two students in their first year at Exeter College, Oxford, read John Ruskin's *Stones of Venice* with a sense of recognition: to both William Morris and Edward Burne-Jones it seemed that here was what they had always believed. They told other undergraduates of their discovery, and there began to be talk of founding a brotherhood. "We must," Morris wrote a friend a year or two later, "enlist you in this Crusade and Holy Warfare against the age."

Morris was the son of a London broker, member of an established firm that made money almost without effort. The family lived in Walthamstow with the most complete middle-class respectability. The father "did something in the City." The mother supervised her household with care. Both adored Queen Victoria and her consort, and Mr. Morris believed in the Manchester School as he believed in the Bible. Their evangelicalism included intense loyalty to the Church of England, for they refused to allow their children to play with dissenters. Unashamed of their class, they nevertheless modeled their lives on those of the gentry, and in 1843 Mr. Morris obtained a grant of arms from the Herald's College. It was the next year that his comfortable income was transformed into wealth by the development of copper mines in which he accidentally held shares.

The life of the Morrises was perfectly Victorian, and yet their Victorianism was not of the sort against which a sensitive boy would be forced to revolt. There was no obsession with money, no passion for display, no struggle for position. And, as a matter of fact, Morris, bitter critic of Victorianism that he became, never turned against his family. He merely grew, in some strange way, into medievalism. At seven he had read all of Scott's novels. At fourteen he was touched by the Anglo-Catholicism prevalent at Marlborough College. At nineteen he was a disciple of John Ruskin. At twenty-one he discovered Malory. His first poems and stories dealt with the Middle Ages, and he seemed at home there as he never did when he wrote of his own times.

Yet Morris carried into medievalism, and for that matter into Socialism, many of the traits of the class from which he came. Though he was content to call himself "the idle singer of an empty day," he demonstrated his energy and shrewdness in each of the many activities he pursued. He greatly preferred the life of the thirteenth century to that of the nineteenth, but the preference, instead of justifying a futile regret for the past, precipitated him into enterprises in which he was surprisingly successful.

When he went to Oxford, Morris had expected to enter the church, but in conversations with the Brotherhood, as he and his friends began to call their group, he abandoned that choice. Eager, as he always was, to do something concrete, he founded and financed the *Oxford and Cambridge Magazine,* which was praised by Ruskin, Tennyson, and Rossetti. Ruskin was still and would remain his master, but already differences were appearing. Ruskin, conventional in religion, saw in the Middle Ages a period of faith and virtue; Morris, already skeptical and indifferent, saw a period in which art was flourishing. Ruskin believed in discipline and obedience, Morris in liberty. Ruskin was chiefly interested in architecture, and Morris began to prepare himself as an architect, but he soon found that his preference was for the decorative arts.

In 1856 Morris and Burne-Jones met Rossetti, who almost superseded Ruskin as an influence, and Morris turned from architecture to painting. Rossetti so dominated his imagination that he forgot much of what he had learned from Ruskin, and wrote: "I can't enter into politico-social subjects with any interest, for on the whole I see that things are in a muddle, and I have no power or vocation to set them right in ever so little a degree. My work is the embodiment of dreams in one form or another." He was never able to embody his dreams in painting, but they soon found expression in poetry. *The Defense of Guenevere,* published in 1858, was generally ignored, and it was nine years later, with *The Life and Death of Jason,* that fame began. The Guenevere poem, however, was not inferior to its successor, and might have been just as popular. There was more than a touch of Browning in it, but its principal distinction was its feeling for the Middle Ages. It did not so much seem to re-create a vanished period as to grow out of it, for, whether Morris knew the Middle Ages thoroughly or not, he had the air of authority. He also had an almost unique facility in verse that made the embodiment of dreams good fun.[1]

Perhaps because Morris found poetry so easy, he had no intention of devoting himself to it. In 1859 he was married and began building and furnishing a house according to his

---

[1] "I once told him that the reason I did not write verse was that instead of saying what I wanted to say in it I had to say something that would rhyme. . . . Morris looked at me exactly as if I had told him that I was blind or deaf or impotent, or at best an utter fool. He could not understand anyone finding any difficulty in finding a rhyme or forcing it in any way." Bernard Shaw, in May Morris' *William Morris, Artist, Writer, Socialist,* II, xxxvii.

own standards. The impossibility of getting from ordinary shops the furniture and decorations he wanted led to the forming of Morris, Marshall, Faulkner and Company in 1861. At first Morris and his associates were principally engaged in church decoration, but soon they were supplying mural decoration, carving, stained glass, metal work, and furniture. Later they added embroidery and wall-paper, which was the most popular of their enterprises. The firm was dissolved in 1875, but Morris continued, adding dyeing to his work and beginning the creation of tapestries. Printing occupied him at the end of his life.

"Have nothing in your houses," Morris preached, "that you do not know to be useful, or believe to be beautiful," and many in the middle class, beginning to be ashamed of their cluttered parlors, listened to his sermons and bought his chintzes and wall-papers. He was glad to raise public taste, just as he was glad that the firm showed a profit, but what he really wanted was a chance to do the kind of work he liked. All his life his greatest pleasure came from using his hands to make something he believed beautiful. Though the mere thought that he was imitating the medieval craftsmen gave him joy, he would have found satisfaction enough in the technical details and the manual labor of the various processes he employed.

His poetry he regarded as another expression of the creative impulse that went into the handicrafts. Although his poems were remote enough from the life his contemporaries led, they were not remote from his own. "If a chap can't compose an epic poem while he's weaving tapestry," he remarked, "he'd better shut up, he'll never do any good at all." All the arts, according to his view, were to be integrated with the daily lives of the people, and it was because art could not be part of life as it went on in his own era that he condemned the era. In the fifties, sixties, and early seventies he did not see any hope of changing the contemporary way of life, but at least he could refuse to lead it.

His reputation as a poet was growing. *The Life and Death of Jason* had pleased Victorian taste,[1] and the first part of *The Earthly Paradise,* which appeared the next year, 1868, gave him a following. *Love is Enough,* a strange and strangely misnamed masque, came in 1873, and *Sigurd the Volsung,* the greatest of his poems, closed the period of story-telling in verse. He had already translated several Icelandic sagas, and in subsequent years translated the *Aeneid,* the *Odyssey,* and *Beowulf.* In original verse, however, he limited himself to shorter poems, often written for special occasions.

If Morris had died in 1875, when *Sigurd the Volsung* was published, his position as a poet would not be very different from what it is now. It is not, certainly, in the front rank, and yet it is a secure position, if only because he has never been fashionable and hence there has been no danger of a critical reaction. Both in content and in manner he is as far from today's taste as a poet could be. His themes are the least complex of emotions—romantic love, physical courage, loyalty to ideals—and his facility seems insipid to a generation that asks its poets for intellectual intensity. Yet his freshness, the vigor of his narratives, and the movement of his lines make his poems readable, and *Sigurd the Volsung* is an epic of which English literature can be proud. Far as he falls short of his master, Chaucer, the comparison is by no means ridiculous.

---

[1] "When the *Pall Mall Gazette,* then the great arbiter of cultured opinion, could find little in 'Jason' to condemn beyond an 'indifference to manners' shown in the passage where 'Medea obtains her first interview with Jason by knocking unexpectedly at his chamber door' (instead, we must infer, of sending him a note by the footman), its fortunes with the critics were secured." J. W. Mackail, *Life of William Morris,* I, 184.

2. *The Road to Socialism.*

If Morris had died in 1875, however much might be said in praise of his poetry, there would be little occasion for speaking of him here, for he would be merely one more late Victorian who could not stomach his own era and did his best to escape from it. But at about the time that he finished *Sigurd the Volsung,* as passages in that poem might be cited to show, he was feeling more actively discontented than he had felt in the twenty years since he abandoned the church and turned to art. He had always lamented the barrenness of the age, but constant activity had solaced his mind. Now, rather dissatisfied with his easy success in poetry, and personally unhappy because of the dissolution of the firm and his rupture with Rossetti, he restlessly looked about him, and paid alarmed attention to conditions he had never quite succeeded in forgetting.

In March, 1874, he wrote a friend: "Suppose people lived in little communities among gardens and green fields, so that you could be in the country in five minutes' walk, and had few wants, almost no furniture for instance, and no servants, and studied the (difficult) arts of enjoying life, and finding out what they really wanted: then I think one might hope civilization had really begun." "But," he added, "as it is, the best thing one can wish for this country at least is, meseems, some great and tragical circumstances, so that if they cannot have pleasant life, which is what one means by civilization, they may at least have a history and something to think of." "Years ago," he wrote a little later, "men's minds were full of art and the dignified shows of life, and they had but little time for justice and peace; and the vengeance on them was not increase of the violence they did not heed, but destruction of the art they heeded. So perhaps the gods are preparing troubles and terrors for the world (or our small corner of it) again, that it may once again become beautiful and dramatic withal, for I do not believe they will have it dull and ugly forever."

This notion of some cleansing catastrophe grew upon him, so that, as he later wrote, "I was in for a fine pessimistic end of life, if it had not somehow dawned on me that amidst all this filth of civilization the seeds of a great change, what we others call Social-Revolution, were beginning to germinate." The hope of a great change could not come from Ruskin. To the end Morris praised Ruskin as the man who had opened his eyes, and said the seventies would have been "deadly dull" without him, but his hard practical sense always balked at such schemes as the Guild of St. George. Ruskin had fostered his discontent with the laissez-faire school of economics and with the politics, art, and morals of the middle class, and he had provided a kind of theoretical basis for the love of the Middle Ages, but Ruskin's various schemes for the salvation of the world could inspire no hope in so keen-sighted a son of the bourgeoisie as William Morris.

The hope did not come from anyone's teachings but, as Morris was wise enough to see, from his own experiences in the seventies and eighties. His first participation in public affairs grew out of his love for the architecture of the Middle Ages. Many of the medieval churches of England were being "restored," and this attempt to imitate the style of an earlier age seemed to Morris pure fraud. To prevent the outrage, he formed the Society for Protection of Ancient Buildings, a name that he and his circle abbreviated to Anti-Scrape. As he lectured and wrote on this cause, and accustomed himself to public activity, his views on popular art grew clearer.

Even more important was the almost simultaneous organization of the Eastern Questions Association, of which he became treasurer. In 1876 Russia had gone to war with Turkey, which was ravishing the Balkans, and the Tories wanted to

bring England into the war on Turkey's side, in order to
weaken their Russian rival. Morris saw that British commercial interests were proposing to strangle liberty in the Balkans
in order to increase their own profits, and he was indignant
that the people of England should be asked to fight for such
a cause. In May, 1877, he addressed a manifesto to the workingmen of England, in which he named the advocates of war:
"Greedy gamblers on the Stock Exchange, idle officers of
the army and navy (poor fellows!), worn-out mockers of the
clubs, desperate purveyors of exciting war-news for the comfortable breakfast-tables of those who have nothing to lose
by war; and lastly, in the place of honor, the Tory Rump,
that we fools, weary of peace, reason, and justice, chose at the
last election to represent us. Shame and double shame, if we
march under such leadership as this in an unjust war against
a people who are not our enemies, against Europe, against
freedom, against nature, against the hope of the world."

He went on, with a sharpness of tone his friends must have
found surprising: "Working men of England, one word of
warning yet: I doubt if you know the bitterness of hatred
against freedom and progress that lies at the hearts of a certain part of the richer classes in this country: their newspapers
veil it in a kind of decent language; but do but hear them talk
among themselves, as I have often, and I know not whether
scorn or anger would prevail in you at their folly and insolence. These men cannot speak of your order, of its aims, of
its leaders, without a sneer or an insult: these men, if they had
the power (may England perish rather!) would thwart your
just aspirations, would silence you, would deliver you bound
hand and foot for ever to irresponsible capital. Fellow-citizens,
look to it, and if you have any wrongs to be redressed, if you
cherish your most worthy hope of raising your whole order
peacefully and solidly, if you thirst for leisure and knowledge,
if you long to lessen these inequalities which have been our

stumbling-block since the beginning of the world, then cast aside sloth and cry out against an Unjust War, and urge us of the middle classes to do no less." He turned to the working class, and he was not disappointed. "More and more," he wrote, "I feel how right the flattest democracy is." He referred to the cowardice of the Liberals and the staunchness and sagacity of "our working-men allies," to whom he attributed the victory for peace.

With the end of the Russian crisis, he found it impossible to drop politics, and he became treasurer of the National Liberal League, which had been formed by London working-class Radicals. Support of the Liberal Party, however, could not satisfy him, especially after the election of 1880 had given it a chance to show its inadequacies in office. When Arnold's "Equality" was published, Morris approved, except that "if he has any idea of a remedy he dursen't mention it." "I think myself," he went on, "that no rosewater will cure us; disaster and misfortune of all kinds, I think, will be the only things that will breed a remedy; in short, nothing can be done till all the rich men are made poor by general consent. I suppose that dimly he sees this, but is afraid to say it, being, though naturally a courageous man, somewhat infected with the great vice of that cultivated class he was praising so much— cowardice, to wit."

Morris continued to lecture on art and architecture, but none of his listeners could fail to realize what problems were occupying his mind. "I do not want art for a few," he declared, "any more than education for a few, or freedom for a few." Again: "The lack of art, or rather the murder of art, that curses our streets from the sordidness of the surroundings of the lower classes, has its exact counterpart in the dulness and vulgarity of those of the middle classes, and the double-distilled dulness, and scarcely less vulgarity of those of the upper classes." Finally: "Luxury cannot exist without some slavery of some kind or other, and its abolition will be blessed, like the abolition of other slaveries, by the freeing both of the slaves and their masters." He had always known, he recorded on the first day of 1881, that society was "founded on injustice and kept together by cowardice and tyranny," but he had hoped for gradual improvement; now he saw that the great cause was "the abasement of the rich and the raising up of the poor." Arnold had urged the working class to lead the struggle for sweetness and light, but he had not offered to join them. Morris asked, "How can we of the middle classes, we the capitalists and our hangers-on, help?" And he answered: "By renouncing our class, and on all occasions when antagonism rises up between the classes, casting in our lot with the victims; those who are condemned at the best to lack of education, refinement, leisure, pleasure, and renown; and at the worst, to a life lower than that of the most brutal of savages." This was the step he was now ready to take.

He joined the Democratic Federation on January 17, 1883, four days after he had been made an Honorary Fellow of his college at Oxford. The Federation was founded in 1881, largely under Hyndman's influence. Its membership was varied: Professor Edward Beesly, a Positivist and a friend of Marx; Helen Taylor, John Stuart Mill's step-daughter; Justin McCarthy, the journalist and historian; H. H. Champion, an officer, who resigned from the artillery in 1882 in protest against the Egyptian war; J. L. Joynes and H. S. Salt, who had been masters at Eton; and a number of workmen, among them Tom Mann, John Burns, and Harry Quelch. Not all were Socialists, but the majority were coming to see, as Morris saw, that Radicalism "is made for and by the middle classes, and will always be under the control of rich capitalists." The organization was in effect Socialist when Morris joined it, and not long after it was re-christened the Social Democratic Federation.

Almost the only reading on Socialism Morris had done before he joined the Federation was a series of critical articles by Mill. After joining, however, he read much of *Capital,* and of course heard Marxian ideas discussed by his associates. He began lecturing on behalf of the Federation, and on March 6, 1883, shocked an audience at the Royal Institution of Manchester by making an appeal for Socialism. The following November, speaking at Oxford, with Ruskin in the chair, he offended the authorities by asking his listeners to support the Federation. He was a member of the executive committee, signed its manifesto, and paid the deficit of *Justice,* its organ. He spent so much time in Federation affairs that the firm suffered, and he almost abandoned poetry, writing only some Socialist verses such as "The Day is Coming." When Mrs. Burne-Jones protested, he told her that poetry was not a sacred duty and work for Socialism was.

Despite his devotion to the Federation, Morris was not unaware of its shortcomings. From the first Marx and Engels had distrusted Hyndman, regarding him as a political adventurer who was eager to create a political party for his own purposes. He himself records that in 1881, after he had presumably become a Socialist, he went to Disraeli and urged upon him a policy of enlightened imperialism and domestic palliation. Subsequently he accepted money from Tory sources to finance Federation candidates, while seeking to strike a bargain with the Radicals. Such tactics, even if Hyndman's intentions were creditable, seemed to Morris the bankruptcy of Socialist ideals. Moreover, his dictatorial conduct was paralyzing the Federation. The majority broke away and founded the Socialist League.

Morris was even more diligent in the League than he had been in the Federation. He edited its paper, the *Commonweal,* and financed it, and he spoke at hundreds of meetings. A record he kept of a tour taken in 1887, shows him speaking twice in Glasgow on Sunday, April 3: at an open air meeting in the morning, and at an evening meeting at which Cunninghame Graham presided. On Monday he spoke at Dundee, and Tuesday at Edinburgh. Wednesday he returned to Glasgow for a meeting of the League branch, and the next day spoke in a neighboring coal district. Friday he was at Paisley, Saturday at Coatbridge, Sunday at Glasgow again, and on Monday he held several meetings in and around Newcastle, where the miners were on strike. Every year for several years he made a number of such tours, and even when he was in London he often noted that five or six evenings in succession had been occupied with League business.

Both the Federation and the League were effective enough with their propaganda to annoy the authorities, and in 1885 a system of petty persecution began, with raids on the headquarters of workingmen's clubs and interference with outdoor meetings. The Christian Socialists and the newly formed Fabian Society joined in the resulting protest, and, since religious bodies also objected to the ban on open air meetings, it was finally lifted. But more stirring struggles soon followed. Hyndman, believing in the value of sensational tactics, had tried to organize a series of unemployment demonstrations. On February 8, 1886, the Fair Trade League, a Tory-inspired organization intended to counteract Socialist propaganda as well as to advocate a protective tariff, called a meeting of the unemployed in Trafalgar Square. Hyndman and his followers gained possession of the meeting, and urged the eight or ten thousand persons in attendance to march to Hyde Park. As the procession entered Pall Mall, there were jeers from some of the upper-class clubs, and the demonstrators began to throw rocks. Criminals had, of course, attached themselves to the crowd—some, indeed, it was suspected, had been hired by the Tories—and there was looting of shops.[1]

[1] Henry James wrote his brother: "The two great public matters here have

What impressed Morris was the terror that had been displayed. "Such abject cowardice," he wrote in the *Commonweal*, "has perhaps seldom been so frankly shown as was shown by the middling bourgeoisie on those two days. Whatever were they afraid of? Of nothing? No; they were afraid of their own position, so suddenly revealed to them as by a flash of lightning; their position as a class dominating a class injured by them, and more numerous than they." This revelation was, he felt, significant, and he was amused by the flood of contributions to the Mansion House Fund for the unemployed, but he saw that the incident had its more sinister meanings. "I have said," he wrote, "that we have been overtaken unprepared, by a revolutionary incident, but that incident was practically aimless." Such displays of the fury of the masses were dangerous unless the masses understood the end for which they were fighting.[1]

been the riot, and the everlasting and most odious —— scandal. (I mean, of course, putting the all-overshadowing Irish question aside.) I was at Bournemouth (seeing R. L. Stevenson) the day of the émeute, and lost the spectacle, to my infinite chagrin. . . . The wreck and ruin in Piccadilly and some other places (I mean of windows) was, on my return from Bournemouth, sufficiently startling, as was also the manner in which the carriages of a number of ladies were stopped, and the occupants hustled, rifled, slapped or kissed, as the case might be, and turned out. The real unemployed, I believe, had very little share in all this: it was the work of the great army of roughs and thieves, who seized, owing to the favorable nature of their opportunity, a day of license. . . . Everyone here is growing poorer —from causes which, I fear, will continue. All the same, what took place the other day is, I feel pretty sure, the worst that, for a long time to come, the British populace is likely to attempt." *Letters of Henry James*, I, 120–1. Later he wrote Charles Eliot Norton: "The condition of that body [the British upper class] seems to me in many ways very much the same rotten and *collapsible* one as that of the French aristocracy before the revolution—minus cleverness and conversation; or perhaps it's more like the heavy, congested and depraved Roman world upon which the barbarians came down. In England the Huns and Vandals will have to come *up*—from the black depths of the (in the people) enormous misery, though I don't think the Attila is quite yet found—in the person of Mr. Hyndman. At all events, much of English life is grossly materialistic and wants blood-letting." *Ibid.*, 124.

[1] Engels agreed. "As to Hyndman," he wrote Bebel, "the way he came out in Trafalgar Square and Hyde Park on February 8 has done infinitely more harm than good. Shouting after revolution, which in France passes off harmlessly as

As soon as the middle class had recovered from its panic, it tried to suppress the Socialists and the unemployed. Morris himself was arrested, and many of his colleagues were given long sentences. Demonstrations were repeatedly held in the autumn of 1887, on behalf of the Haymarket martyrs and in the interests of free speech, both for Socialists and for advocates of Irish independence. London merchants demanded the closing of Trafalgar Square, and on November 8 Sir Charles Warren complied. The Radical Clubs of London called a meeting for November 13, to demand the release of Irish patriots, and all Socialist bodies took part, Shaw and Morris being among the scheduled speakers. Four thousand police, three hundred mounted police, three hundred grenadiers, and three hundred Life Guards were sent to stop the meeting. One hundred and fifty persons were arrested, and seventy-five held for trial, among them John Burns and Cunninghame Graham, both of whom were sentenced to prison. Police brutality went beyond anything that had been seen since the days of the Chartists, and one worker, Alfred Linnell, died from the wounds he received. At his funeral Morris said: "Our friend who lies here has had a hard life and met with a hard death; and if society had been differently constituted, his life might have been a delightful, a beautiful, and a happy one. It is our business to begin to organize for the purpose of seeing that such things shall not happen; to try and make this earth a beautiful and happy place."

stale stuff, is utter nonsense here among the totally unprepared masses, and has the effect of scaring away the proletariat, only exciting the demoralized elements. It absolutely cannot be understood here as anything but a summons to looting, which accordingly followed and has brought discredit which will last a long time here, among the workers too. . . . The first alarm of the bourgeois was certainly very funny, and brought in about £40,000 in contributions for the unemployed—in all about £70,000—but that has been disposed of and nobody will pay more and the distress remains the same. What has been achieved—among the bourgeois public —is the identification of Socialism with looting, and even though that does not make the matter much worse still it is certainly no gain to us." Marx-Engels, *Selected Correspondence*, 447-8.

With the organization of the Law and Liberty League, in which Radical and Socialist workmen united to secure freedom of speech, Socialism achieved measurable influence, and the dock strike of 1889 presented it with fresh opportunities. But unfortunately neither the Social Democratic Federation nor the Socialist League was able to give British labor effective Socialist leadership. Hyndman's curious combination of sectarianism and opportunism kept the Federation aloof from labor struggles, and the League had fallen into the hands of anarchists.

Socialism had missed one of its great chances, but Socialists could not feel wholly downhearted, as Morris pointed out in a statement he published when he resigned from the League in 1890. "Those who set out 'to make the revolution,'" he wrote, "were a few working-men, less successful even in the wretched life of labor than their fellows; a sprinkling of the intellectual proletariat, whose keen pushing of Socialism must have seemed pretty certain to extinguish their limited chances of prosperity; one or two outsiders in the game political; a few refugees from the bureaucratic tyranny of foreign governments; and here and there an unpractical, half-cracked artist or author." Yet great changes had taken place from 1883 to 1890: "No one who thinks is otherwise than discontented with things as they are. The shouts of triumph over the glories of civilization which once drowned the moans of the miserable (and that but a dozen years ago at most) have now sunk into quavering apologies for the existence of the horrors and fatuities of our system." Capitalism was on the defensive. But now there was a danger that, finding the capitalists ready to make concessions, many professed Socialists would content themselves with palliative measures. That the reforms were good in themselves Morris would not deny, but they should not be allowed to blind men to the need for getting rid of capitalism itself. The constant preaching of this need remained the task of true Socialists.

This was Morris' aim during the remaining six years of his life. He organized an independent body, the Hammersmith Socialist Society, and was active in its work. If he was less pre-occupied with the movement than he had been in the preceding seven years, this was not because his convictions had changed. He lectured some, though his health would not permit extensive travel, and he wrote many articles. He joined Hyndman and Shaw in preparing a manifesto that was intended to encourage co-operation among all Socialist groups. In January of 1896, the year of his death, he re-affirmed his belief in Socialism, and although he was seriously ill, he wrote a brief article for the May Day number of *Justice*.

The character of the Socialist movement was changing, and even if he had been capable of his former activity, he would not have taken a decisive part in the new phase. The major aim now was to permeate the labor movement, and in 1890, when nearly two hundred thousand persons gathered in Hyde Park to celebrate May Day, it seemed, even to Engels himself,[1] that a beginning had been made. But, because of the anarchistic theories of the League and the sectarian policies of the Federation, and perhaps for other reasons as well, Fabianism was increasingly guiding the thinking of the working class. Morris himself was so afraid of forgetting the ultimate goal of Socialism that, in practice if not in theory, he was likely to keep aloof from the labor unions, and in any case neither temperament nor experience fitted him to work with them. It was in the eighties, when the great need was to introduce the idea of Socialism into England, that his kind of work could be done.

[1] Engels wrote in the Vienna *Arbeiterzeitung:* "On May 4th, 1890, the English proletariat, newly awakened from its forty years' winter sleep, again entered the movement of its class." Quoted by Allen Hutt, *This Final Crisis,* 123.

3. What Morris Believed.

Enough has been said to show that Morris was not a dilettante Socialist. He called himself and he was a Marxist. According to his friend Bruce Glasier, he once said, "I put some emphasis on Marx—more than I ought to have done, perhaps. The fact is that I . . . have never been able to make head or tale of his algebraics. He is stiffer reading than some of Browning's poetry. But you see most people think I am a Socialist because I am a crazy sort of artist and poet chap, and I mentioned Marx because I wanted to be upsides with them and make believe that I am really a tremendous Political Economist—which, thank God, I am not!" Morris would have said something like that, and meant it too, for he was not and never pretended to be a master of Marxian economics, but his essays show how consistently he was guided by Marxism. May Morris reports that, though her father was often bewildered by the chapters on economic theory in *Capital,* he was excited and impressed by the historical sections. Two essays in *Signs of Change,* called "Feudal England" and "The Hopes of Civilization," show how useful Morris found Marxism in reconsidering the period he loved so well. At last he understood how feudalism had developed and why it declined.

In the same way, though he may have been baffled by the labor theory of value, he grasped clearly enough the mechanics of exploitation. In such lectures as "True and False Society," "Monopoly," and "Useful Work versus Useless Toil," he expounded the nature of the capitalist system. Always he gave his exposition the particular emphasis that his own pre-occupation with the future of art required, and in this way he made his lectures the more persuasive for the audiences to which they were addressed, but he was talking Marxism, and he knew it.

Since he had no desire to minimize the class struggle, he looked to the proletariat to destroy capitalism. He told C. E. Maurice that only "the antagonism of classes, which the system has bred," could establish Socialism. When he spoke to middle-class audiences, he urged his listeners to renounce their class and join the proletariat in its fight. "You will run the risk of losing position, reputation, money, friends even," he told one audience. "Nor can I assure you that you will forever escape scotfree from the attacks of open tyranny. It is true that at present capitalist society only looks on Socialism in England with dry grins. But remember that the body of people who have for instance ruined India, starved and gagged Ireland, and tortured Egypt, have capacities in them, some ominous signs of which they have lately shown, for openly playing the tyrants' game nearer home."

He thought it unlikely that Socialism would come without the use of force. "I am quite sure," he wrote Maurice, "that the change which will overthrow our present system will come sooner or later; on the middle class to a great extent it depends whether it will come peacefully or violently." "It is no use prophesying," he said in one of his lectures, "as to the events which will accompany that revolution, but to a reasonable man it seems unlikely to the last degree, or we will say impossible, that a moral sentiment will induce the proprietary classes—those who live by *owning* the means of production which the unprivileged classes must needs *use*—to yield up this privilege uncompelled; all one can hope is that they will see the implicit threat of compulsion in the events of the day, and so yield with a good grace to the terrible necessity of forming part of a world in which all, including themselves, will work honestly and live easily."

Apparently he believed in the early eighteen-eighties that the transition to Socialism was about to begin. On the one hand he saw what seemed to him conclusive evidence of the collapse of capitalism and the demoralization of the ruling class. On the other he noted the increasing militancy of the workers and the growth of Socialist sentiment. When Hyndman talked, as he often did, of the upheaval that would take place in England on the one hundredth anniversary of the French Revolution, Morris was skeptical, but he did expect both the uninterrupted decline of capitalism and the steady growth of Socialist strength, with inevitable revolutionary results in a not very distant future.

These convictions determined his conception of Socialist strategy. He was not one to favor a temporizing policy in any situation, and in the eighties he felt obliged to condemn any talk of compromise. In 1887 he opposed Socialist participation in Parliament on the ground that Socialist M.P.'s would only serve the capitalists' purpose by "propping the stability of robber society." He favored, of course, the building of a strong labor movement, but he was inclined to emphasize its ultimate aims rather than its immediate demands. He was even rather sympathetic to anarchism at the time the Socialist League broke away from the Federation, but association with the League's anarchistic members quickly cured him.

In the nineties he was less intransigent than he had been at the outset, but he was suspicious—and with plenty of reason—of the Independent Labor Party. There is only a narrow path between the kind of fanatical loyalty to principle that cuts revolutionaries off from the working class and the kind of amiable flexibility that results in working-class betrayal. Morris did not find that path, but neither did any of his contemporaries except the little group directly associated with Friedrich Engels.[1] What he did see was the true nature of the problem. In 1893, commenting on reform measures

---

[1] John Strachey says: "While the Social Democratic Federation failed to do the right thing, the Fabian Society succeeded in doing the wrong thing." *What Are We to Do?*, 71. See Chapter III of Allen Hutt's *This Final Crisis*.

adopted by the London County Council, he said that what interested him was whether these reforms contributed to the preparation of the working class for Socialism. If not, if they were merely a successful attempt to buy out the militant workers, then "we had best try if we can't make terms with intelligent Tories and benevolent Whigs, and beg them to unite their intelligence and benevolence, and govern us as kindly and wisely as they can, and to rob us in moderation only." If, however, such measures could contribute to the education of the workers in the long period of transition that he now saw stretching before the Socialist movement, they were good. Which end they served, he suggested, depended in large measure on the wisdom and sincerity of the Socialists themselves.

What distinguishes Morris' writings on Socialism from those of his contemporaries is not so much his views on the means by which Socialism was to be established as his persistent interest in the ultimate end of the process. Again, he got his cue from Marx. But whereas Marx had merely defined Communism as the goal, and had, indeed, warned against too detailed speculation on the character of the classless society, Morris dreamt of the future. He knew he was dreaming, but he did not want men to forget their dreams. "The great mass," he wrote, "of what most non-Socialists at least consider at present to be Socialism, seems to me nothing more than a *machinery* of Socialism, which I think it probable that Socialism *must* use in its militant condition; and which I think it *may* use for some time after it is practically established; but does not seem to me to be of its essence." In "The Society of the Future" he made clear what he wanted: "I demand a free and unfettered animal life for man first of all: I demand the utter extinction of all asceticism. If we feel the least degradation in being amorous, or merry, or hungry, or sleepy, we are so far bad animals, and therefore miserable men." Both asceticism and luxury must go, but let no one expect monotony to result. "What is simplicity?" he asked. "Do you think by chance that I mean a row of yellow-brick, blue-slated houses, or a phalangstere like an improved Peabody lodging-house; and the dinner-bell ringing one into a row of white basins of broth with a piece of bread cut out nice and square by each, with boiler-made tea and ill-boiled rice-pudding to follow? No; that's the philanthropist's idea, not mine."

As an artist he anticipated the flowering of art in the classless society of the future. "For myself," he said at Oxford in 1883, "I am so discontented with the present conditions of art, and the matter seems to me so serious, that I am forced to try to make other people share my discontent, and am this evening risking the committal of a breach of good manners by standing before you, grievance in hand, on an occasion like this, when everybody present, I feel sure, is full of good-will both towards the arts and towards the public." In going on to explain the degradation of the arts, Morris maintained that the workman was exploited in many ways in the Middle Ages but not, as under capitalism, by the private ownership of the means of production. As a producer the workman was relatively free, and he could therefore take the creative interest in what he was doing that is natural to any human being. This gave to the ordinary objects of daily living the quality of art, and art flourished, for it was rooted in the needs and tastes and capacities of the masses of the people. But with the rise of capitalism and the division of labor, workers were required to turn out the largest possible amount of goods in the shortest possible time. The majority of the people lost their joy in their work and their eagerness for beauty, and art, becoming something for the leisured few, was corrupted. You cannot, Morris argued, have beautiful pictures if you have ugly homes. In a civilization that deliberately commits millions of people to squalor, that destroys natural beauty for the sake of profits, and that regards joyless work and hideous products as natural, no kind of art is possible.

Morris never saw either the social or the artistic possibilities of machinery, but he did not indulge in a romantic rejection of the machine. He would use machines, but only to eliminate the labor in which there is no element of creation. Finding his own greatest satisfaction in work, he could not believe that the aim of life was to reduce labor to a minimum. Once men were freed from the necessity of killing drudgery, he was sure they would recognize the joy of true work. In the same way, once they had overcome the terror of starvation, they would be interested in making life better rather than in amassing things. "They will discover," he wrote, "or rediscover rather, that the true secret of happiness *lies in the taking of a genuine interest in all the details of daily life,* in elevating them by art instead of handing the performance of them over to unregarded drudges, and ignoring them; and that in cases where it was impossible either so to elevate them and make them interesting, or to lighten them by the use of machinery, so as to make the labour of them trifling, that should be taken as a token that the supposed advantages gained by them were not worth the trouble and had better be given up."

If he had not believed Socialism a step to a freer and more joyous life, Morris would not have been interested in working for it. The mere raising of the masses to a level of comfort seemed to him good, but not good enough. In his pre-occupation with the more distant future he differed, no doubt, from most Socialists, but only in degree. His conception of the future was his own, but he was not alone in believing that the end of capitalism would bring an enriching of human life on every level. And in his analysis of the steps by which the transformation would be accomplished he followed the scientific guidance of Marx and Engels.

If we make it clear that Morris was a Marxian Socialist,[1] this is not to establish orthodoxy for the sake of orthodoxy. He has frequently been misunderstood, and not unnaturally so. An admiration for the Middle Ages has so often been identified with some brand of either Guild or Tory Socialism that it is hard to realize he was not of that breed. As a matter of fact, he was full of contempt for "the last pessimist prig who has written a bad novel to prove that some new and vague form of Toryism is the only thing that can save us." Much as he admired the Middle Ages, he had not the remotest idea that civilization could return to the conditions of feudalism. He laughed at "attempts, more or less preposterously futile, to graft a class of independent peasants on our system of wages and capital." He hoped, to be sure, that the future would restore some of the virtues that he believed had existed in feudal times, but not because he expected the economic system of the future to resemble that of the past.

Without Marx, Morris would not have been a Marxist. That is, he had neither the knowledge nor the patient logic to have arrived by himself at an understanding of the laws of capitalism. He learned of Marxism from Marx, and he learned of Marx from the Socialist movement that the economic decline of the late seventies had brought into existence. So much is clear, and yet, when one has explained how Morris came in contact with Marxism, it is still hard to understand why he recognized its truth so promptly. His literary contemporaries, even when they went so far as to grant the advisability of Socialism, quarreled with Marx's interpretation of history, his emphasis on the class struggle, and his analysis of capitalism. Morris, as we have seen, was willing to take the analysis of capitalism on faith, and he wholeheartedly

---

[1] There is, of course, a formal exposition of his views in *Socialism, Its Growth and Outcome* (1893). His collaborator, E. Belfort Bax, was probably the dominant partner, but obviously there is nothing in the book with which Morris disagreed.

agreed with the interpretation of history and the conception of the dynamic role of the proletariat.

This can be explained only in terms of the philosophy that Morris had developed before he discovered the Socialist movement. From Ruskin, as he always insisted, he had learned that the Manchester economists were not infallible, and that the condition of art was closely related to the condition of the masses of the people. But Ruskin's reactionary opinions never touched Morris, and even his disgust with capitalism merely re-enforced a disgust that Morris had begun to feel in his earliest youth. This complete contempt for the bourgeoisie and all the results of industrialism was the key to his acceptance of Socialism, for it led him to contemplate without reservation or regret the destruction of the capitalist system and the wiping out of the middle class. Most intellectuals, even when they were professing Socialists, wanted to preserve many of the achievements of capitalism. Strictly speaking, they were often right and Morris wrong, but their affection for this or that aspect of the system they opposed tempered their opposition, whereas Morris' hatred preserved him from compromise. In a real sense, he was, despite his comfortable income, like the proletariat: he had nothing to lose, nothing, that is, that he valued.

Even Morris' medievalism contributed, in a curious way, to his acceptance of Marxism. For most people, he wrote, "it seems a part of the necessary and eternal order of things that the present supply and demand Capitalist system should last for ever; though the system of citizen and chattel slave under which the ancient civilizations lived, which no doubt once seemed also necessary and eternal, had to give place, after a long period of violence and anarchy, to the feudal system of seigneur and serf; which in its turn, though once thought necessary and eternal, has been swept away in favor of our present contract system between rich and poor." Always conscious of the fact that the capitalist system had a beginning, he was able to realize that it might have an end. The thing he most admired in Marx was his description of the decay of feudalism and the beginning of capitalism, and, as "Feudal England" and "The Hopes of Civilization" show, he learned from Marx the dynamics of a change he had long recognized. Morris' curious remoteness from the nineteenth century, his amazing ability to domesticate himself in the thirteenth, freed him from an intellectual bondage in which most of his contemporaries were held.

4. *The Socialist Writer.*

William Morris was not a professional man of letters in the ordinary sense. From the beginning the writing of poetry had been but one of many activities, and by no means the most important in his own mind. In the late seventies, moreover, the flood of inspiration, hitherto so profuse, had almost ceased, and, even if he had not become a Socialist, there would have been some kind of change in his literary career. As it was, the conviction held him that, as he wrote Mrs. Burne-Jones, the principal contribution a poet could make to poetry was to create a world in which the arts would eventually flourish. "Our business is now, and for long will be," he wrote in 1891, "not so much attempting to produce definite art, as rather clearing the ground to give art its opportunity." Many means might be used to this end, but Morris, being a practical man, relied chiefly on the efficacy of direct agitation. Consequently, during the seven years of active Socialism, his lectures and his articles for *Justice* and the *Commonweal* exceed in bulk all other work. The lectures, which fill several volumes in the *Collected Works,* have no literary pretensions. Morris wanted above all else to make his lectures clear and convincing, and they were fashioned for the ear rather than the eye.

He was eager to use his talents in any way that would serve the cause, even turning out an amusing satirical farce, and it was natural that he should write political verse. In 1878, during the campaign of the Eastern Question Association, he wrote "Wake, London Lads," his first political ballad. Soon after he joined the Federation he wrote "The Day Is Coming," still the best known of his Socialist songs. "A Death Song," written for the funeral of Alfred Linnell, "The Voice of Toil," "All for the Cause," and other poems followed. These verses, intended to evoke and express the emotions of militant, purposeful workers, could scarcely win the admiration of the critics, but they were as appropriate to the needs and convictions of the Socialist movement as sailors' chanties are to the life of ships. Morris found his models in the ballads of the Middle Ages, and he had always known how to speak simply and directly.

It was not his poetry, however, that gave him his reputation as a Socialist writer. Of his two Socialist prose romances *The Dream of John Ball,* though less well known than *News from Nowhere,* is the more perfectly integrated and the better written. It is a dream of the past as the other is a dream of the future. The dreamer finds himself in a Kentish village, where he is impressed by the fineness of the church, the beauty of the inn, the plain dignity of clothes and furnishings. John Ball appears in the village and speaks to a group of laborers: "What else shall ye lack when ye lack masters? Ye shall not lack for the fields ye have tilled, nor the houses ye have built, nor the cloth ye have woven; all these shall be yours." The sheriff comes with troops, and Morris gives a lively description of the victory of Ball and his followers. Ball summons the men to march on London. That night the dreamer talks with him, and the next morning the expedition sets forth.

In the first part of the romance is all Morris' love of the thirteenth and fourteenth centuries. The book throbs with what must have been the deepest regret of his later life: that the evils of feudalism, which he never minimized, were not overcome in such a way that humanity could pass directly into a classless society. Gladly would Morris have spared mankind the centuries of capitalism. But history did not take, and could not have taken, this course. The poignant moment of the story comes when John Ball, after he has been told by the dreamer of all that must happen before his ideal of fellowship can be realized, nevertheless goes to die for that ideal.

John Ball is good Socialist propaganda, but its message is less obvious than that of *News from Nowhere,* which followed it as a serial in the *Commonweal. News from Nowhere* adopts the familiar pattern of Utopian romances, with a slight and not very convincing story as the vehicle for long passages of exposition. It is only in the later chapters, when Morris is describing the trip up the Thames, that the book has the emotional force of *John Ball.* Morris had so often rowed up the river to his house at Kelmscott, had so often cursed the plague of industrialism that was blighting the stream and its banks, that this account of the same trip in the twenty-first century was transfused with the eloquence of his hopes.

News from Nowhere grew out of Morris' instant and strong dislike for Edward Bellamy's *Looking Backward.* To Bruce Glasier he said, "Thank you, I wouldn't care to live in such a cockney paradise as he imagines." Reviewing the book in the *Commonweal,* he praised it for its description of the evils of capitalism but deplored its conception of the future. Bellamy's temperament, he said, "may be called the unmixed modern one, unhistoric and unartistic; it makes its owner (if a Socialist) perfectly satisfied with modern civilization, if only the injustice, misery, and waste of class society could be got rid of; which half-change seems possible to him." Bellamy predicted that monopoly would become more and

more inclusive until finally it had organized the entire productive process, when it could and would be taken over by
the people. This seemed to Morris an unrealistic kind of formula. What he anticipated was "the recurrence of breaks-up
and re-formations of this kind of monopoly, under the influence of competition for privilege, or war for the division
of plunder, till the flood comes and destroys them all." He
could not, therefore, expect the easy transition that Bellamy
predicted. On the other hand, he felt that Bellamy made the
more distant future much too difficult, for, still thinking in
terms of scarcity, he projected into the future evils that a classless society could readily abolish. Essentially the trouble was
that he lacked imagination. "Mr. Bellamy's ideas of life are
curiously limited; he has no idea beyond existence in a great
city; his dwelling of man in the future is Boston (U.S.A.)
beautified." "I believe," Morris reiterated, "that the ideal of
the future does not point to the lessening of man's energy
by the reduction of labor to a minimum, but rather to the
reduction of *pain in labor.*"

In an essay called "How We Live and How We Might
Live" Morris had stated the four qualifications of the good
life: health, education, a fair share of the world's rough work
and a chance to do pleasant work, and agreeable surroundings. It is to satisfy these qualifications that the England described in *News from Nowhere* is organized. The dreamer
notices first the handsome buildings, the fine furnishings, and
the attractive clothing of the people among whom he suddenly finds himself. Then he is struck by their happiness.
Each is doing work that he likes to do. There is no competition, no financial worry, no greed. The state has withered
away. Machines are used only to perform tasks that would
otherwise be drudgery. Prisons have vanished, but most people are well-behaved. Schools have gone, but people are better educated than they used to be. Life is free and happy.

It is easy to pick the flaws in Morris' Utopia. In the first place, despite his statement to the contrary, it is obvious that England has been depopulated, and the needs of even a diminished population are met with remarkable ease, for everyone in the book seems to be engaged in making pottery or bronze doors or pipes or hay. Somehow, despite the use of very little machinery, and with only a few hours a day being devoted to the fundamental tasks of production, there is not only an abundance of all the necessities of life but an actual shortage of work. This is a situation that not even the elimination of capitalist wastefulness and the encouragement of the simple life can quite explain.

Such criticisms are easy, and they were made in Morris' time. He disregarded them, and rightly.[1] Marx and Engels deplored the building of Utopias, and Lenin did no more than hint at the character of the classless society in *State and Revolution*. But if one is going to depict a Utopia, then surely one is right in doing as Morris did and giving the imagination play. Morris is as incisive as Bellamy in his attack on capitalist folly; his account of the transition to Socialism is considerably more plausible; and who is to say that his conception of the future is not just as likely to be realized? At least he had the courage to believe that the revolution would really transform human beings. At least he dared to say that men could create the kind of society they wanted. As the book rises, after the inevitable pedestrianism of the middle section, to a climax of

---

[1] "As there were dozens of Utopian paper constitutions and economic schemes in the market, all unreadable and repulsive, and not one credible and attractive picture of what life might be under Communism, there was no reason to reproach Morris for supplying exactly what was needed instead of wasting his time in building political castles in the air. The experience of Russia has now shown us that nobody in the nineteenth century could possibly have foreseen the new shapes in which the social machinery would be forced by the abolition of 'real' property and the transfer of the profit incentive from the proprietors to the proletariat. Morris knew that all this would do itself one way or another when once people wanted it; the difficulty was to make them want it." May Morris, *William Morris*, I, 504.

passionate longing, the reader is moved to sympathy if not belief. It is no bad omen that, with all its impracticality, *News from Nowhere* has remained a classic of the Socialist movement.

There is a passage in the romance on the nature of literature, a topic on which Morris seldom expressed himself. A young woman complains because literature and art do not deal with the present. Hammond, the antiquarian, answers: "It always was so, and I suppose always will be, however it may be explained. It is true that in the nineteenth century, when there was so little art and so much talk about it, there was a theory that art and imaginative literature ought to deal with contemporary life; but they never did so; for, if there was any pretence of it, the author always took care . . . to disguise, or exaggerate, or idealize, and in some way or another make it strange; so that, for all the verisimilitude there was, he might just as well have dealt with the times of the Pharaohs." Dick comments, "Surely it is but natural to like these things strange; just as when we were children, as I said just now, we used to pretend to be so-and-so in such-and-such a place. That's what these pictures and poems do; and why shouldn't they?" "Thou hast hit it, Dick," Hammond answers; "it is the child-like part of us that produces works of imagination."

"My work," Morris had said more than thirty years earlier, "is the embodiment of dreams in one form or another." More than anything else he admired the romances and sagas of the Middle Ages, and for recreation his favorite reading was Dumas. In *News from Nowhere* Ellen says, "As for your books, they were well enough for times when intelligent people had but little else in which they could take pleasure." That was Morris' attitude. Literature was either a poor substitute for life or a pleasant occupation for idle moments.

Except as his own writing might serve the cause in which he believed, he thought of it as a kind of salutary amusement for himself and his readers.

This will explain why, after the writing of *News from Nowhere,* he turned to the composing of long prose romances based on folk themes of the Middle Ages. He thought it good for people to look back to those heroic times, but chiefly *The House of the Wolfings, The Roots of the Mountain,* and *The Well Beyond the World's End,* with their curious vocabulary and style, were intended to amuse. "He needed a refuge from reality," Shaw says, "and there was a limit to the number of times he could read the novels of Dumas père, his usual way of escape when his Socialist duties involved some grimy job in the police court or at the meetings of the League. I have used the Morris stories in that way myself, and found them perfectly effective."

Usually those who have used their writing as a refuge have been afraid of reality. Morris, as we have seen, spent the last twenty years of his life in the roughest kind of struggle with contemporary society. But he could not write about nineteenth century England. At least twice, according to his biographer, he tried, and both times he failed. He had nothing to say about his own century except that he hated it, and that scarcely seemed worth saying in a poem or a novel and could in any case be better said in a lecture. Before he became a Socialist, his imagination dwelt in the past, and afterwards it dwelt in the past and the future, though as a man he was active enough in the present.

Nothing quite like Morris had ever appeared in English literature or was likely to appear again. In his energetic, impersonal way he strode through the Victorian years, doing the things that he wanted to do and thought needed to be done. To the Socialist movement he brought a resourceful mind, an indefatigable body, and an impetuous imagination,

and with *John Ball, News from Nowhere,* and the poems he
created a beginning for the literature of Socialism. No other
Socialist writer, it is true, would be likely to take Morris'
work as his model, but the example the man had set was a
different matter. Thereafter it would not only be permissible
to ask a writer why he was not a Socialist; it would be impossible not to raise the question.

5. *Socialist Men of Letters.*

Morris was not the only English writer who was thinking
about Socialism in the eighties and nineties. Edward Carpenter, author of *Towards Democracy,* had helped to found
the Sheffield Socialist Society, which he invited Morris to
address in 1886. In 1887, as we have already seen, Morris,
touring Scotland, found in Cunninghame Graham a sympathetic chairman for his Glasgow meeting. In London many
young men, including William Butler Yeats, came to Hammersmith to talk with Morris about Socialism, and in the rival
Fabian Society George Bernard Shaw, with whom Morris
was on the friendliest terms, already had his group of literary
disciples.

The two main streams of nineteenth century thought had
not yet exhausted themselves. Morris, as we have seen, came
to Socialism by the way of the interventionists, and retained
many of their beliefs.[1] Edward Carpenter, though less specifically indebted to the anti-utilitarians, was in the romantic
tradition. Though his father was a Liberal with Radical lean-
ings, he fell under the influence of Frederick Denison Maurice
and his Broad Church mysticism, and his transcendentalism
was later strengthened by his admiration for Whitman. Socialism was for him part of a broad—and vague—humanitari-

---

[1] When Yeats asked him what led up to his movement, Morris replied, "Oh,
Ruskin and Carlyle, but somebody should have been beside Carlyle and punched
his head every five minutes." Yeats, *Autobiography,* 127.

anism, which embraced vegetarianism and theosophy as well
as what he believed to be Marxism. Like Morris he had little
use for the achievements of which his contemporaries boasted
so much, and he wrote *Civilization: Its Cause and Cure* to
express and justify his scorn.

It is contempt for nineteenth century civilization that unites
Morris, Carpenter, and Cunninghame Graham. Morris turned
to the thirteenth century. Carpenter lived the simple life and
reflected on the wisdom of the East. Graham, after the brief
Parliamentary career in which he acted as an ally of the Socialists, spent much of his time in Africa and South America,
and most of what he wrote concerns people uncursed by industrialism. "The world," he once wrote, "is to the weak.
The weak are the majority. The weak of brain, of body, the
knock-kneed and flat-footed, muddle-minded, loose-jointed,
ill-put together, baboon-faced, the white-eye-lashed, slow of
wit, the practical, the unimaginative, forgetful, selfish, dense,
the stupid, fatuous, the 'candle-moulded,' give us our laws,
impose their standards on us, their ethics, their philosophy,
canon of art, literary style, their jingling music, vapid plays,
their dock-tailed horses. . . ." But this heroic scorn, not inappropriate in a man who, as Shaw said, was authentically both
a Spanish Hidalgo and a Scottish Laird, was directed, not
against the masses, but against the traditional enemy of the
aristocracy, the middle class. In 1887, a year after his election
to Parliament, he protested against the interference with
Socialist meetings: "England is a free country—thanks to
Heaven! It is a free country for a man to starve in—that is a
boon you can never take away from him—but it appears in the
future it is not going to be a free country to hold meetings in."
A month later he declared: "We look confidently for the time
when the Government will take possession of the mines and
machinery of this country, and work them for the benefit of
the country, and not in the selfish interests of capitalists." In

the following November he was arrested at the famous Trafalgar Square meeting, beaten by the police, kept for twenty-four hours without food or drink, and sentenced to two months of hard labor. He became chairman of the Scottish Parliamentary Labor Party in 1888, and spoke for Socialist measures until he left Parliament in 1892. In what he wrote thereafter, if he seldom advocated Socialism, he often attacked imperialism and exploitation and often satirized middle-class hypocrisy. Usually, however, his disgust with capitalist society was such that he turned his back on it.

Bernard Shaw, though he paid a pleasant tribute to Graham in his note on *Captain Brassbound's Conversion,* and though, as everyone knows, he could be sharp enough about the follies of the contemporary world, did not share the passionate hostility to nineteenth century institutions that united Graham, Morris, and Carpenter. Shaw wanted Socialism, but not at the sacrifice of whatever capitalism had accomplished in the way of order and comfort. The romantics, anyone would grant, were all too eager for destruction. Shaw was too insistent on conservation. That is why he became a Fabian.

The Fabian Society was born while Edward Pease, long its secretary and its official historian, was ghost-hunting with Thomas Davidson. Davidson, as they whiled away their time in a haunted house, suggested the formation of the Fellowship of the New Spirit. The Fellowship, which aimed at "the cultivation of a perfect character in each and all" and "the subordination of material things to spiritual," soon had many members who wanted to formulate a more definite policy. These members, on January 4, 1884, created the Fabian Society. Shaw joined it in September of that year and Sidney Webb the following May. Under their influence and that of Graham Wallas and Sidney Olivier, its aims and methods were clarified.

As the society gained shape, it took as definite a place in the utilitarian tradition as Morris had taken in the tradition of interventionism. John Stuart Mill, as Webb was pleased to point out, had died a Socialist—of a strangely qualified kind—and it was his spirit that presided over the Fabians. They owed something to Spencer, though he was their arch-enemy, much to Henry George, more than they liked to admit to Marx, almost nothing to Ruskin.[1] Shaw was indebted to Jevons, whose theory of marginal utility he adopted, turned to Fabian account, and constantly preached.

A gradual transition to Socialism was, according to the Fabians, not merely possible but inevitable. Such a revolution as the Social Democratic Federation and the Socialist League preached simply could not take place. "There will never be a point," Mrs. Besant declared in *Fabian Essays,* "at which a society crosses from Individualism to Socialism. The change is ever going forward; and our society is well on the way to Socialism. All we can do is to consciously co-operate with the forces at work, and thus render the transition more rapid than it would otherwise be." Shaw traced in detail the steps in what he called "this inevitable, but sordid, slow, reluctant, cowardly path to justice." "The Socialists," he wrote, "need not be ashamed of beginning as they did by proposing militant organization of the working classes and general insurrection," though "the proposal proved impracticable" and "has now been abandoned."

In their various ways—Shaw with at least a show of regret, most of the others with frank rejoicing—the Fabians agreed that the coming of Socialism would be accomplished in a slow, peaceful manner by the whole population, led by the middle class. They expected the steady growth of capitalism, which would give them unlimited time for the education of

---

[1] Shaw says of the Fabian attitude towards Ruskin: "My explanation is that, barring Olivier, the Fabians were inveterate Philistines." In Pease, *History of the Fabian Society,* 263.

the British voters. The cities would take over water works and power plants and trolley lines, and thus would prove the efficiency of public ownership. Nationalization of basic industries would come next, and the owners would not object, for they would be compensated and would be too stupid to realize that the Fabians would take away in taxes what they gave as compensation. The process might take decades, even centuries, but it was the only possible way.

Nothing could be more at odds with what Marx had taught and Engels was at the moment teaching. Nor were the Fabians unaware of this: they were conscious anti-Marxists. Mr. Pease goes out of his way to make it clear that the original Fabians had not read *Capital,* and he insists that the society's great achievement was "to break the spell of Marxism in England." "Marx," he wrote, "demonstrated the moral bankruptcy of commercialism and formulated the demand for the communal ownership and organization of industry; and it is hardly possible to exaggerate the value of this service to humanity." If that were all Marx had done, its value might easily be exaggerated, for the interventionists had dwelt on the immorality of commercialism not only during Marx's lifetime but long before the *Communist Manifesto,* and the Utopians had anticipated his demand for the socialization of the means of production. What Marx had really contributed to Socialism the Fabians rejected, and they were therefore completely unprepared for the actual course capitalism has taken.[1]

The Fabians did not so much attempt to refute Marx's theories as to disparage them. He was, after all, a German,

[1] Harold Laski says of Fabianism: "Accepting the fundamental economic postulates of liberal capitalism, it saw no reason to anticipate that collapse of the postwar years which would not only set definite limits to taxable capacity under a system based upon the predominant motive of profit-making, but would also, once the making of profits was in jeopardy, persuade, as in Italy and Germany, the owners of economic power to overthrow the democratic foundations of society in the interest of their right to make profit." *Rise of Liberalism,* 276.

they insisted, whereas Fabianism emerged from and was adapted to British conditions. Or, as Max Beer argued, he was a product of the mid-nineteenth century, whereas Fabians were up-to-date. The Fabians rather distrusted the workers, to whom he attached chief importance, and were sure that middle-class intellectuals were called to serve as midwives of the new society. He talked about the class struggle, and the Fabians loved order.[1] Finally, his followers were often dogmatic and difficult, and he himself was said to have been highly irascible.

Shaw says that he joined the Fabian Society, rather than any other Socialist organization, because he realized that he would be happier with intellectuals of his own class. At the outset the Fabians addressed themselves primarily to the middle class, and it was not until they were confident of their ability to impose their ideas on the labor movement—of being leaders rather than followers—that they allied themselves with the trade unions and helped form the Independent Labor Party. Yet the fact that Fabian ideas did come to dominate the labor movement indicates that Fabianism is not to be explained in terms of individual whims or even of middle-class psychology. Max Beer argues that Webb's theories were more appropriate to the two or three decades before the war than Marx's, and in a superficial sense he is right. The only trouble was that Webb's theories were based on an incomplete view of certain transitory phenomena, whereas Marx had understood the laws underlying the whole development

---

[1] Engels wrote Friedrich Sorge in 1893: "The Fabians are an ambitious group here in London who have understanding enough to realize the inevitability of the social revolution, but who could not possibly entrust this gigantic task to the rough proletariat alone and are therefore kind enough to set themselves at the head. Fear of the revolution is their fundamental principle. . . . With great industry they have produced amid all sorts of rubbish some good propagandist writings as well, in fact the best of the kind which the English have produced. But as soon as they get on to their specific tactics of hushing up the class struggle it all turns putrid. Hence too their fanatical hatred of Marx and all of us—because of the class struggle." Marx-Engels, *Selected Correspondence*, 505–6.

of capitalism. Events were to prove, with sad consequences for British labor, that Marx was right, but in the meantime Fabianism was triumphant.

It triumphed also in literary circles. At one time or another the society numbered among its members Granville Barker, Edward and Constance Garnett, Cecil Chesterton, G. D. H. Cole, St. John Ervine, Aylmer Maude, J. C. Squire, H. G. Wells, Clutton Brock, Arnold Bennett, A. R. Orage, Jerome K. Jerome, and Rupert Brooke. The writings of some were considerably influenced by Fabian ideas, whereas others were only slightly affected. What happened to them is not part of our story, but we must notice that they testify to the strength —and the weakness—of Fabianism.

Shaw and Wells were the major Fabian men of letters. Their careers principally belong, like those of most of the Society's converts, to the twentieth century, but we must not forget the Fabian plays Shaw wrote in the nineties. *Candida, You Never Can Tell, Widowers' Houses,* and *Mrs. Warren's Profession* are not merely satires, pleasant or unpleasant, on late Victorian stupidities; they teach the Socialist lesson that we cannot have moral individuals in an immoral society. It is better Socialism than you will find in the Fabian tracts, or, rather, it is the better part of the Socialism that can be found there, for it points to the need for the complete transformation of society. Shaw's feeling for dramatic effectiveness made him direct himself to essential issues, ignoring some of the fallacies he was contemporaneously preaching in his pamphlets.

Wells did no Socialist writing before 1900, but, coming to London as a bright young man, he did attend Fabian meetings and meetings of Morris' Hammersmith Society as a matter of course. The doctrines of the Social Democratic Federation and the Socialist League made no impression on him. In 1885, he tells us, "Fabianism was Socialism, so far as

the exposition of views and policy went. There was no other
Socialist propaganda in England worth considering." This
extraordinary statement may be intended to explain his complete ignorance of Marxism. He did not, as a matter of fact,
join the Fabian Society until much later, for at the moment
he was concerned with making his way in the world. A little
of what he had picked up entered into the scientific romances
he wrote in the nineties, but for the most part the allusions
to Socialism one finds there seem merely part of the stock
in trade of a young man who likes to be in fashion and en-
joys shocking the bourgeoisie.

A glance at the Fabian writers increases our respect for
Morris. "He was our one acknowledged Great Man," Shaw
has recently written, and Shaw is right in more senses than
he realizes. Morris could not be satisfied with less than real
Communism, and that was fortunate, for many who could
be satisfied with less deceived themselves into believing that
they had got or were about to get all they wanted. The
Fabians, as they drew up their careful plans for municipal
water works, called themselves scientific, and smiled con-
descendingly over the romanticism of *News from Nowhere,*
but it constantly becomes clearer that Morris was right on
fundamentals and the Fabians simply not right at all. Whatever his limitations as part of a usable Socialist tradition in
literature, it is good that England's first Socialist poet was
a Great Man and a Marxist.

Chapter III

THE PESSIMISM OF THOMAS HARDY

WHEN William Butler Yeats said that, if some angel offered him the choice, he would choose to live William Morris' life rather than his own or any other man's, he must have been thinking, at least in part, of Morris' surprising freedom from the doubts that troubled most literary men in the later nineteenth century. Apparently Morris abandoned the faith of his parents without the slightest pang. The progress of science interested him little and troubled him not at all. His acceptance of what men were calling a bleak and terrifying concept of nature was complete and tranquil, and the whole problem, so far as one can judge, seemed to him less interesting and less important than the affairs of the firm or the Socialist League.

In this as in other ways Morris was nearly unique, for the majority of his contemporaries were alarmed, and some of the more thoughtful were in despair. Their pessimism was, or seemed to them to be, of a new kind. Gloomy men of the eighteenth century—Swift, for example, or Dr. Johnson, or the hypersensitive Cowper—never lost their belief in a just God. The Deists and the rebels of the period of the French Revolution, though they had rejected the Christian revelation, were convinced that they had fathomed the secret of the universe and found it good. But now science was revealing a universe that did not seem to be the work of a benevolent and just God and that was apparently indifferent to all men's hopes and fears. Though the weight of social approval was still heavily on the side of orthodoxy, the onus of proof in intellectual circles was shifting from the skeptics to the believers. If a man was not to be a pessimist, it was necessary for him to show cause for his belief in the beneficence of the universe or, failing that, to justify his hopes on other grounds.

Some men were, of course, more acutely conscious of the dilemma than others. If few could achieve the indifference of William Morris, there were not many who were so exclusively pre-occupied with it as Thomas Hardy. He thought and wrote of little else. Other writers might be gloomier, more savage, or more desperate; none addressed himself so constantly to this particular problem or saw it so consistently as a problem that science had created.

1. What Hardy Believed.

As he insisted again and again, Hardy was not a systematic philosopher, but he was so often misunderstood that he had to try to give some clear and precise statement of his beliefs. He believed, he said, that the Cause of Things was "neither moral nor immoral, but *un*moral." In a constant process of change the human race had appeared, one of countless species, of no more concern to the universe than any of the others. It was partly adapted to its environment, for otherwise it would not survive, but it occupied no privileged position. He saw no evidence of a power not ourselves that makes for righteousness, no sign of an order corresponding to man's moral values.

Among the qualities of the race that contributed to man's misery Hardy placed consciousness first. "A woeful fact," he wrote, "that the human race is too extremely developed for its corporeal conditions, the nerves being evolved to an activity abnormal in such an environment. Even the higher animals are in excess in this respect. It may be questioned if

Nature, or what we call Nature, so far back as when she crossed the line from invertebrates to vertebrates, did not exceed her mission. This planet does not supply the materials for happiness to higher existences. Other planets may, though one can hardly see how."

From this emphasis he drew what he regarded as the only original part of his philosophic scheme. By the time at least that he wrote *The Dynasts,* he had concluded that the Cause of Things might eventually become conscious. A portion of the universe having developed consciousness, it was believable that this quality might be extended until the laws of nature were dictated by design. This thesis, he maintained, settled the question of free will: "The will of a man is, according to it, neither wholly free nor wholly unfree. When swayed by the Universal Will (which he mostly must be as a subservient part of it) he is not individually free; but whenever it happens that all the rest of the Great Will is in equilibrium the minute portion called one person's will is free."

The logic of this does not much concern us, for all that is necessary is that we should distinguish what Hardy really believed from the fantastic views attributed to him. "It is my misfortune," he wrote in 1920, "that people *will* treat all my mood-dictated writing as a single scientific theory." It was also his misfortune that his readers insisted on regarding his parables and allegories as philosophical formulas. He could pretend, as in "God-Forgotten," that the earth had been overlooked by a pre-occupied but well-intentioned God, or, as in "By the Earth's Corpse," that it was a careless creation the deity would some time regret. He could imagine God dying, as in "A Plaint to Man," or already dead, as in "God's Funeral." He could have God marvel at man's development of an ethics "I never knew or made provision for," promise to learn from man's higher thoughts, or try to justify His unconsciousness. He might suggest that the thrush was sustained by "some blessed hope" that the poet could not know. He might, as in "Agnosto Theo" and "The Aerolite" offer theories to explain human consciousness. These were all no more than ways of telling what the universe seemed to him to be like. In "Nature's Questioning" he propounds four theories, each of them elaborated in other poems, and none of them more than a figure of speech:

> Has some Vast Imbecility,
>> Mighty to build and blend,
>> But impotent to tend,
> Framed us in jest, and left us now to hazardry?

> Or come we of an Automaton
>> Unconscious of our pains?
>> Or are we live remains
> Of Godhead dying downwards, brain and eyes now gone?

> Or is it that some high Plan betides,
>> As yet not understood,
>> Of Evil stormed by Good,
> We the Forlorn Hope over which Achievement strides?

Well might Hardy complain when some critic wrote, "To him evil is not so much a mystery, a problem, as the wilful malice of his god." Hardy commented: "As I need hardly inform any thinking reader, I do not hold, and never have held, the opinions here assumed to be mine—which are really, or approximately, those of the primitive believer in his man-shaped tribal god." Not even the automatism of *The Dynasts* is more than a metaphor. When, as in certain scenes, Hardy speaks of the Immanent Will as a puppet-master, or when he displays "the anatomy of the Immanent Will," "exhibiting as one organism the anatomy of life and movements in all humanity and vitalized matter," he is merely stating in his own way his consistent monism. Man is part of a universe whose changes seem, to man's limited perceptions, to follow certain sequences that he calls laws. These laws, whatever they may be, are binding upon him as well as upon the rest of nature, even when he does not detect their operation.

His theories can and must be understood, but—and this is what he never seemed to grasp—it was not his theories that gave him the name of pessimist. In 1922, in his preface to *Late Lyrics and Earlier,* he said that he believed in "the exploration of reality, and its frank recognition stage by stage along the survey, with an eye to the best consummation: briefly, evolutionary meliorism." "But," he went on, "it is called pessimism nevertheless; under which word, expressed with condemnatory emphasis, it is regarded by many as some pernicious new thing." By 1922 there were many to agree with him that the way to the Better demanded "a full look at the Worse," but, in spite of all Hardy's protests, they could not help feeling that his look was not only full but exclusive.

In one of his earliest poems, "Hap," Hardy wrote:

> These purblind Doomsters had as readily strown
> Blisses about my pilgrimage as pain.

His readers noticed that the Doomsters seldom did strew blisses. Anyone could observe in *The Mayor of Casterbridge* and *The Return of the Native* how repeatedly disaster hung upon a mere throw of the dice and how inevitably the dice fell against the heroes and heroines. Anyone could see how surely Hardy selected for examination in *Life's Little Ironies* incidents in which the best intentions had the worst results —often in the face of what the reader felt to be the probabilities. Anyone could sense Hardy's predilection as a poet for the more melancholy moods and more harrowing incidents.

Not only does unhappiness overwhelmingly predominate over happiness in his accounts of life; Hardy's own estimate of man's lot is clearly registered. Scores of passages will rise to any reader's mind. The famous description of Egdon Heath in *The Return of the Native* comes to this conclusion: "Fair prospects wed happily with fair times; but alas, if times be not fair! Men have oftener suffered from the mockery of a place too smiling for their reason than from the oppression of surroundings oversadly tinged. Haggard Egdon appealed to a subtler and scarcer instinct, to a more recently learnt emotion, than that which responds to the sort of beauty called charming and fair. Indeed, it is a question if the exclusive reign of this orthodox beauty is not approaching its last quarter. The new Vale of Tempe may be a gaunt waste in Thule: human souls may find themselves in closer and closer harmony with external things wearing a sombreness distasteful to our race when it was young." And in *Jude the Obscure,* after Little Time has hanged the other children and himself, Jude reports: "The doctor says there are such boys springing up amongst us—boys of a sort unknown in the last generation—the outcome of new views of life. They seem to see all its terrors before they are old enough to resist them. He says it is the beginning of the coming universal wish not to live."

The growing preference for bleak scenery and the tendency to youthful suicide seem to have existed only in Hardy's mind, and his melodramatic insistence upon them makes us feel the quality of his pessimism. He might maintain that his views were strictly in accordance with the discoveries of science, but his state of mind was so nearly unique that it could not have been the necessary outcome of scientific revelations. Other men of letters were forced to abandon orthodox views of the world and yet neither felt nor found evidence of "the coming universal wish not to live." Exceptional as Morris may have been, he was closer to the norm than Hardy. Frederic Harrison, Leslie Stephen, and John Morley, for example, were all born in the same decade as Morris—that is, just a little before Hardy—and each was brought up, as Hardy was, in an orthodox Church of England family. All three of them met in their twenties with scientific conceptions of the universe, skeptical analyses of theology, and the higher criticism of the Bible, and they all abandoned Christianity. Yet none of them ever came to be, or to be regarded as, an apostle of despair. Frederic Harrison accepted Comte's Positivism, became a reformer, and was a lifelong critic of Hardy's position. Morley, looking back on the decades that seemed to Hardy to be breeding a taste for melancholy landscapes and suicide, wrote, "These years—say from 1860 to 1890—were an animated, hopeful, interesting, and on the whole, either by reason of or in spite of, its perpetual polemics, a happy generation." Even Leslie Stephen, who seems closer to Hardy than the others, was willing to guess "that happiness predominates over misery in the composition of the known world."

That such men could accept the idea of an unmoral, distinterested universe without feeling that it would be better for the human race to sink back into nescience, that they would never have written "I Said to Love," "Mad Judy," or "Sine Prole," is enough to convince us that Hardy's pessimism was not the simple product of new modes of thought he believed it to be. Since pessimism has become one of the recognizably modern modes of thinking and feeling, it is worth asking what, in addition to the impact of nineteenth century science, made Hardy the kind of pessimist he was. Quite different from his formulated opinions, which he shared with many contemporaries, was the view of life that found expression in his novels and poems, nor was there the necessary relationship between his opinions and his attitudes that he supposed.

2. *The Making of a Pessimist.*

If we knew more about Hardy's life between 1862 and 1866, we should be better able to answer the questions that have been posed. In the former year, when he went to London, he had scarcely begun to question the orthodoxy of his family. By the latter, from which his earliest published writings come, he had arrived at the convictions he held during the remainder of his life. It was in 1866 that he wrote "Hap" and "A Young Man's Epigram on Existence":

> A senseless school, where we must give
> Our lives that we may learn to live!
> A dolt is he who memorizes
> Lessons that leave no time for prizes.

Because of his reticence, we do not know what he was like when he went to London or what happened to him there. We do know that he began to read scientists, theological heretics, and Biblical critics, and we can gather that he was a sensitive young man, interested in the arts, unwilling to push himself forward, sympathetically aware of the frustrations and sufferings of others. He was studying architecture in London, and apparently he was not wholly satisfied with his chosen profession. In 1865 he considered entering the ministry, and gave up the idea only because his theological doubts were taking shape. A little later it was literature that seemed more desirable than architecture. One suspects that he had wanted to find a life-work that demanded less aggressiveness and gave more scope to the imagination than anything normally open to the son of a small contractor and had seized the opportunity to study in an architect's office. He was beginning to believe that he had chosen unwisely. At least architecture neither gave him personal pleasure nor promised much to his shy ambitions. In 1863 he wrote: "The world does not despise us; it only neglects us." In 1865: "My 25th birthday. Not very cheerful. Feel as if I had lived a long time and done very little."

Hardy was always bitter at those critics who insisted on finding autobiography in his novels, but no one can suppose that he kept his experiences and moods out of his books. Though he specifically told Ernest Brennecke, Jr., that Edward Springrove in *Desperate Remedies* was drawn, not from himself, but from "a youth I once knew quite well," Brennecke was unconvinced. Springrove is "a man of rather humble origin," "a thorough bookworm," and "a poet himself in a small way." He is disillusioned with regard to architecture: "Worldly advantage from an art doesn't depend on mastering it. I used to think it did; but it doesn't. Those who get rich need have no skill at all as artists." All the acquisition of wealth requires is "a certain kind of energy which men with any fondness for art possess very seldom indeed—an earnestness in making acquaintances, and a love for using them." He tells the heroine: "If anything on earth ruins a man for useful occupation, and for content with reasonable success in a profession or trade, it is the habit of writing verses on emotional subjects, which had much better be left to die for want of nourishment." His father says of him: "I am sometimes afraid that he'll never get on—that he'll die poor and despised under the worst mental conditions, a keen sense of having been passed in the race by men whose brains are nothing to his own, all through his seeing too far into things —being discontented with makeshifts—thinking o' perfection in things, and then sickened that there's no such thing as perfection."

Hardy may have chosen a friend as the model for Springrove, but he put much of himself into the character. He was in other characters too. We know well enough that Jude's story was not his, and yet the origin of *Jude the Obscure* may be found in a note of April 28, 1888: "A short story of a young man—'who could not go to Oxford'— His struggles and ultimate failure. Suicide. There is something the world ought to be shown, and I am the one to show it to them—though I was not altogether hindered going, at least to Cambridge, and could have gone up easily at five-and-twenty." Can we not conclude that some of the bitterness that Jude comes to feel towards Christminster was at one time felt by Hardy, if not at the moment he wrote the novel? And perhaps he was right in feeling that he had lost much by not going to a university. It is worth remembering that Harrison and Morley made the transition to agnosticism at Oxford and Leslie Stephen at Cambridge. The process of disillusionment was one that they shared with a group of associates, and it took place at a time when new activities were occupying their attention, whereas Hardy made his discoveries in solitude and while he was engaged in a profession he did not like.

The novels give us another hint. Hardy says of Angel Clare: "Early association with country solitudes had bred in him an unconquerable and almost unreasonable aversion to modern town life, and shut him out from such success as he might have aspired to by entering a mundane profession in the impracticability of the spiritual one." We know that much of the time Hardy was not happy in London and that by 1867 he "was beginning to feel that he would rather go into the country altogether." Blomfield urged him to stay in London, but when his first master, John Hicks, wanted an assistant, he returned to Dorsetshire, and almost immediately began to feel better for having escaped "the fitful yet mechanical and monotonous existence that befalls many a young man in London lodgings."

We must remember also that, in the process of becoming an agnostic, Hardy had lost more than a comforting belief in the benevolence of the universe. Late in life he remarked that instead of being called atheist and pessimist he might well have been called churchy. The remark is less surprising than it may sound. He repeatedly regretted that the Church of England was not so reconstructed as to admit agnostics. The church meant more to him than its doctrines. His father and grandfather had been interested in church music, and his own love of music was closely associated with church-going in his mind. The church as an institution so deeply impressed him that he preached sermons as a small boy and his first ambition was to enter the ministry. The church provided a bond with society and a link with the past. Since he believed that views such as his must be more and more common, he could not see why the church should not adapt itself to them, and its failure to do so deprived him, unnecessarily as he saw it, of something he would have cherished.

A final suggestion comes from his concern with the position of his family. *A Pair of Blue Eyes* shows that he was not unaware of class distinctions, but it was not merely his father's relatively low estate and his own lack of worldly success that bothered him; he mourned the decline of the Hardys. Once the family had been of some importance in Dorsetshire. A sixteenth century Thomas Hardy had founded the primary school in Dorchester, and, in a collateral branch, there had been a number of naval heroes, including the Captain Hardy who is introduced in *The Trumpet-Major* and whose part in the battle of Trafalgar is portrayed in *The Dynasts*. Hardy's wife and biographer calls the Hardys "an old family of spent social energies," a phrase that might well be his. In 1888 he wrote in his journal, "The decline and fall of the Hardys much in evidence hereabout. . . . So we go down, down, down."

We can see Hardy, then, in the late sixties, as a young man with a sense of personal loss, little confidence in his own powers, and a certain number of social grievances. He had lost a faith and a church. He had been denied a university education, and had seen less worthy men succeed in architecture. He was thinking of marriage, we may surmise from some of the early poems and from repeated situations in the novels, and knew he could not afford it. And to his own misfortunes was added his awareness of the misfortunes of others. He had seen plenty of misery in London, and he was not one who could turn his back on it.

Many other young men have been conscious of their own sufferings and the sufferings of others, and have set out to make a better world. So did Thomas Hardy, by writing a book. His first novel, *The Poor Man and the Lady,* was read by John Morley for Macmillan and by George Meredith for Chapman and Hall. Macmillan rejected it. Chapman and Hall accepted it, but Meredith consulted with the author and advised against publication. Hardy subsequently revised the novel but never published it.[1] What we know about it we know from letters and from Mrs. Hardy's description. She calls it "a sweeping dramatic satire of the squirearchy and nobility, London society, the vulgarity of the middle class, modern Christianity, church restoration, and political and domestic morals in general; the author's views, in fact, being obviously those of a young man with a passion for reforming the world—those of many a young man before and after him; the tendency of the writing being socialistic, not to say revolutionary." Alexander Macmillan, writing Hardy about it, speaks of "the utter heartlessness of *all* the conversation you give in drawingrooms and ballrooms about the working-classes," and says, "Will's speech to the workingmen is full of wisdom."

We may be a little dubious about the Socialism if Sir Alexander Macmillan could find wisdom in a speech to workingmen, and may suspect that Hardy went no further than, say, George Eliot in *Felix Holt.* But he did make a bitter attack on the upper classes, and he did set forth some program,

---

[1] A short story published in the *New Quarterly Magazine* has been identified as part of this novel. See *An Indiscretion in the Life of an Heiress,* edited by Carl J. Weber. Naturally this fragment contains none of the passages in which we should be interested. See also Edmund Gosse, "Thomas Hardy's Lost Novel," London *Times,* Jan. 22, 1928.

however vague, of social reform. Gloomy as he might be about the nature of the universe, he believed that mankind could improve its lot, and was willing to advocate and work for drastic change.

Precisely this note was never struck again. That Hardy should not immediately attempt another novel in advocacy of reform is natural enough, but there is not even a hint of rebelliousness. If he made any political entries in his journal in the seventies, Mrs. Hardy does not repeat them. It is not until 1881 that his views are recorded, and then they are of this kind: "Conservatism is not estimable in itself, nor is Change, or Radicalism. To conserve the existing good, to supplant the existing bad by good, is to act on a true political principle, which is neither Conservative nor Radical." In 1888 he writes: "I find that my politics really are neither Tory nor Radical. I may be called an Intrinsicalist. I am against privilege derived from accident of any kind, and am therefore equally opposed to aristocratic privilege and democratic privilege. (By the latter I mean the arrogant assumption that the only labor is hand-labor—a worse arrogance than that of the aristocrat—the taxing of the worthy to help those masses of the population who will not help themselves when they might, etc.) Opportunity should be equal for all, but those who will not avail themselves of it should be cared for merely —not be a burden to, nor the rulers over, those who do avail themselves thereof." And in 1890: "Democratic government may be justice to man, but it will probably merge in proletarian, and when these people are our masters it will lead to more of this contempt, and possibly be the utter ruin of art and literature."

If we had all Hardy's letters and journals, perhaps we could see just how he lost the eagerness for reform that he expressed in *The Poor Man and the Lady*. As it is, only hazardous surmises are possible. His departure from London doubtless had something to do with it. Once back in Dorsetshire, in an environment that he knew and loved and that was as yet only remotely affected by the growth of industrialism,[1] Hardy not only felt more at ease but was less likely to believe in the possibility of change. Not only was the labor movement, with which he had apparently had a brief sympathy, a product of the cities;[2] the cities were the centers of the middle-class Radicalism that attracted Meredith, Morley, Harrison, and, for a brief time, Morris. In Dorsetshire it was easier than it had been in London to look on most evils as fixed in the nature of things.

Somehow the change took place. Hardy, already driven by science and his own experience, to take a somewhat melancholy view of life, had acquired and lost a belief in the possibility of revolutionary change. When he wrote *The Poor Man and the Lady,* he must have believed that, evil as the world was, improvement could be hoped and worked for. In a few years he had concluded that this was a delusion. Only slight changes were conceivable, and these, though he favored them, could not rouse his enthusiasm. If his energies had been absorbed in practical labors for reforms that seemed attainable, if he had shared with earnest companions the hope of obliterating some of the world's suffering, if, in short, he had been concerned chiefly with the remediable rather than the irremediable evils, his mood must have been dif-

---

[1] "In comparison with cities, Weatherbury was immutable. The citizen's Then is the rustic's Now. In London, twenty or thirty years ago are old times; in Paris ten years or five; in Weatherbury three or four score years were included in the mere present, and nothing less than a century set a mark on its face or tone. Five decades hardly modified the cut of a gaiter, the embroidery of a smock-frock, by the breadth of a hair. Ten generations failed to alter the turn of a single phrase." *Far from the Madding Crowd,* 167.

[2] In 1883, in an article for *Longman's Magazine* on "The Dorsetshire Laborer," Hardy commented, not unsympathetically, on Joseph Arch's attempts to organize the agricultural workers, calling Arch "rather the social evolutionist than the anarchic irreconcilable." *Life and Art,* 40. This movement came too late to have any influence on his thinking.

ferent, even though he could not deny that the universe cared nothing for his aims. As it was, the loss of the faith he had had when he wrote *The Poor Man and the Lady* underscored the loss of the other faith he had had as a boy. In Dorsetshire solitude he had plenty of time to think of all that was wrong with the world and all that could not be done to mend it.

We can see why Hardy's mood differed from that of many of his contemporaries. Frederic Harrison was, when compared with Hardy, an insensitive person. His own life's program was quickly mapped out, and he found in Positivism an adequate chart for the race. John Morley passed from an active life in Oxford to an active life in literature, and from this to an active life in politics. Leslie Stephen, though his course was less certain, enjoyed a period of intense satisfaction at Cambridge, before his years of theological difficulties, and thereafter quickly found his way into a career. All three came from prosperous middle-class families, went to Oxford or Cambridge as a matter of course, and except for Stephen, had no hesitation over the choice of a profession. They mingled with people who shared their interests and strengthened their conviction that England's ills could soon be set right. Hardy, on the other hand, took satisfaction neither in his family nor in his profession, and he was denied a university education. He was unhappy in the great cities and isolated in the country. The loss of his God and his church came at a time when he had reason enough for his unhappiness and when he was miserably aware of the unhappiness of others. And somehow he could not hold to a brief and perhaps always fragile hope in concerted effort for change.

3. *The Thin-Skinned Man of Letters.*

One may doubt if there was ever an artist of equal talent so susceptible to suggestion and criticism as Thomas Hardy.

George Meredith, after reading *The Poor Man and the Lady,* advised him to "attempt a novel with a purely artistic purpose, giving it a more complicated 'plot.'" He immediately set to work and wrote *Desperate Remedies,* modeling it on the novels of Wilkie Collins and even surpassing Collins in the contrivance of coincidences. The next novel, *Under the Greenwood Tree,* was undertaken because Morley had praised a scene in *The Poor Man and the Lady* having to do with tranters and rural folk. Leslie Stephen liked the novel, and wrote Hardy, asking for something for the *Cornhill Magazine,* but specifying that it must have more incidents: "Though I do not want a murder in every number, it is necessary to catch the attention of readers by some distinct and well-arranged plot." Hardy, who was working on *A Pair of Blue Eyes* for Tinsley, turned his attention as soon as he could to Stephen's request, and wrote *Far from the Madding Crowd,* which is filled with incidents that are not essential to its theme. The success of this novel would seem to have established him so that he should have felt free to write as he wished, but he was now worried because critics had pigeonholed him as a novelist of rural life, and he abandoned *The Woodlanders* to write *The Hand of Ethelberta,* a comedy of society.

Thus Hardy was nearly forty years old and the author of five novels before he ceased trying to shape his work according to somebody else's interpretation of what the public wanted. And by this time he had formulated for himself rigid theories of the art of popular fiction. "The real, if unavowed purpose of fiction," he wrote in 1881, "is to give pleasure by gratifying the love of the uncommon in human experience, mental or corporeal. This is done all the more perfectly in proportion as the reader is illuded to believe the personages true and real like himself. Solely to this latter end a work of fiction should be a precise transcript of ordinary life: but the uncommon would be absent and the interest lost. Hence the writer's problem is, how to strike the balance between the uncommon and the ordinary so as on the one hand to give interest, on the other to give reality. In working out this problem, human nature must never be made abnormal, which is introducing incredibility. The uncommonness must be in the events, not in the characters; and the writer's art lies in shaping that uncommonness while disguising its unlikelihood, if it be unlikely." "A story must be exceptional enough to justify its telling," he later wrote. "We tale-tellers are all Ancient Mariners, and none of us is warranted in stopping Wedding Guests (in other words, the hurrying public) unless he has something more unusual to relate than the ordinary experience of every average man and woman."

This is enough to explain the abuse of coincidence that has disturbed most of Hardy's critics. In *Desperate Remedies, A Pair of Blue Eyes,* and *Far from the Madding Crowd* coincidences are used, by and large, as Hardy's predecessors and contemporaries used them, even Dickens, Thackeray, and George Eliot; that is, to provide variety of incident and to shape the story towards the desired end. It is in *The Return of the Native* and *The Mayor of Casterbridge* that Hardy's peculiar use of coincidence appears in recognizable form. In these novels the coincidences develop cumulatively, so as to bring the doom of certain characters. In *The Mayor of Casterbridge,* for example, there is an almost mechanical sequence: Henchard's quarrel with Farfrae, the discovery of Susan's letter to Elizabeth-Jane, Elizabeth-Jane's association with Lucetta, the revelation of the furmity woman, the reading of Henchard's letters to Lucetta, and the return of Newson. Commenting on the novel, Hardy admits that, in the interests of serial publication, he tried to "get an incident into almost every week's part." And he says, "I fear it will not be so good as I meant, but after all, it is not improbabilities of incident but improbabilities of character that matter." Thus he adapts a literary convention to his own philosophy. If other writers interested their readers by a generous use of coincidence, which they manipulated to achieve a happy ending, why should he not win the same interest, but employ his coincidences, in accordance with his views of the universe, to bring about his characters' destruction?

With his lack of self-confidence and his constant preoccupation with what he was told the public wanted, it is no wonder that Hardy held a low opinion of the novelist's function. The opinion was strengthened by the apparent impossibility of candor. Macmillan rejected *The Poor Man and the Lady* in part at least because of the author's opinions, and Meredith warned him that the book would injure his reputation. The *Spectator* attacked *Desperate Remedies* because Hardy dared "to suppose it possible that an unmarried lady owning an estate could have an illegitimate child." Leslie Stephen asked him to make many changes in *Far from the Madding Crowd:* "Remember the country parson's daughters," he said. "*I* have always to remember them." And he would not publish *The Return of the Native* because of the part sexual passion played in the story. *Two on a Tower* was called "repulsive," "little short of revolting," and "a studied and gratuitous insult," and Hardy was enough troubled by these criticisms to defend himself against them when the book was republished thirteen years later. He modified the end of *The Woodlanders* because of "the conventions of the libraries," and altered *Jude the Obscure* to adapt it to serial publication.

Plagued by the practical problems abuse created, Hardy gloomily explored the possibilities of candor in an article he wrote for the *New Review* in 1890. The magazine and the circulating library, he pointed out, both catered to entire households and therefore barred whatever parents might regard as harmful for their children. "The crash of broken commandments," he wrote, "is as necessary an accompaniment to the catastrophe of a tragedy as the noise of drum and cymbals to a triumphant march." He did not countenance the relaxation of conventional morals: "Nothing in such literature should for a moment exhibit lax views of that purity of life upon which the well-being of society depends." But art was impossible without honesty, and honesty was forbidden the artist. "If the true artist ever weeps it probably is then, when he first discovers the fearful price that he has to pay for the privilege of writing in the English language—no less a price than the complete extinction in the mind of every mature and penetrating reader, of sympathetic belief in his personages."

Hardy could not respect his own craft. He had begun by wanting to be a poet, and had turned to the novel chiefly because it paid better. He often thought, as the years went on and the attacks continued, of ceasing to write fiction, and, after the fury roused by *Tess,* the decision became more and more attractive. "Well," he wrote in his journal, "if this sort of thing continues no more novel-writing for me. A man must be a fool to deliberately stand up to be shot at." *Jude the Obscure* brought him abusive anonymous letters; the Bishop of Wakefield announced that he had burned the book; Jeannette Gilder wrote in the New York *World,* "Aside from its immorality, there is coarseness which is beyond belief." "Perhaps," the journal recorded in 1897, "I can express more fully in verse ideas and emotions which run counter to the inert crystallized opinion—hard as a rock—which the vast body of men have vested interests in supporting."

For a mature man of letters to surrender to hostile criticism, at a time when his reputation was growing steadily among men whose opinions he could value, would be inexplicable if we did not know how bitterly Hardy suffered with every onslaught. In mid-career he wrote, "What Ruskin says as to the cause of the want of imagination in works of the present age is probably true—that it is the flippant sarcasm of the time. 'Men dare not open their hearts to us if we are to broil them on a thorn fire.'" Soon after the belaboring of *Jude,* he wrote in his journal, "Every man's birthday is a first of April for him; and he who lives to be fifty and won't own to it is a rogue or a fool, hypocrite or simpleton." Swinburne's death led him to ask, "Was there ever such a country —looking back at the life, work, and death of Swinburne— is there any other country in Europe whose attitude towards a deceased poet of his rank would have been so ignoring and almost contemptuous?" No doubt he remembered that he and Swinburne had laughed together at their having been "the two most abused of living writers." Even as late as 1922 Charles Morgan was astonished by the bitterness with which Hardy discussed the critics, and in the same year, in the preface to *Late Lyrics and Earlier,* the poet addressed the reviewers of his earlier volumes with some impatience.

It was no ordinary vanity that made Hardy wince. He regarded himself as a serious artist, trying to describe the world he saw. That he should be so often misunderstood, and so often condemned when he was understood, could scarcely encourage him. He did not feel that he personally was being persecuted but that honesty was impossible. His career as man of letters proved to him year by year that his estimate of man's chances for happiness erred if at all by being on the bright side.

4. *The Remediable Ills.*

"I am a meliorist," Hardy wrote, "not a pessimist as they say." "What are my books," he asked William Archer, "but one plea against 'man's inhumanity to man,' to woman, and to the lower animals? . . . Whatever may be the inherent good or evil of life, it is certain that men make it much worse than it need be. When we have got rid of a thousand remediable ills, it will be time enough to determine whether the ill that is irremediable outweighs the good." Late in his life he said, "As to pessimism. My motto is, first correctly diagnose the complaint—in this case human ills—and ascertain the cause: then set about finding a remedy if one exists." There are many poems that come from this mood. "To Sincerity" ends:

> Yet, would men look at true things,
> And unilluded view things,
> And count to bear undue things,
>
> The real might mend the seeming,
> Facts better their foredeeming,
> And Life its disesteeming.

And in the fine "Plaint to Man" God says:

> But since I was framed in your first despair
> The doing without me has had no play
> In the minds of men when shadows scare;
>
> And now that I dwindle day by day
> Beneath the deicide eyes of seers,
> In a light that will not let me stay,
>
> And tomorrow the whole of me disappears,
> The truth should be told, and the fact be faced,
> That had best been faced in earlier years:
>
> The fact of life with dependence placed
> On the human heart's resource alone,
> In brotherhood bonded close and graced
>
> With loving-kindness fully blown,
> And visioned help unsought, unknown.

This perhaps deserves the name of meliorism, but it is not a robust kind of hopefulness, and we cannot be surprised that Hardy spent little time in work for reform. After the disillusionment that presumably followed the writing of *The Poor Man and the Lady,* there were almost twenty years in which he had nothing to say about proposals for social change, and even in the latter half of his life it was only rarely that he committed himself on particular measures. In 1893, asked by a Paris paper for his conception of an ideal social system, he suggested, obviously rather casually, that society might be divided into groups of temperaments, each with its own code, in order to preserve individual spontaneity. Not uncharacteristically, he urged, when asked how war might be humanized, that horses should not be used except for transport, since "soldiers, at worst, know what they are doing, but these animals are denied even the poor possibilities of glory and reward as a compensation for their suffering." Though he seldom expressed himself on the subject, he felt strongly about the marriage laws, and in 1912 went so far as to attribute to them half the misery in England. Always opposed to war, he supported Great Britain in 1914, saying that "we are fighting to save what is best in Germany." Although, according to Mrs. Hardy, the war destroyed a growing hope that the race might be able to improve its lot, it did not alter his conviction that improvement would be possible if men would face evils and intelligently set about remedying them. "I might say," he wrote at the time of the war, "that the Good-God theory having, after some thousands of years of trial, produced the present infamous and disgraceful state of Europe—that most Christian Continent!—a theory of a Goodless-and-Badless God (as in *The Dynasts*) might perhaps be given a trial with advantage."

It is on his writings, rather than on any labor for reform, that Hardy's claim to be a meliorist must rest. There is no whining in that work, no self-pity, often as it appears that Hardy is going out of his way to have his full look at the worst. Nor is there any cheap pessimism at the expense of human nature. On the contrary. Almost without exception circumstances are responsible for sufferings in his novels, and one is invariably given the impression that in a different sort of universe even his least admirable men and women would prove worthy of some respect. There is not a villainous villain in his works. Sergeant Troy, Damon Wildeve, Edred Fitzpiers, and Alec D'Urberville are all weak men, but Hardy seems to say that they are no weaker than many others and, with better fortune, their weaknesses might have done little damage to themselves or their acquaintances. He does not so much seek to explain their defects, in ordinary deterministic fashion, as to attribute the misfortunes in which those defects resulted to the nature of the world. Man, he repeatedly seems to be saying, even at his worst deserves a better universe than this. There is almost melodramatic fitness in his asking, on his deathbed, to be read from the *Rubaiyat*:

> O Thou, who Man of Baser Earth didst make,
> And ev'n with Paradise devise the Snake:
>   For all the Sin wherewith the Face of Man
> Is blacken'd—Man's forgiveness give—and take!

His estimate of human nature is the more remarkable and attractive because it embraced the great majority of mankind. It is true that he once wrote, "You may regard a throng of people as containing a certain small minority who have sensitive souls; these, and the aspects of these, being what is worth observing. So you divide them into the mentally unquickened, mechanical, soulless; and the living, throbbing, suffering, vital." But in practice he found that most men did their share of living and suffering. He set out in his article, "The Dorsetshire Laborer," to combat the conventional idea of the country dweller as "a degraded being of uncouth manner and aspect, stolid understanding, and snail-like movement." Experience showed that there was no typical Hodge, but "a number of dissimilar fellow-creatures, men of many minds, infinite in difference, some happy, many serene, a few depressed; some clever, even to genius, some stupid, some wanton, some austere; some mutely Miltonic, some Cromwellian."

It was this varied and animated group that he so often undertook to portray in his novels. In *Under the Greenwood Tree* rustics compose the entire dramatis personae, and certainly there is no lack of variety, animation, and charm in the story. Some of the characters are less than normally intelligent, but others are full of wisdom. As Hardy describes the singing of carols, the Christmas party, the interview of the choir with the vicar, and the wedding, he makes the reader feel his joy in Wessex customs, speech, and character. But he is not merely a lover of the picturesque; he respects the tranter and his associates, and respects them for what they are, without a trace of condescension.

Except in *The Trumpet-Major,* Hardy never repeated the experiment of limiting himself to rural characters, but the country people appear in most of his novels, and always are treated with the same dignity. There could not be a more attractive group than Edward Springrove's father, John Smith, Gabriel Oak, Giles Winterbourne, and others of their kind, sturdy, hard-working men, thoughtful, generous, brave. Even the clowns are self-respecting and shrewd. In *A Pair of Blue Eyes* Martin comments on the wide black edges that adorn announcements of Lady Luxellian's death: " 'Tis out of the question that a human being can be so mournful as black edges half-an-inch wide. I'm sure people don't feel more than a very narrow border when they feels most of all." When the farm-workers in *Far from the Madding Crowd* are discussing the chapel-goers' interest in dogma and their making of prayers, Coggan says: "Yes, we know very well that if any-body do go to heaven, they will. They've worked hard for it, and they deserve to have it, such as 'tis. I baint such a fool as to pretend that we who stick to the Church have the same chance as they, because we know we have not. But I hate a feller who'll change his old ancient doctrine for the sake of getting to heaven. I'd as soon turn king's evidence for the few pounds you get." They have a feeling, too, these country people, for the sadness of things, never more touchingly expressed than in Mother Cuxsom's comments on Mrs. Henchard's death: "And all her shining keys will be took from her, and her cupboards opened; and little things a' didn't wish seen, anybody will see; and her wishes and ways will be as nothing!"

Hardy admires the versatility of John Smith, Gabriel Oak's knowledge of sheep and his skill in tending them, Donald Farfrae's sound judgment of wheat. He respects even the roughest kind of labor, and in describing the shearing in *Far from the Madding Crowd,* the bark-gathering in *The Woodlanders,* or the milking in *Tess,* gives full value to the skill required and to the satisfaction of good work. The least rewarding and most arduous toil, such as the swede-hacking in *Tess,* is not without nobility in Hardy's account of it.

He has not the same feeling for the work that is done in cities. Late in his life he observed, "The spontaneous goodwill that used to characterize manual workers seems to have departed." That was the effect, he felt, of crowding workers in cities and breaking down the old traditions. In *A Pair of Blue Eyes,* describing John Smith, he wrote: "In common with most rural mechanics, he had too much individuality to be a typical 'workingman'—a resultant of the beach-pebble attrition with his kind only to be experienced in large towns, which metamorphoses the unit Self into a fraction of the unit Class." The same feeling led him to satirize the specialization of the city worker in *The Hand of Ethelberta*. Julian tells Sol and Dan, who are thinking of going to London, that the carpenter must learn to attend to doors but not windows and be able to turn screws but not drive nails, while the painter might limit himself to the color blue. Later, when the two have been in London for some time, Hardy says of them: "The brothers were by this time acquiring something of the airs and manners of London workmen; they were less spontaneous and more comparative; less genial, but smarter; in obedience to the usual law by which the emotion that takes the form of humor among country workmen becomes transmuted to irony among the same order in town."

No group, as a matter of fact, is treated with anything like the tender appreciation given the plain people of Wessex. Not only urban workers but country gentlemen fare badly by comparison. Although there is nothing in Hardy's published works to resemble the forthright satire that we are told he introduced into *The Poor Man and the Lady,* there is a constant, if cautious, criticism of the characters and manners of the highly born. *Desperate Remedies, A Pair of Blue Eyes, The Hand of Ethelberta,* and *A Laodicean* all ridicule class distinctions and poke fun at the affectations of polite society. The tragedy of *The Woodlanders* hinges upon Melbury's eagerness for his daughter to make a good marriage, and Alec D'Urberville is the son of a father who, for the sake of social prestige, assumed a family name to which he had no right.

Hardy did not lose his good opinion of human nature, even when he was dealing with classes he could not admire, but his warmest sympathies were restricted to the common country people. His heroes and heroines, however, are usually either persons just above this class—Elfrida Swancourt, Bathsheba, Christopher Julian, Eustacia Vye, Angel Clare—or, more frequently, persons in the process of rising out of it—

Edward Springrove, Stephen Smith, Clym Yeobright, Jude, and, in a slightly different sense, Ethelberta, Grace Melbury, and Donald Farfrae. A publisher's reader had said of *The Mayor of Casterbridge* that "the lack of gentry among the characters made it uninteresting," and Hardy always distrusted his ability to interest the public in the working classes. But the more important reason, in all probability, for his preoccupation with a slightly higher social stratum was that he belonged to it. Born the son of a stone-mason, he had aspired to success, first in architecture and then in letters. He chose to write of the type of character that he best understood, setting it against a background that he both knew and loved.

Hardy's heroes and heroines are worth looking at. Many of them are passive creatures, accepting with patience whatever fate brings them. In *Far from the Madding Crowd* Hardy speaks of "the simple lesson which Oak showed a mastery of by every turn and look he gave—that among the multitude of interests by which he was surrounded, those which affected his personal well-being were not the most absorbing and important in his eyes. Oak meditatively looked upon the horizon of circumstances without any special regard to his own standpoint in the midst." Giles Winterbourne is his fit companion; Thomasin, Diggory Venn, and Elizabeth-Jane are of their school, and Tess, except for her last desperate act, exhibits this stoicism in its most tragic aspects.

But there are other types of character. Bathsheba Everdene and Eustacia Vye are impatient women, determined to shape their own lives and resist the glowering onset of circumstance. Sue Bridehead, also, before she is broken by the death of the children, will not submit to the injustices of the world, and Michael Henchard dies a rebel. Between this group and their passive associates is an intermediary group, composed chiefly of men who began with hope and courage but learned to submit. Edward Springrove introduces the type in Hardy's first published novel. He is followed by both Stephen Smith and Edward Knight in *A Pair of Blue Eyes* and in *The Hand of Ethelberta* by Christopher Julian, who became "so well accustomed to the spectacle of a world passing him by and splashing him with its wheels that he wondered why he had ever minded it." The purest example of the type is probably Clym Yeobright, but Angel Clare and Jude Fawley have many of its characteristics. In short, it is the pattern for almost all the young men whose outward circumstances bear some resemblance to Hardy's own.

Naturally Hardy shows the deepest sympathy with this group, but it is by no means certain that he admires it. His admiration vacillates between the other two. In *The Mayor of Casterbridge,* where the conflict is at its sharpest, it is Farfrae and Elizabeth-Jane who find happiness. Farfrae, bending easily to circumstance, deeply affected by neither pleasure nor pain, has a tranquil passage through life. Elizabeth-Jane, after bearing her misfortunes without complaint, accepts with equal calm the peace that she cannot believe has come to one "whose youth had seemed to teach that happiness was but the occasional episode in a general drama of pain." She has learned to make life endurable through "the cunning enlargement, by a species of microscopic treatment, of those minute forms of satisfaction that offer themselves to everybody not in positive pain." Her qualities are those that, Hardy's philosophy taught him, ought to be cultivated. But, in spite of this, his admiration and sympathy go out, not to Elizabeth-Jane, certainly not to Donald Farfrae, but to Michael Henchard. More cruelly harassed by fate than any other character in Hardy's novels, Henchard never yields an inch, rebellion crying out to an indifferent heaven in the will that he pins upon the head of his deathbed. And it is to this defiant, impulsive, unphilosophical man that Hardy's tribute is paid.

Whether passive or rebellious, Hardy's characters find

themselves in a disastrous world, and some of their disasters are traceable to conditions that might be remedied, some to conditions that are inherent in the nature of a faulty universe. In the earlier novels social conditions, especially stupid conventions, share with fate responsibility for the misfortunes of the characters. In *The Mayor of Casterbridge* and *The Return of the Native,* on the other hand, the tragedy is largely, though not entirely, independent of forces that are within human control. In *The Woodlanders,* in *Tess,* and particularly in *Jude,* the remediable, man-made evils are placed in the foreground and Hardy makes a direct attack upon them.[1]

The Woodlanders, for example, makes explicit the criticism of the laws and conventions governing marriage that had been hinted at in earlier books, and the criticism is given an ironic twist by Melbury's mistaken trust in the new divorce law. In 1895, in a preface he wrote for the novel, Hardy laid aside whatever caution he had retained and wrote: "In the present novel, as in one or two others of this series which involve the question of matrimonial divergence, the immortal puzzle—given the man and woman, how to find a basis for their sexual relation—is left where it stood; and it is tacitly assumed for the purposes of the story that no doubt of the depravity of the erratic heart who feels some third person to be better suited to his or her tastes than the one with whom he has contracted to live, enters the head of reader or writer for a moment. . . . Yet no thinking person supposes that on the broader ground of how to afford the greatest happiness to the units of human society during their brief transit through this sorry world, there is no more to be said on this covenant; and it is certainly not supposed by the writer of these pages."

[1] It is interesting to note how the assumptions of critics lead them to give pre-eminence to either *The Return of the Native* and *The Mayor of Casterbridge* on the one hand or *Tess* and *Jude* on the other. See, for example, J. F. A. Pyre's introduction to the edition of *The Mayor of Casterbridge* in Harper's Modern Classics. The preference is usually justified on esthetic grounds.

In *Tess* there are coincidences, of course, and Hardy exploits them in the interests of his irony, but they are not ultimately responsible for what happens. As if to call attention to the increased openness of his criticism, Hardy belligerently subtitled *Tess* "A Pure Woman Faithfully Presented," and he did not hesitate, throughout the novel, to underscore his thesis. For Tess's original downfall the predatory traditions in sexual relations of men of Alec's class are responsible, and it is the narrowness of the social code that makes her misfortune a tragedy by marking her as a fallen woman. Her second disaster comes because Angel Clare, "with all his attempted independence of judgment," is nevertheless "the slave to custom and conventionality when surprised back into his early teachings."

Much as Hardy winced at the attack on *Tess,* he made *Jude* even more emphatically critical of contemporary society. He again attacks marriage laws. Because youths like Jude and Arabella are in the grip of "the strongest passion known to humanity," they are forced to swear that "at every other time of their lives they would assuredly believe, feel, and desire precisely as they had believed, felt, and desired during the few preceding weeks." From this marriage and Sue's marriage to Mr. Phillotson and the difficulty of dissolving them springs much of the tragedy. Because Jude and Sue are living out of wedlock, he loses one of the few satisfactions his life brings him, his office in an Artisans' Mutual Improvement Society, and Sue's relapse into conventional views after the shock of the children's death destroys any possibility of happiness for the pair.

Yet more is involved than matrimonial disasters. *Jude,* it must be remembered, is the book that was to show the world what it ought to be shown about a young man who couldn't go to Oxford. Sue, who is less conventional than Jude when they meet, tells him, "You are one of the very men Christ-minster was intended for when the colleges were founded; a man with a passion for learning, but no money, or opportuni-ties, or friends. But you were elbowed off the pavement by the millionaires' sons." Jude gets work in Christminster to be near the men of learning he admires. "Yet he was as far from them as if he had been at the antipodes. Of course he was. He was a young workman in a white blouse, and with stone-dust in the creases of his clothes; and in passing they did not even see him, or hear him, rather saw through him as through a pane of glass at their familiars beyond." When he writes to the masters of the colleges, the only one who bothers to reply tells him, "You will have a much better chance of success in life by remaining in your own sphere and sticking to your own trade." As Jude dies, he hears the cheering that greets the bestowal of honorary degrees on "the Duke of Hamptonshire and a lot more illustrious gents of that sort."

So clear is it that tragedy could have been avoided if Jude had been allowed to develop his talents, and if his life with Sue had not been wrecked by stupid conventions, that ex-pressions of pure despair, common in earlier novels and there not inappropriate, seem almost grotesque in *Jude*. That Jude and Sue should be melancholy is natural enough, but that Hardy should pause to bemoan the character of the universe in a story that points directly to the removal of specific evils seems not much more than the survival of an old habit. Little Time's saying, "I should like the flowers very, very much, if I didn't keep on thinking they'd be all withered in a few days," comes close to bathos; to present the boy as a typical "outcome of new views of life" is ridiculous.

We can now see how much truth there was in Hardy's statement to William Archer that his books were "one plea against 'man's inhumanity to man,' to women, and to the lower animals." [1] There is another quality of his character that must be considered before the case for his meliorism is closed. We must recognize his strong and enduring devotion to truth, and see it in its proper setting, his timidity and lack of self-confidence. We must remember that he always exaggerated the opposition to truth-telling, though it was strong enough, and that every attack upon his work made deep and abiding wounds. Yet, though he might make minor compromises, he never concealed his views of society and the universe. "It is so easy nowadays," he wrote, "to call any force above or under the sky by the name of 'God'—and so pass as orthodox cheaply, and fill the pocket!" Of this kind of insincerity, which he called "the besetting sin of modern literature," he was never guilty. He proceeded cautiously, as much because of his own uncertainty as because of fear of public opinion, but he would neither hide nor misrepresent his beliefs. As time went on he spoke more boldly, and, much as he resented the attacks on *Tess* and *Jude,* he did not think of repudiating the views he had expressed or returning to his earlier discretion. He felt that verse might make it easier to oppose "inert crystallized opinion"; it did not occur to him to give up opposition.

This devotion to truth speaks in all the hundreds of poems, from the earliest to the latest. It is the rock on which all the novels are founded. It is the force that drove Hardy ahead in his greatest enterprise, *The Dynasts,* his attempt to interpret a vast historical event in the light of his understanding of the universe. It is, perhaps, his greatest claim to the name of meliorist. He if anyone had the right to say:

[1] Hardy believed that the theory of evolution, by proving our kinship with animals, required us to expand our ethics to include them. This was probably little more than a rational defense of a tenderness that he had always felt, and that led him to oppose vivisection and, as we have seen, to urge that horses should not be used in war. This tenderness was responsible for many fine passages in the novels, and for one of the most extraordinary lyrics in *The Dynasts,* the description of the effect of the battle of Waterloo on the animals that lived in its fields.

Yet, would men look at true things,
And unilluded view things,
And count to bear undue things,

The real might mend the seeming. . . .

5. *The Indivisible Hardy.*

Hardy's conception of the nature of the universe was not incompatible with a mood of hopefulness: other men, holding the same conception, escaped his kind of despair, and he himself, in theory and to some extent in practice, held to the doctrine that improvement is possible through man's efforts and worth struggling for. He did not believe for a moment that human nature was incurably bad; on the contrary he felt tenderness towards all men and admiration for many. So far as his theories went, he might perfectly well have engaged in any one of a dozen struggles for human betterment.

What kept him from enlisting in those struggles was temperament and circumstance. He distrusted himself too much to mingle easily with other men, and the difficulties and failures of his early years increased his aloofness. It happened that he had grown up in a region that was remote from the dominant influences of the nineteenth century, and to that region he naturally retired when London proved, on so many grounds, to be unendurable. Hardy could not have identified himself with the Liberal Party as Morley did, nor even have taken as much interest in its activities as Meredith took, for the issues it raised had little relevance in Dorsetshire. As for the labor movement, to which the mood of *The Poor Man and the Lady* might have driven him, that was equally remote from Wessex. It was, moreover, being in its least idealistic stage, incapable of appealing to an outsider who had little natural sympathy with urban workmen. Hardy could give his approval to the aims of either the labor movement or the

Liberal Party, but he could not identify himself with them, could not feel their human reality, could not share in their struggles and their hopes.

There was little, therefore, despite his theoretical meliorism, to modify the tone of his pessimism. No one wants to minimize the actual shock of his religious disillusionment, or to disparage the logic with which he built upon the discoveries of science, but the shock might have been cushioned, and there might have been other facts for his logic to take into account. On New Year's Day, 1902, he wrote in his journal: "A Pessimist's apology. Pessimism (or rather what is called such) is, in brief, playing the sure game. You cannot lose at it; you may gain. It is the only view of life in which you can never be disappointed. Having reckoned what to do in the worst possible circumstances, when better arise, as they may, life becomes child's play." Here for once Hardy admitted that he was a pessimist, not so much because God had been taken out of his universe as because he was the kind of person who liked to play safe. Many devout believers in Christian revelation could have understood and sympathized with him.

To say that Hardy could, with exactly the same beliefs about the universe, have been a very different kind of person may help us to define his pessimism. It does not warrant us in assuming that he would have been a greater writer if he had, let us say, remained in London, entered upon a career of active journalism, become closely associated with such men as Morley and Stephen, and taken part in various movements to alter church and state. To be able to do this he would have had to be a very different Hardy from the despondent architect we have seen in London in the sixties, and in doing it would have become even less like the Hardy we know. His work, whether better or worse, would have been the work of another man.

As a matter of fact, the temperament and the circumstances that made him a pessimist also made him great as a writer. His isolation, for example, may have checked his intellectual development, but it gave him a world that he could compass. He knew every heath and cliff and woodland in Dorsetshire. He had grown up with the farm laborers he wrote about, and could share without effort their thoughts and feelings. Even his style, when it is at its simplest and most flexible, carries the rhythms that had grown through centuries of country speech. He had known Wessex as a boy, and he came back, as a young writer, to find it unchanged and, at least in comparison with London, unchanging. It was his world, already half mastered and wholly masterable.

The very limitations of his intellect, which kept his mind unaltered through sixty years, blessed his writing. It was a pity, no doubt, that he paid little attention to historical developments, philosophical controversies, even scientific discoveries, but a groping author could not have had his clarity and his certainty of direction. The unity of Hardy's work— poems, short stories, novels—cannot be matched in contemporary literature. Perhaps his mind was closed, but he believed that he had come to terms with the universe, and out of that belief came not only the precision of the lyrics and the firmness of the novels but also the unique achievement of *The Dynasts*. The orderly marshaling of hundreds of characters in their myriad activities, the unwavering grip of men, events, and forces, the sustained vision that sweeps heaven and earth and turns with unshaken dignity from Napoleon to the moles under the battlefield of Waterloo—all this grows from the philosophy that took shape in Hardy's mind when Christianity was driven out.

Robbed of the Victorian faith in God's plans for the British nation, Hardy, unlike Morris, found no other faith to take its place. Less conscious than Morris of the terrible extent of the remediable evils, he was almost completely ignorant of the struggle to remedy them. He had nothing to believe in but clear-sightedness and courage and the decency of the human race, but this was enough for him to go on for more than sixty years. Too often the bleaker view of the universe has been an excuse for mere whining over personal misfortunes. Hardy never whined. If his weaknesses were fully apparent to a later generation, his virtues proved hard to emulate.

Chapter IV

SAMUEL BUTLER, CAUTIOUS REBEL

IN 1859, three years before Thomas Hardy went to London, Samuel Butler set sail for New Zealand. The first night out he did not say his prayers, and he never said them again. What later bothered him, as well as his astute friend, Miss Savage, was that he had reached the age of twenty-four before he seriously questioned the dogmas of the Church of England. Subsequently he tried to explain this by pointing out that there was singularly little discussion of religion at Cambridge in the years he was there. It may be doubted, however, whether the currents of theological thought had so much to do with his beliefs as he pretended. Like Ernest in *The Way of All Flesh,* he was so dominated by his father that the least degree of skepticism would have been a rebellion against parental authority, and, when he did begin to express doubts, it was a conscious declaration of civil war. In the letter to his father in which he announced his determination not to enter the ministry, one senses his fumbling search for some rational justification, and the half-apologetic discussion of baptism and grace suggests no deep conviction one way or the other. One might say that Butler became a skeptic because he did not want to take orders, and he stopped saying his prayers when he did because he was escaping from his father's control.

It was, nevertheless, the general progress of infidelity that gave Butler his chance. If his break with orthodoxy was not so clearly thought out as Hardy's, and if it was neither so painful nor so complete, that makes him the more representative. Orthodoxy was not so much being battered down as undermined. Hardy found, to his dismay, that a break with the church was necessary; Butler learned with relief that it was possible. Once he had his freedom, however, he did not quite know whether he wanted it or not, and there again he was typical of the majority of his unbelieving contemporaries.

1. The Ambiguous Heretic.

The Way of All Flesh tells us all we need to know about Butler's boyhood. Whatever exaggerations malice may have suggested, we cannot doubt that Canon Butler was much like Theobald Pontifex or that his son suffered quite as deeply as did Ernest. From the canon's tyrannical household, Butler went to Shrewsbury, where he was subjected to the bullying of both teachers and fellow-students. At Cambridge he was somewhat more independent and a good deal happier, and at last he worked up courage enough to challenge his father's wishes. The outcome of their long debate was his migration to New Zealand.

Freed from parental control, Butler gave up the forms of religion, but he hesitated to go further. In 1861, writing to his aunt, who, as a Unitarian, was not likely to be shocked, he said that he had "felt an immense intellectual growth shortly after leaving England," and that, where once he had regarded her as a dangerous heretic, he would now assent to most of her doctrines. He hinted, indeed, at greater depths: "The worst of it is that in the total wreck of my own past orthodoxy I fear I may be as much too skeptical as then too orthodox." But it was not until the next year that, after having considered the evidence for the resurrection, he ventured to say, "For the present I renounce Christianity altogether."

Just at this time, in the midst of his sheep-raising, Butler read *The Origin of Species*. Completely convinced, he wrote

for a New Zealand paper, the *Canterbury Press,* an article
called "Darwin on the Origin of Species," stating the Darwinian position so well that Darwin himself asked an English
periodical to reprint the little dialogue. The conception of
evolution continued to fascinate Butler, but his restless mind
began moving in a new direction. In 1863 he wrote "Darwin
Among the Machines," later incorporated in *Erewhon.* As he
explained in the introduction to the second edition of that
book, his satire was not aimed at Darwin, who had merely
supplied him with his theme, but at a writer guilty of "the
specious misuse of analogy," presumably Joseph Butler, whose
Analogy of Religion was a university text. That this was
really Butler's aim is suggested by his writing a companion
piece, "Lucubratio Ebria," in which he defended a contradictory thesis with the same ingenious show of logic.

His success with these satires, and the pleasure he took in
them, encouraged him to go on to the writing of *Erewhon.*
Butler was by no means sure of his position, and obliqueness
had a protective value for him, but he loved it for its own sake.
How much, then, he must have enjoyed the writing of *Erewhon,* with its adroitly misleading introductory chapters, its
double-edged satire, and all its incidental and elusive jibes.
What satisfaction he must have taken in ridiculing simul-
taneously the treatment of criminals and the treatment of the
sick, or the rites of baptism and the attitude of parents toward
their children. How he must have relished paying his tribute
to Cambridge as he worked out the details of the Colleges
of Unreason, and how he must have chuckled as he buried his
attack on Puritanism in his discussion of the rights of vegetables. Not until he wrote *The Way of All Flesh* were his peculiar gifts again to have such play.

Perhaps *Erewhon* is not great satire. The attacks on the
home, the university, and the church—three institutions that
had caused Butler personal unhappiness—are often petulant

and occasionally roguish. "Darwin Among the Machines," in spite of the effort of critics to find in it an astute analysis of industrialism, is, as has been said, merely the recreation of an agile mind. When one thinks how much of Victorianism invited irony, *Erewhon* seems ingenious rather than profound. But it was a useful book in its own time and it remains an entertaining one in ours.

It is strange that Butler, who could hit so hard and straight in minor issues, seldom landed direct blows in major controversies. The question of the resurrection continued to plague him, and after the success of *Erewhon* he returned to this topic. In an anonymous pamphlet he had already indicated the contradictions in the gospel accounts, and now, in *The Fair Haven,* he reviewed his case by the characteristic method of pretending to refute his own arguments. In the introductory memoir of the supposed author, John Pickard Owen, Butler showed the skill in semi-autobiographical fiction that had given *Erewhon* much of its interest and was to distinguish *The Way of All Flesh.* In the book proper he began by affirming the crucial importance of the resurrection, contradicted—apparently sincerely—Strauss's hallucination theory, offered his own account of the discrepancies in the records, suggested that Jesus had not really died on the cross, and finally proposed a completely unsatisfactory refutation of this view.

Butler was delighted because several reviewers were deceived by *The Fair Haven* and praised Mr. Owen's ingenious defense of orthodoxy. But the gullibility of the pious might have given him less satisfaction than it did, for *The Fair Haven* is, to say the least, an ambiguous book. In view of the fact that Owen is supposedly the butt of the satire, it is surprising that Butler made him, just as he had made Higgs in *Erewhon,* so much in his own image. And when we realize that Owen is arguing for the poetic, rather than the literal, truth of Christian dogmas, we cannot help wondering if he is not much like his creator in his beliefs as well as his character. He became, the memoir tells us, a broad churchman "in the true sense of being able to believe in the naturalness, legitimacy, and truth *qua* Christianity even of those doctrines which seem to stand most widely and irreconcilably asunder." If Butler had been one to scorn such equivocations, the satire would be obvious enough, but, recalling that he too called himself a broad churchman, we are not sure whose leg is being pulled.

Even if we make full allowance for the subtlety that Butler's admirers attribute to him, and for the sheer mischievousness that we have already observed, *The Fair Haven* is a puzzle. Butler did not accept Owen's arguments for the physical resurrection, and wanted, indeed, to make them seem ridiculous, but when he made Owen plead for a flexible Christianity, he was coming close to his own position. Either because of continued fear of his father or because of concern with public opinion, he did not want to make an outright break with the church, and he clung to his ambiguity, even though he became almost as ridiculous as his John Pickard Owen.

The retreat was to continue, though in fundamentals he remained a skeptic. Paradoxically, it was the revival of his interest in science that took him several steps on the way back to the faith he had abandoned. By 1876 he was looking about for a subject for another book. He had already, on Miss Savage's advice, begun *The Way of All Flesh,* but he knew that he would never publish it during his father's lifetime. He needed money, because of unwise investments, and he was not hopeful about the artistic career he had undertaken on his return from New Zealand. Having published two books and had some success with one, he could not help thinking of letters.

The idea he wanted suddenly came to him, and he wrote

Miss Savage: "I have got a very dry but exceedingly (to me) interesting subject—something like the machines in *Erewhon* —on which I am now working steadily; but what it will come to I do not know. At any rate it has the merit of not being aimed directly or indirectly at Christianity, and not being satirical save incidentally. It is on the force of habit." What this led to was the publication in December, 1877, of *Life and Habit*. As Butler had said, the work could not offend the orthodox, but it had the result—apparently quite unpremeditated—of involving him in controversy with the followers of Charles Darwin. This controversy he carried on in many magazine articles and in three books—*Evolution, Old and New* in 1879, *Unconscious Memory* in 1880, and *Luck, or Cunning?* in 1886. And in the end, though he was still far from a position acceptable to orthodox church members, he conceived of himself as a defender of religion against Darwinian infidelity.

Butler stumbled upon the theme of *Life and Habit*. His telling Miss Savage that the subject was "something like the machines in *Erewhon*" suggests that it originally attracted him by the opportunity it gave for the play of fancy. Twenty-five years later, re-reading his letter, he felt that it indicated too clearly the casualness of his approach, for he wrote on the margin: "Then I was not sure that the *Life and Habit* theory was more than ingenious paradox; but by February 14th I had gripped my meaning, and knew it to be sound." In August, 1876, he wrote Miss Savage, "The theory frightens me—it is so far-reaching and subversive."

The theory is that instinct is simply habit and that all inheritance is unconscious memory. To support it, Butler described the role of the unconscious in human life, and it is here, if anywhere, that his book is of value. His next step was to maintain the identity of parents and children, to argue that sperms and ova partake in the experiences of the parent bodies, unconsciously remember these experiences, and are influenced by them in their subsequent careers. We all know, he says, that a process that has been repeated many times can be remembered without conscious effort, though the steps by which it was learned are forgotten, and so it is with the experiences in which the germ plasm has shared. We know how to digest when we are born; we learn to breathe and to eat with little trouble; walking comes somewhat harder. These are processes that our ancestors have been repeating for various lengths of time. Recapitulation in the embryo is evidence of memory, and only memory can explain instinct. Memory is, then, the means by which descent with modification is brought about. It is the key to evolution.

Butler had gone a long way with his theory before he realized that it conflicted with Darwinism. When he read *The Origin of Species,* he had been impressed by the general idea of evolution, and, as he later maintained, had not paid much attention to the theory of natural selection. Darwin had admitted the possibility of the inheritance of acquired characteristics, but had denied that it was of primary importance in the evolutionary process. Butler's reasoning, on the other hand, made this the chief force in the creation of new species. He was distressed at finding himself thus opposed to a man whom he had publicly praised and whose good will he valued, and he took a semi-apologetic tone in the book and in a letter to Darwin's son.

Butler was, however, even at the outset, encouraged in his opposition to Darwin by the discovery that the theory of evolution had been proposed a hundred years earlier and in a form much like his own. When, in the course of his controversy in the *Canterbury Press,* an opponent had charged Darwin with warming over his grandfather's exploded theories, Butler had ridiculed the notion. But now, just as he was finishing *Life and Habit,* he learned more about Erasmus Darwin and Lamarck. As a result, he identified himself as a Lamarckian and asked why Charles Darwin had ignored the works of his predecessors. As soon as *Life and Habit* had been published, he began to study Buffon, the elder Darwin, and Lamarck, and wrote *Evolution, Old and New,* in which he restated his theories, gave a detailed account of the work of the earlier evolutionists, and attacked Darwin for claiming credit for the general theory of evolution and for confusing the issue by his faulty and misleading arguments in favor of natural selection.

In the first two books Butler carried on the controversy with some moderation, but just at this time Charles Darwin sponsored the translation from a German periodical of an article on Erasmus Darwin. The author undertook to revise his article before it was translated, and he included in the revision criticisms of *Evolution, Old and New,* a copy of which Darwin had sent him. A note calling attention to the introduction of new material was omitted when the article was published, and Butler scented a conspiracy to discredit his book without mentioning it. Darwin, on the advice of friends, refused to answer Butler's attacks, and the latter, his suspicions confirmed, promptly wrote *Unconscious Memory,* in which he reviewed the progress of the quarrel. "If it appears," he said, "that I have used language such as is rarely seen in controversy, let the reader remember that the occasion is, so far as I know, unparalleled for the cynicism and audacity with which the wrong complained of was committed and persisted in. I trust, however, that, though not indifferent to this, my indignation has been mainly roused, as when I wrote *Evolution, Old and New,* before Mr. Darwin had given me personal ground of complaint against him, by the wrongs he has inflicted on dead men, on whose behalf I now fight, as I trust that some one—whom I thank by anticipation—may one day fight on mine."

Six years later, in *Luck, or Cunning?,* he took up the fight once more, and, though Darwin had died in the meantime, did not abate the sharpness of his tone. Darwin, he charged, had put forth the preposterous theory of natural selection because he wanted to take credit for originating the whole idea of evolution. And why had he received so much praise? Not because he was a person of unusual powers: "On the whole I should doubt his having been a better observer of nature than nine country gentlemen out of ten who have a taste for natural history. . . . It was in his business qualities—and these, after all, are the most essential to success, that Mr. Darwin showed himself so superlative. . . . Mr. Darwin played for his own generation, and he got in the very amplest measure the recognition which he endeavored, as we all do, to obtain." "He was heir," Butler concluded, "to a discredited truth; he left behind him an accredited fallacy."

Luck, or Cunning? was Butler's last book on evolution, but he wrote a series of articles in 1890 called "The Deadlock in Darwinism," in which he repeated all the old charges. To the end Darwin was Butler's devil. Only four months before he died, Butler held Darwin responsible for the failure of his books to impress the public: "With *Erewhon,*" he wrote, "Charles Darwin smelt danger from afar. I knew him personally; he was one of my grandfather's pupils. He knew very well that the machine chapters in *Erewhon* would not end there, and the Darwin circle was then the most important literary power in England."

The manner in which Butler conducted his controversy with the Darwinians gives us a picture of the man. We see him drifting, half-unwittingly, into the position of opposing a person he had always admired and perhaps envied. We observe how embarrassed he is by his own temerity, and how shrill his self-consciousness makes him. Then the miracle happens: his opponent puts himself in the wrong. Butler is no

longer the persecutor but the victim, and his conflict is resolved in a passion of righteous indignation. It never occurs to
him to ask what is to be gained by his furious vituperation.
He is what he wants to be, a crusader attacking the enemies
of truth.

As for Butler's theories, all a literary critic can say is that
modern science has turned steadily against them.[1] Even vital-
ists accept the general Lamarckian hypothesis rather than
Butler's specific innovations. And Butler's arguments do not
commend themselves to the attentive reader. There is much
sheer quibbling and not a little fancifulness. Nor is there any
evidence, as all his contemporary opponents pointed out, of
adequate equipment for the discussion of scientific problems.
Butler admitted that he had no scientific training, saying it
was unnecessary because he based his conclusions entirely on
data furnished by his opponents, but this is more than a little
disingenuous. The crux of the controversy, as even an outsider can understand, is the question whether acquired characteristics can be inherited. Yet Butler never seems to see the
problem clearly, for he offers as evidence illustrations from
history that can obviously be explained by what is called social
inheritance and that have nothing to do with biology. Moreover, when Weismann's work forced him to consider the
actual biological basis of inheritance, he could do no better
than point out that Darwin himself had believed acquired
characteristics to be inheritable, which was true but not rele-
vant. Although he had insisted again and again that inherited
change is gradual and therefore cannot be disproved by experiments of the Weismann type, he snatched at such straws
as Hartog's astigmatic man whose habit of holding his hand

---

[1] Bernard Shaw is the best known of the defenders of the Lamarck-Butler position; see his preface to *Back to Methuselah*. C. E. M. Joad states the case for vitalism in his *Samuel Butler*, and Clara Gruening Stillman, in *Samuel Butler—A
Mid-Victorian Modern*, 161–3, mentions various scientists who are more or less in
agreement with Butler.

over one eye was allegedly inherited by his non-astigmatic children.

On the whole, it is clear that, even if Butler's theories were defensible, he was not able to defend them, and we become even more suspicious of them when we observe that they permitted him to take a position in the shadow of the church. Butler did not become a Lamarckian so that he could call himself religious. His Lamarckism was a kind of accident, and it was only after he had taken his stand that he realized its theological advantages. If, moreover, he had not been so anxious to find allies in his fight against Darwin and Huxley, he might have been less interested in the church. But we have seen his unwillingness to declare himself unequivocally against religion, and we can surmise that he was not sorry to have the support of what he regarded as sound science.

Butler ended *Life and Habit* with these words: "Will the reader bid me wake with him to a world of chance and blindness? Or can I persuade him to dream with me of a more living faith than either he or I had yet conceived as possible? As I have said, reason points remorselessly to an awakening, but faith and hope still beckon to the dream." This appeal, coming strangely at the end of a work supposedly devoted to scientific investigation, suggests not only his desire for some kind of religious security but also his lack of confidence at this stage in his own theories. Indeed, he wrote to Francis Darwin—perhaps in an excess of courtesy, but perhaps not—that he fully expected to be proved wrong. If, however, reason might awaken him, in the meantime he intended to enjoy his dream.

Opposition, of course, had the effect of strengthening his belief in his theories and forcing him to accept the conclusions to which they pointed. In *Evolution, Old and New* he printed an appendix on "Rome and Pantheism," in which he said, "If the Church of Rome would only develop some doctrine or,

I know not how, provide some means by which men like myself, who cannot pretend to believe in the miraculous element of Christianity, could yet join her as a conservative stronghold, I, for one, should gladly do so." He believed, he said, in "the omnipresence of mind and design throughout the universe," and asked, "What is this but God?" The church might well recognize that such men as he are her strongest bulwark against Darwinian infidelity. To combat that infidelity had been his highest aim. "The unscrupulousness with which I have been attacked, together with the support given me by the general public, are sufficient proofs that I have not written in vain."

By the time he wrote *Luck, or Cunning?* Butler seems to have known quite well what he was doing. "What convention or short cut," he asked, "can symbolize for us the results of labored and complicated chains of reasoning or bring them more aptly and concisely home to us than the one supplied long since by the word God?" He ended the book by saying: "The theory that luck is the main means of organic modification is the most absolute denial of God which it is possible for the human mind to conceive—while the view that God is in all His creatures, He in them and they in Him, is only expressed in other words by declaring that the main means of organic modification is, not luck, but cunning." "Orthodox," he wrote a friend, "the book is not, religious I do verily believe and hope it is; its whole scope is directed against the present mindless, mechanical, materialistic view of nature, and, though I know very well that churchmen will not like it, I am sure they will like it much better than they like the opinions now most generally accepted, and that they will like it much better than men of science will." A little later he wrote, "Do I—does any free-thinker who has the ordinary feelings of an Englishman—doubt that the main idea underlying and running through the ordinary orthodox faith is substantially sound? . . . I want the Church as much as I want free-thought; but I want the Church to pull her letter more up to date or else to avow frankly that her letter is a letter only." "If," he wrote in the preface to *Erewhon Revisited*, "I may be allowed to speak about myself, I would say that I have never ceased to profess myself a member of the more advanced wing of the English Broad Church. What those who belong to this wing believe, I believe. What they reject, I reject."

It is not easy to say how much Butler meant by all this. He never once indicated the slightest willingness to reconsider his disbelief in the resurrection and other miracles, nor did he express the slightest sorrow over his inability to believe in them. "No sincere man," he wrote, "will regret having attained a truer view concerning anything which he has ever believed. . . . I hope no one will say I was sorry when I found out that there was no reason for believing in heaven and hell." Furthermore, though he was less intransigent on the point, he continued to criticize Christian ethics. "As an instrument of warfare against vice," he wrote in his notebook, "or as a tool for making virtue, Christianity is a mere flint implement"—a thesis he elaborated in *The Way of All Flesh*.

There was a point, then, beyond which Butler refused to retreat, but he did want to keep on good terms with the church, and he did desire a bulwark against materialism. One of his disciples, C. E. M. Joad, has written of Darwinism: "It will be readily apparent how adversely this view reflects upon man's natural belief in the special significance of life in general and of human life in particular." Shaw calls creative evolution "the genuinely scientific religion for which all wise men are now anxiously looking." If Lamarckism has survived, it is because of its appeal to "natural belief" and the desire for "a genuinely scientific religion." Butler had that belief and felt that desire.

Hardy also wanted to re-unite with the church, and there were moments when he hoped that modernism, in either the

Church of Rome or the Church of England, might make it possible for agnostics like himself to join the religious community. His passion for the church, moreover, was deeper than Butler's, for he had a stronger sense of the value of historical continuity as well as pleasanter personal associations. But it never occurred to Hardy to ask for re-admission to the church as anything but an agnostic. He never professed to believe, in some esoteric sense, in God. Even if he had accepted Butler's vitalism, he would have scorned the pretense that it could be reconciled with Christian theology. And he did not accept vitalism, for he recognized it as a feeble concession to tender-mindedness. When he was eighty, he wrote a poem called "Our Old Friend Dualism":

All hail to him, the Protean! A tough old chap is he:
Spinoza and the Monists cannot make him cease to be.
We pound him with our "Truth, Sir, please!" and quite appear
    to still him:
He laughs; holds Bergson up, and James; and swears we cannot
    kill him.
We argue them pragmatic cheats. "Aye," says he. "They're deceiving:
But I must live; for flamens plead I am all that's worth believing."

"Faith and hope" might beckon to the dream, but Thomas Hardy was not to be deluded.

2. *The Snob and the Bad Boy.*

"I am the enfant terrible of literature and science," Butler wrote in his notebook. "If I cannot, and I know I cannot, get the literary and scientific big-wigs to give me a shilling, I can, and I know I can, heave bricks into the middle of them." From "Darwin on the Origin of Species," which irritated the Bishop of Wellington, to the posthumous *Way of All Flesh,* he did heave his bricks. Not only did he attack preachers and scientists; not only did he challenge Victoria's moral code; he fought with art critics on a dozen different points, wrote oratorios that defied contemporary theories of music, produced a new and, to Victorian sensibilities, shocking interpretation of Shakespeare's sonnets, and contended that the *Odyssey* was written by a woman. It is true that the big-wigs paid little attention to the bricks, perhaps because, as Butler insisted, they regarded silence as the best means of defense, more probably because they did not know the bricks were being thrown. This was a pity, for Butler counted on the spectacle of wincing victims.

And yet we may doubt whether Butler really got so much fun out of his bricks as he thought he did. Mrs. R. S. Garnett, a distant relation, was shrewd enough to say: "He had then no trace of the moral robustness that does not care a jot what is thought, which welcomes opposition, and is unmoved by vituperation. So far from standing unmoved, strong in his own opinion, he felt vividly and even to excess the effect he was producing upon his opponents. He stabbed himself with every thrust at his enemies." He was not, in other words, very well equipped for the role of bad boy. He had, moreover, a kind of caution that does not go well with the throwing of bricks. We scarcely know what to make of an iconoclast who convinces himself, and tries to convince others, that he is the savior of religion. It is not a question of sincerity; it is a problem of temperament, and a difficult one.

After he returned from New Zealand, Butler wrote for G. J. Holyoake's *The Reasoner* an article surprisingly entitled "Precaution in Free Thought." "He who rejects the belief in a personal Deity," he said, "sees that he is opposed to almost all the wealth and learning of the country. I put wealth first and do so on purpose. It is an august symbol. The Universities, the public schools, the rampant Sabbatarianism of the age, the countless churches, the huge organization of the various Christian creeds, are visible signs of one's own audacity. Fairly convinced a man cannot change, and yet if he does not change, he must seem to rate the average intellectual morality of the world very low. The arguments in favor of the Christian miracles are such as should satisfy no candid and inquisitive mind. . . . By our rejection of them we virtually bring a charge against our age of being either very stupid, or very indolent, or very cowardly." Nothing, we should suppose, would please an enfant terrible more than to bring just such a charge, but the substance of the article is that the skeptic should proceed cautiously, remembering that "an atheist may be a very good Christian," and being careful not "to look down on those who perhaps may not be so strictly logical as himself."

The reader of *Erewhon* and *The Way of All Flesh* will not be unprepared to find Butler suggesting that the opinion of the majority is not to be lightly challenged. Bad boy or not, he was a respecter of conventions. In *Erewhon* he says of Ydgrun, "She was a beneficent and useful deity," and he singles out for admiration the "high Ydgrunites," those who "seldom spoke of Ydgrun, or even alluded to her, but would never run counter to her dictates without ample reason for doing so." "They," he declares, "were gentlemen in the full sense of the word" and "more like the best class of Englishmen than any whom I have seen in other countries." When in 1902 a reviewer of the new edition of *Erewhon* wondered if this passage was intended seriously, Butler stated that his aim was "to uphold the current conscience of a man's best peers as his safest moral guide. I intended this, intend it, and I trust always shall intend it. What sane man will uphold any other guidance as generally safer—*exceptis,* of course, *excipiendis?*" Doubtless there is irony here, as Butler's admirers would insist, but it is irony only for the admirers' benefit. This is the half-candid, half-disingenuous way of

speaking of a man who wanted all of the intellectual satisfactions and none of the practical inconveniences of non-
conformity.

Nothing would be easier than to make a case for Butler as
a conservative. In the first place, he was, for what that may
signify, a Conservative in politics. He speaks of himself as
"an avowed Conservative" and "intolerant of Liberals," and
"Gladstonian" was with him an abusive epithet. He never
once referred directly to labor conditions or indicated the
slightest sympathy with the working class.[1] Indeed, the only
time that he seems to run counter to the political views of
the average Conservative is when, in *Erewhon,* he satirizes
imperialism, and even there his primary aim is to poke fun
at missionaries. Certainly he never doubted the propriety or
the permanence of the capitalist system, and paid little attention to those who did.

Much of his writing is concerned with money and personal
property. In "Lucubratio Ebria," the essay with which he
answered his own "Darwin Among the Machines," he wrote:
"We observe men for the most part (admitting, however,
some few abnormal exceptions) to be deeply impressed by the
superior organization of those who have money. It is wrong
to attribute this respect to any unworthy motive, for the feeling
is strictly legitimate and springs from some of the very highest impulses of our nature. . . . He alone possesses the full
complement of limbs who stands at the summit of opulence,
and we may assert with strictly scientific accuracy that the
Rothschilds are the most astonishing organisms that the
world has ever yet seen."

The irony here is directed rather against those who pretend

[1] It is true that he delivered several lectures at the Working Men's College,
Great Ormond Street, but this seems to be because an acquaintance asked him to
and because opportunities for self-expression were few. Neither the character of the
lectures nor any of his comments on them suggest interest in working-class education.

to disregard wealth than against those who regard it highly. So it is in *The Fair Haven,* where he asks, "Why are we to interpret so literally all passages about the guilt of unbelief, and insist upon the historical character of every miraculous account, while we are indignant if any one demands an equally literal rendering of the precepts concerning human conduct? He that hath two coats is not to give to him that hath none: that would be 'visionary,' 'Utopian,' 'wholly unpractical,' and so forth." These teachings, he insists, must be intended "for the ill-instructed and what we are pleased to call 'dangerous' classes." "How many a humble-minded Christian while reflecting upon the hardness of his lot, and tempted to cast a longing eye upon the luxuries which are at the command of his richer neighbors, is restrained from seriously coveting them by remembering the awful fate of Dives, and the happy future which was in store for Lazarus." But, fortunately for the privileged members of society, "modern criticism forbids us to believe that the parable of Dives and Lazarus was ever actually spoken by our Lord—at any rate not in its present form."

The irony is undeniably two-edged, but Butler would have been distressed if he had thought it might lead readers to question the system of private property. What he was arguing for, quite frankly, was the candid recognition of the importance of money. "A man will feel loss of money," he recorded in his notebook, "more keenly than loss of bodily health, so long as he can keep his money. . . . Money losses are the worst, loss of health is next worse, and loss of reputation comes in a bad third." Everyone remembers how large a part money plays in *The Way of All Flesh,* and it was just as important in Butler's life. Money was the constant theme of his quarrels with his father. His "ever-present anxiety about money" affected, he believed, all his books from *Erewhon* to *Luck, or Cunning?* His suggestion in *The Way of All Flesh* that speculation be taught in the schools may well have come out of his difficulties with his investments, which forced him to spend considerable time in Canada in the early seventies.

He respected not only money but also the leisure, the prestige, and the graces that money can help to secure. "People ask complainingly what swells have done, or do, for society that they should be able to live without working. The good swell is the creature towards which all nature has been groaning and travailing together until now. He is an ideal. He shows what may be done in the way of good breeding, health, looks, temper, and fortune. He realizes men's dreams of themselves, at any rate vicariously. He preaches the gospel of grace. The world is like a spoilt child, it has this good thing given it at great expense and then says it is useless!" The high Ydgrunites are swells, and Towneley is a swell. "The people like Towneley," says Ernest, "are the only ones who know anything that is worth knowing." The swell makes a final appearance as George, Higg's illegitimate son, in *Erewhon Revisited*.

Overton, who speaks for Butler in *The Way of All Flesh*, is a snob, and acknowledges his snobbishness. "A man," he comments at one point, "can give up father and mother for Christ's sake tolerably easily for the most part, but it is not so easy to give up people like Towneley." Towneley himself, of course, is a snob, and that is one of his virtues in Ernest's and in Overton's eyes. Overton, having told him of the money Ernest has, without knowing it, been left by his aunt, says, "Towneley was doing all he could before this, but I knew that the knowledge I had imparted to him would make him feel as though Ernest was more one of his own class, and had therefore a greater claim upon his good offices."

Butler did not carry off his own snobbishness as well as he made Overton carry off his, but it was just as obvious. Bishops, for example, figure largely in his correspondence. Having made a not very pertinent quotation from the Bishop of Carlisle, who had been at Cambridge with him, Butler sent the bishop a copy of *Unconscious Memory*. When he acknowledged the gift, Butler wrote him, "I believe that a purposive theory of evolution may help to bring the two main opposing currents of English thought into a more complete harmony than has for some time past seemed likely, and a rapprochement between them must be desired by every well-wisher of his country." In 1883 he wrote Miss Savage: "Thank you for telling me about Bishop Tozer's speaking warmly of *Alps and Sanctuaries*. It is not the bishops and archbishops I am afraid of. Men like Huxley and Tyndall are my natural enemies, and I am always glad when I find church people recognizing that the differences between them and me are, as I believe myself, more of words than of things." In 1886 he confided in her: "I think bishops generally are rather nice." And in 1893: "What do you think? The Bishop of Peterborough has written and asked me to spend from Saturday to Monday. What a Sunday I shall have, to be sure. Of course I must go."

Butler's first break with the church came because that was the most obvious way of escaping parental plans for the ministry. Once he had taken a stand, he would not abjure it, but he did not like its social consequences. The nice people, after all, did support the church. Like Aunt Alethea, although they "disliked equally those who aired either religion or irreligion," they were regular in church attendance. Butler wanted to emulate them, but, because he was too sincere or too proud to repudiate his heresies, he could not do so. The only way to save his face was to reconcile his heresies with orthodoxy, so that he could return to the church by a kind of private entrance. Especially after he had begun his feud with the Darwinians, and had thus severed himself from another influential group, he desired the social prestige the church could give.

He was neither unaware nor ashamed of his motives. In 1886 he went to a dinner of graduates of the Shrewsbury school. "Why should I," he asked, "knowing that I do not particularly like these people, nor they me, why should I, who never liked my school nor got much good from it, go and pay a guinea for a bad dinner, and eat and drink what it takes me a whole day to recover from? It does not seem a very sensible thing to do, and yet people tell me I ought to go. I wish I knew whether they are right, or I, who think the whole thing a nuisance. I think that, considering the Ishmaelitish line which I have been led and driven to take in literature, the less I venture into the enemy's camp the better. They say that the more I take the Ishmaelitish line the more incumbent it is upon me to do the correctest of correct things occasionally, when time and the occasion serve. I believe they are right, and this is why I went, and shall hope to go upon a future occasion, but like it I do not." Deep in his heart Butler almost certainly wanted to go to that dinner and associate with the Archbishop of York and other prominent Shrewsbury alumni, but his discussion of policy is in itself significant. The only necessary comment is the one he inscribed on the margin of the letter in 1898—a note saying that he had been to every dinner since that of 1886.

It was the same way with his biography of his grandfather. We can believe that Butler did come to admire the famous headmaster of Shrewsbury, for he began his study with all the prejudices that are revealed in his characterization of George Pontifex, and he was bound to find that Dr. Butler was better than he had expected. Moreover, Bishop Butler was both a financial and a social success, and his grandson was too candid not to give credit where credit was due. But the biography is nonetheless the product of deliberate calculation. It is a conventional piece of eulogy, and it eulogizes not only the bishop but also Shrewsbury and its later master, Dr. Kennedy, the original of Dr. Skinner in *The Way of All Flesh*. Butler was bidding for the approval of respectable society, and he spared himself no pains.

His behavior was quite in accordance with his professed principles. "If morality is that which, on the whole, brings a man peace in his declining years—if, that is to say, it is not an utter swindle, can you under these circumstances flatter yourself that you have led a moral life?" "For most men and most circumstances, pleasure—tangible material prosperity in this world—is the safest test of virtue." "It is all very well for mischievous writers to maintain that we cannot serve God and Mammon. . . . If there are two worlds at all (and that there are I have no doubt) it stands to reason that we ought to make the best of both of them, and more particularly of the one with which we are most immediately concerned. It is as immoral to be too good as to be too anything else." This was utilitarianism in its most realistic terms. Butler's criticism of most people was that though they acted on these principles, they refused to acknowledge them. For his part, he would like to see ethics brought up to date: "Someone should do for morals what that old Pecksniff Bacon has obtained the credit of having done for science." He personally had a rule to follow: "There are two classes of people in this world, those who sin and those who are sinned against; if a man must belong to either, he had better belong to the first than to the second."

Why, then, was Butler as much of an enfant terrible as he was? We have wondered why an avowed heaver of bricks should be so cautious, but perhaps we should be asking how the pursuit of self-interest could permit the throwing of bricks. If only Butler had obeyed his father and concealed his doubts, he might have had a good income and a position in society. Why did he have to offend the bishops, and then go out of the way to attack the Darwinians, and then shy rocks at art critics, music critics, professors of the classics, and other dignitaries? Why, for that matter, did he have to advertise his principles? If men were getting on well enough in their worship of Ydgrun, what was the use of complaining because they did not acknowledge their deity?

Butler's history helps to explain why he could be neither a consistent enfant terrible nor a consistent conservative and hedonist. The years in Canon Butler's household and in Shrewsbury School had implanted in him an irresistible need for self-assertion. Indeed, his desire for literary prestige and social success may be interpreted not primarily as a rational desire for comfort but rather as a passionate urge to prove to his family and his associates that he could impress the right people. Unfortunately for him, however, the need for self-assertion found expression in many ways. He had been bullied so much that he could not believe in himself unless he was challenging other people. From his pseudonymous controversies in the *Canterbury Press* to his pseudonymous controversies in the *Examiner,* he curiously combined caution and defiance. Even when he alone knew who was doing the challenging, he had to do it.

Both *Erewhon* and *The Fair Haven* were, as we have seen, marked by ambiguity. In the former, of course, he paid off a number of old scores. He was thinking of his mother and father, and how they had treated him, when he wrote "The World of the Unborn," and the fact that they would never understand the satire added to his pleasure. His father and his father's clerical associates inspired "The Musical Banks," and Cambridge was responsible for "The Colleges of Unreason." This was great fun, but Butler could not help worrying about the effect of his satire. Eager as he was for self-assertion and revenge, he had a career to think of. He asked Miss Savage if he would be committing an indiscretion in publishing the book, and, on the advice of another friend, omitted from the first edition the passage about the young man who was cheated by his guardian, a passage aimed at Canon Butler. To make himself quite safe, he at first published the book anonymously.

Erewhon had its brief popularity—it was the only book of Butler's published during his lifetime that paid for itself—but it did not start him on a career. Nor did success of any kind come during his lifetime. If he had been consistently bold, he would have offended the nice people he envied, but he might have made them fear and respect him. If he had been consistently cautious, he was clever enough to have made money and a kind of reputation. But he was neither one nor the other for long, and his writings were easy to ignore.

His social as well as his literary ambitions were thwarted, and he seems the loneliest of British men of letters. Others have lived in greater solitude, but they did not want companionship and social recognition as he did. He wanted them, and he made them impossible. On the one hand, the tyranny he had suffered in his youth fostered a desire for physical independence and freedom from obligations to other persons. He preferred to live alone, and would not have his meticulous routine disturbed. On the other hand, his deep need for self-assertion made him, in spite of many likeable traits, a difficult companion, and limited his intimate circle to ardent admirers.

As one goes through Henry Festing Jones's vast *Memoir,* one finds almost no names that are familiar. Hardy was scarcely a sociable person, but he knew most of the literary men of his time. Butler knew almost none. Richard Garnett he saw frequently at the British Museum, and Francis Darwin was surprisingly pleasant to him, but he was closely acquainted with neither, and there are no other prominent names in his correspondence. As for his personal friends, Pauli, Miss Savage, Hans Faesch, and a few others, his relations with them were almost pitiful. Indeed, the story of Butler and Charles Paine Pauli, in all its implications, is tragic. Butler met Pauli in New Zealand and was immediately impressed. "Everything that he had was good," he wrote of Pauli, "and he was such a fine handsome fellow, with such an attractive manner, that to me he seemed everything I should like myself to be but knew very well that I was not. I knew myself to be plebeian in appearance and believed myself to be more plebeian in tastes than I probably in reality was." This is frank enough and touching enough. Pauli was Butler's swell—Towneley is modeled upon him—and Butler was flattered by his friendship and glad to help him with money. That there was a homosexual basis for Butler's attitude seems clear, though that is as far as we can go with confidence.[1] From 1864 to his death in 1897, Pauli tortured Butler, while taking large sums of money from him, and only at his funeral was it discovered that he had been taking money from other men as well and had died comparatively wealthy.

Butler's other friendships could not be so fraudulent, but were not wholly satisfactory. Miss E. M. A. Savage, the model for Aunt Alethea in *The Way of All Flesh,* was shrewd, loyal, and helpful, but Butler's friendship with her was overcast by his feeling that he ought to marry her, which he did not want to do. And when she died, of a painful cancer that she had never told him about, he was, as he might well have been, filled with remorse. His relations with Hans Faesch were on

---

[1] Pryer in *The Way of All Flesh* is homosexual, and in view of this fact and of his financial dishonesty, we might suspect that Butler gave Pryer Pauli's distressing qualities, as he gave Towneley his admirable ones. This is merely a guess, but what seems certain is that Butler interpreted Shakespeare's sonnets in terms of his own relations with Pauli. Malcolm Muggeridge in *The Earnest Atheist* was the first critic to explore the subject of Butler and Pauli, and on this, as on various other topics, he seems essentially right. On the whole, however, his book gives a false picture of the man and his work.

much the same emotional level as those with Pauli, and, though they were neither so expensive nor so disillusioning, were quite as one-sided. With Jones Butler's position was that of a master condescending to a favored disciple, and Jones's boundless admiration for the great man made intimacy easy; but even this friendship was strained at the end. Perhaps his relations were entirely equable only with Madame Dumas, whom he visited weekly for fifteen years, and with Alfred Cathie, his servant, a person who had real affection for Butler and too much hard common sense to be much disturbed by his vanity.

In time Butler had to accept his isolation, and could talk about the "Ishmaelitish line" he had been driven to take. He began to believe that he had planned everything exactly as it had turned out. His obliqueness, for example, was part of his tactics, and in *Evolution, Old and New* he explained its advantages. Writing of Buffon, he says: "Free-thinker though he was, he was also a powerful member of the aristocracy, and little likely to demean himself—for so he would doubtless hold it—by playing the part of Voltaire or Rousseau. He would help those who could see to see still further, but he would not dazzle eyes that were yet imperfect with a light brighter than they could stand. He would therefore impose upon people, as much as he thought was for their good; but, on the other hand, he would not allow inferior men to mystify them." Butler casts himself in the role of Buffon, and Darwin and Huxley in the role of the inferior men. He will impose upon people by contending that his beliefs are not much different from those of the church, but he will not allow the Darwinians to deceive the public.

Butler convinced himself that he did not care if he was neglected; posterity would recognize him. "Of course," he wrote in his notebook, "I don't expect to get on in a commercial sense at present, I do not go the right way to work for this; but I am going the right way to secure a lasting reputation and this is what I do care for. A man cannot have both, he must make up his mind which he means going in for. I have gone in for posthumous fame and I see no step in my literary career which I do not think calculated to promote my being held in esteem when the heat of passion has subsided." He proceeded to describe his recipe for getting on, and one might assume that he thought popular success could easily have been his; but he had the candor to add, "Perhaps it is better that I should not have a chance of becoming a hack-writer, for I should grasp it at once if it were offered to me." He knew well enough that he was concerned with the future because the present had failed him.

3. *The Jericho Blast.*

The extraordinary thing is that Butler did get his posthumous fame and his lasting reputation. He had begun *The Way of All Flesh,* at Miss Savage's urgent suggestion, in 1873, and by 1885 it was in its present form. He had apparently intended that it should not be published until after the death of his sisters, but R. A. Streatfeild, whom he had appointed literary executor when he was piqued with Jones, decided that he was not bound by such considerations, and brought out the book in 1903, the year after Butler died. Immediately Butler's reputation soared. *Erewhon Revisited* and the new edition of *Erewhon* that had been published in 1901 were revived. Shaw, in the preface to *Major Barbara,* belabored the public for not appreciating Butler. From 1907 to 1910 the *Note-Books* appeared in the *New Quarterly,* increasing his reputation for irony. Jones, though he had been disinherited, organized Butler dinners, which notables attended. Gilbert Cannan published a biography in 1915, and the Jones *Memoir* appeared in 1919. Apotheosis came in the twenties with the elaborate and costly Shrewsbury edition of the *Works,* and meanwhile there were scores of editions, cheap and expensive, of *The Way of All Flesh*.

The excitement over Butler has been kept at a high pitch, for he has been re-discovered every few years, first as a novelist, then as a critic of Darwinism, then as an art critic, then as a student and translator of Homer. Despite all this, he owes the immortality he so greatly coveted to *The Way of All Flesh,* which has been as widely read as any novel of our times, and more widely imitated. It is the ancestor of most of the family chronicles of the past thirty-five years. Butler went back to Ernest's grandfather and great-grandfather because he had peculiar views on the subject of heredity. It was not the Lamarckism, however, that interested readers, but the sense that the novel gave of the changes that could take place from generation to generation in nineteenth century England. There had been earlier novels of the same sort, but *The Way of All Flesh* dramatized a phenomenon that men were just becoming conscious of, and it established the genre. Furthermore, it has influenced most of the twentieth century novels that deal with the spiritual growth of the hero. Again Butler had predecessors, but again he seems to be the author who fixed the pattern in the literary mind. One has only to read *Of Human Bondage,* in which Butler was beaten at his own game, to realize how pervasive his influence has been. *The Way of All Flesh* was peculiarly a novel for the beginning of the new century. Just as Hardy had celebrated the apparent changelessness of the country, so Butler recorded the rapidity of change in middle-class life, and, as men became more and more conscious of that exciting process, they were more and more impressed by the model he had given them.

Butler was fortunate in many ways. The device of making Overton, representing the old Butler, comment on Ernest, the author as a young man, permitted the introduction of all the wry epigrams that had been worked over in conversation, in correspondence with Miss Savage, and in the notebooks. They were admirably quotable, and few qualities can contribute more to a book's success. What he said in these epigrams and what he showed of family relationships served as a kind of emancipation proclamation for the young men and women of the twentieth century. Mrs. R. S. Garnett, using various documents as well as family recollections of Butler's parents, maintains that he exaggerated the narrowness and cruelty of Canon Butler and his wife. One agrees that there is much malice in the novel, but on the whole her book is the best possible defense of *The Way of All Flesh.* What she argues is that the Butlers were not much different from the average parents of their age and class, and this is exactly what admirers of the book have always claimed. When she says that "whippings were the order of the day," or that "this harshness was due to a theory of life and not to aversion," when she points out that "there was even less of domestic tyranny, of household gloom and feminine cattishness, about the Butler family than in the commonplace parsonage," when she defends Thomas Butler because "he had been formed in a school which taught parents it was not only excusable, it was their duty, to be tyrants," she is saying that, in spite of minor malicious exaggerations, Butler was right in his attack on the Victorian family and has been rightly applauded by his hundreds of thousands of readers.

The Way of All Flesh has helped to keep *Erewhon* alive, and that is good, for the variety and ingenuity of the satire make it still worth reading. *Erewhon Revisited,* as Butler realized, is a better organized book but a less interesting one. As for his other works, they are good only in fragments. One has to read many dull pages to find the bits of revealing criticism in *The Authoress of the Odyssey,* and his shrewdness is spread rather thin in *Alps and Sanctuaries* and the *Note-Books.* The four Lamarckian treatises contain some prophetically revealing comments on the unconscious [1] and some useful remarks on definitions and contradictions and the general laws of reasoning, but marginal suggestiveness of this kind, though fairly common, has to be searched for in a mass of argumentation that is often dull as well as dubious. Despite the efforts of disciples to find virtue in all the various exercises of his versatile mind, Butler remains a man of one book.

In *The Way of All Flesh* Butler said something that a large public was glad to hear. "The successful man," he wrote, "will see just so much more than his neighbors, as they will be able to see too when it is shown them, but not enough to puzzle them." By his own standards he was not a success, but he had miscalculated only by a small margin. By 1903 the public was ready to see what he was trying to show it.

Butler wanted, first of all, the destruction of the sentimental ideas that made parental tyranny possible. Second, he wanted to free organized religion from its commitments to the obviously incredible. Third, he wanted a realistic, common sense utilitarianism in morals; he wanted more freedom and less bother, particularly less bother, for he knew that freedom had always, to a great extent, taken care of itself.[2] Realism was what he advocated all down the line, in domestic life, in religion, in morals, in education. People were doing certain things, were living in certain ways, and he wanted them to stop pretending otherwise.

Butler would have been amazed if he could have lived to realize how many persons agreed with him. They felt as he

[1] Butler's interest in the unconscious led him to introduce into *The Way of All Flesh* something very much like the stream-of-consciousness technique. See, for example, Chapter XXIX.

[2] He was no crusader for the single standard or for any other drastic change, except a change in attitude. In *The Way of All Flesh* he says complacently: "The bitter fact remains that if a young girl does certain things she must do them at her peril, no matter how young and pretty she is nor to what temptation she has succumbed. This is the way of the world, and as yet there has been no help found for it."

did, and there was good reason why they should. Victorianism had been, in a manner of speaking, imposed on England by the middle class, and its standards were adapted to the processes by which that class was gaining wealth and power. When, however, the victory was won, it was only natural for the sons and daughters of the triumphant bourgeoisie to ask why they should be bound by the discipline of their parents. Before and after the depression of the eighties, England seemed prosperous enough, and, even during the depression, there were plenty of prosperous people. What sense could there be in refusing to enjoy life for the sake of unnecessary earthly rewards or dubious heavenly ones? The younger men and women welcomed every exposure of the false sentimentality that acted as the cement of family life now that economic necessity was not effectively cohesive. They were glad to see the church challenged and its authority weakened. Like Butler, they wanted to live their own lives. Like him, too, they were made uncomfortable by the hyprocrisy that surrounded them, and, even in defiance of their own theories of self-interest, they were willing to struggle to get rid of it.

We have already seen how Victorian morality had been criticized, subtly by such men as Meredith, aggressively by such men as Swinburne. At least forty years of dissent preceded the appearance of *The Way of All Flesh*. But no critic had found so deadly a method of attack. There were no extraneous issues with Butler. He did not demand a complete reform of the social order; on the contrary, he looked down on the poor, believed in laissez-faire, and regarded wealth as a sign of grace. He did not want to abolish the church; he sought to preserve it as a social institution. He did not propose to do away with classes; he asked only to belong to the swells. He had no silly ideas about defying society by living openly in sin; he was a defender of conventions. All that he asked was an honest revision of attitudes that would make theories square with practice. The surviving Victorians were dismayed, but their juniors recognized a prophet.

Perhaps, in spite of his smug conservatism, the older generation was right in finding his views subversive. Some of them at least were wise enough to realize that the compromise he proposed could not endure, and they asked themselves with alarm what would take its place. It was a question, surely, whether the church could survive on any such basis as he proposed for it, and whether a moral code that rested merely on "the current conscience of a man's best peers" could be expected to have any authority. Even what seemed to be the most safely orthodox of Butler's teachings, his insistence on the value of money, could be dangerous in the hands of the wrong people, as Shaw proved when he turned it into an argument for Socialism.

At the moment, however, those who were revolting against Victorianism did not care to look so far ahead, and their vision was matched by Butler's. During the slow disintegration of the Victorian system more than one writer became popular because he saw what his neighbors could see and felt what they realized they felt when he had pointed it out to them. Of these Butler was perhaps the most fortunate. In his curiously blundering life he was driven, against his own wishes and contrary to his own theories, to take an Ishmaelitish line, to become a gadfly, an enfant terrible. His need for asserting himself, for getting even with his enemies, spoiled all his plans for a comfortable success. And then a new generation discovered that it had a spokesman.

Chapter V

THE CHANGING NOVEL

THE novel could not help but be affected by the disintegration of Victorianism, for it had been the chief Victorian mode of expression. Many of the favorites of the nineteenth century's new reading public have fortunately been forgotten, but Thackeray, George Eliot, and especially Dickens were also favorites. They had carried the public away from the historical romanticism of Scott and the wilder romanticism of "Monk" Lewis and Udolpho, persuading it to take an interest in a more or less faithful reflection of its own way of life. They had traversed the greater part of England, finding comedy and tragedy wherever they went. They had explored social, ethical, and psychological problems. And they had, for good or for evil, made the novel a great instrument for the shaping of public opinion. The didacticism of the British novel shocked Taine, as it shocked most French critics, and there were signs of a revolt against it in England, but it was and for a long time would remain quite acceptable to readers and very tempting to writers.

The Victorian novel was prevailingly neither romantic nor realistic according to the usual definitions. Hardy had said, "The writer's problem is, how to strike the balance between the uncommon and the ordinary so as on the one hand to give interest, on the other to give reality." But he had become increasingly conscious that the appearance of reality was almost unobtainable. Not only was it imperative to write about the uncommon; it was impossible to write about the ordinary. The restrictions that had troubled Dickens and Thackeray became intolerable to a generation that could not accept the view of life on which they were founded. Evangelical tabus were an outrage once evangelical doctrines had been rejected.

The demand for realism, the insistence that truth was the only justification the writer needed, took two forms, as, on the strength of Hardy's formula, one might have predicted it would. In the first place, there was the inevitable and in time rather tedious battle to give fiction what might be called its physiological rights. In the second place, there was the determination to deal with the common, in both senses of the term. Even as far back as *Pamela,* it had been clear that the middle-class public had an insatiable appetite for hearing about its social superiors, and its taste had been slow to alter.

George Gissing and George Moore, out of very different impulses and with very different results, turned to the lower strata of the population for themes. Gissing wrote as a disciple of Dickens, trying to do what he felt his master had not done. Moore presented himself as a follower of the French school of naturalism. After a few years and a few novels both changed, in ways and for reasons that are worth examining, but literature did not therefore cease to move in the direction they had indicated. Even if there had been no influence from France, all the various kinds of change we have seen would have operated to alter the character of the novel. Morris' desire for social re-organization, Hardy's view of the universe, Butler's attack on hypocrisy—these had become literary forces. The novel was to play no less important a part in the early decades of the twentieth century than it had played in the nineteenth, and in the eighties and nineties it was being shaped for its new functions.

1. George Gissing and the Working Class.

In *The Private Papers of Henry Ryecroft,* the last of his books to be published in his lifetime, George Gissing makes his alter ego a man who has escaped from poverty through the inheritance of money. This motif recurs in fully half the novels Gissing wrote, including his earliest, *Workers in the Dawn.* Its recurrence makes us feel how passionately the author had himself hoped for such an immediate and simple release from his own miseries. But, so far as can be discovered, no one ever left him a cent of money, and if eventually he had enough to live on, it was because of his own efforts. That is the difference between George Gissing and Henry Ryecroft. Ryecroft is the man Gissing would have liked to be and felt that he would have been had he been more fortunate. The book, as Gissing admitted, is "much more an aspiration than a memory." Ryecroft, the serene old man, calmly waiting for death amid his books and the rural beauties he loves, is a portrait not of the artist but of the artist's ideal.

Yet Ryecroft does speak for the Gissing of 1903, and it is what he has to say that has endeared the book to the American humanists, two of whom, Paul Elmer More and Robert Shafer, have written in praise of it. "I am no friend of the people," Ryecroft tells us. "As a force, by which the tenor of the time is conditioned, they inspire me with distrust, with fear; as a visible multitude, they make me shrink aloof, and often move me to abhorrence. . . . Every instinct of my being is anti-democratic, and I dread to think of what our England may become when Demos rules irresistibly." Instinctive Gissing's opposition to democracy may have been, but he could not take it for granted. There was a time, he says in the person of Ryecroft, when his prosperity would have given him a guilty conscience. "I have hungered in the streets; I have laid my head in the poorest shelter; I know what it is to feel the

heart burn with wrath and envy of 'the privileged classes.'"
He has not grown callous, he insists, and, if he were to walk
into the slums of London, indignation would again rise in
him. "If I hold apart and purposely refuse to look that way,
it is because I believe that the world is better, not worse, for
having one more inhabitant who lives as becomes a civilized
being." He knows that his leisure is paid for by some man's
toil, and he is grateful, but he has no desire to meet that man
or his fellows. There is an insuperable barrier between him
and the working class, and he is amazed that he once believed he could ally himself with it: "To think that at one
time I called myself a socialist, communist, anything you like
of the revolutionary kind!"

Behind these autobiographical glimpses is a pathetic story.
The son of a pharmaceutical chemist, Gissing won a scholar-
ship to Owens College, Manchester, where he achieved distinction in Latin and Greek, but, before he could get his degree, he became involved in a sexual escapade, and was sent
by his family to America. There he underwent the sufferings
attributed to Whelpdale in *The New Grub Street,* and there
also he observed democracy as it existed in the Gilded Age.
Writing to his brother of the railroads, he says with a certain
pride, "Our democratic notions do not allow of division into
classes," but it is clear that already he was not quite at ease
with "our democratic notions."

After his return to England he lived in poverty and began
the writing of his first novel, *Workers in the Dawn.* He proclaimed himself a Radical in politics and an agnostic in religion. He rebuked his brother for his conservatism, joined
a Positivist society, hoped for a working-class revolution in
Germany, and lectured on Socialism. More than that, he
planned his first novel as "a very strong (possibly too plain
spoken) attack upon certain features of our religious and
social life which to me appear highly condemnable," and

thought of himself, in writing the novel, as "a mouthpiece of the advanced Radical party." "I mean," he said, "to bring home to people the ghastly conditions (material, mental, and moral) of our poor classes, to show the hideous injustice of our whole system of society, to give light upon the plan of altering it, and, above all, to preach an enthusiasm for just and high ideals in this age of unmitigated egotism and 'shop.' "

Workers in the Dawn suffers from a plot too complicated for the author to handle. The irony is usually feeble, and the attempt to reproduce Dickens' humor, especially in the portrayal of the Rev. Mr. Whiffle, is distressing. Bathos and melodrama are common, reaching a climax when, in a livid passage, the despairing hero plunges into Niagara Falls—as, it must be said, Gissing had contemplated doing. Yet from the opening description of Saturday night in the London slums the reader knows that here is a man who is trying to do something new and important, and in some measure succeeding. Earlier authors, and primarily Dickens, of whose example Gissing was always conscious, had portrayed the ghastly material conditions of the poor, but they had never shown what poverty did to the mind. Later Gissing wrote, "With the working class household, Dickens, I think, is never entirely successful; one reason among others being that he shrinks from criticizing the very poor." Gissing did not. From Mrs. Blatherwick and her sadistic son to Carrie and her cronies, most of the poor in *Workers in the Dawn* are incurably brutalized.

Yet it must be made clear that, in this novel, Gissing does not place the blame upon the poor themselves. At the end of his introductory description he writes, "We suffer them to become brutes in our midst, and inhabit dens which clean animals would shun, to derive their joys from sources from which a cultivated mind shrinks as from a pestilential vapor."

"What," he asks, "if Bill Blatherwick himself, bestially drunk as he now is, were to be transported bodily into one of these mansions and then thrown down upon the carpet—a novel excitement for these Christmas guests! Would it strike any of them, with the terrific force of a God-sent revelation, that to them individually was due a share of the evil which has bred such an unutterable abomination?" [1]

Knowing that a considerable section of the rich would not be receptive to such a revelation, Gissing criticizes the hard-hearted wealthy far more bitterly than he does the brutalized poor. He shows, for example, Gilbert Gresham, an artist with a considerable income, whose brilliant cynicism lapses into mere callous bad nature. Gresham insists that the poor are "not to be classed with human beings, but rather with the brutes." "It is my firm belief," he says, "that their degeneration is actually and literally physical; that the fine organs of virtue in which *we* possess all that we have of the intellectual and refined, have absolutely perished from their frames; that you might as well endeavor to teach a pig to understand Euclid as to teach one of these gaol-birds to know what is meant by honesty, virtue, kindness, intellectuality." Mr. Gresham himself has none of these qualities, except a superficial kind of intellectuality, and his daughter has not even that attribute. Her first husband and her lover, who is the son of a peculiarly pretentious and obnoxious minister, descend beneath her own and her father's level.

Contrasted with the Greshams, Waghorns, and Whiffles are the working-class friends of the hero. Tollady, the printer who takes him in charge, gives away the greater part of his meager income. Tollady's friend, Mark Challenger, works for the cause of social justice. Will Noble, a pure idealist, organizes a club of workingmen to devote themselves to the

---

[1] Passages from *Workers in the Dawn,* by George Gissing, reprinted by permission of Doubleday, Doran and Company, Inc.

improvement of their class. None is a revolutionary. Will Noble says: "I am convinced there *must* be a rich class and a poor class. But shall I tell you what I am *not* convinced of? I am not convinced that, of these rich and poor, the one must be a class of brute beasts—of ignorant, besotted, starving, toil-worn creatures—whilst the other must be a class of lords and princes, spending in profitless luxuries—luxuries which perish with them and are of no further good in the world—riches which would suffice to put every poor man at his ease." Tol-lady asks Arthur, "Did you ever reflect that there are men in England whose private wealth would suffice to buy up every one of the vile slums we have just been traversing, and build fresh, healthy streets in their place, and the men still remain wealthy? To me it is one of the most fearful marvels of the time, that among such countless millionaires scarcely one arises in a generation actuated with the faintest shade of phil-anthropic motives, and *not* one worthy of the name of a true philanthropist."

It is under the influence of these men that the hero, Arthur Golding, falls. At times he seems to go beyond them, though never so far as John Pether, the fanatical revolutionary, who has been crazed by his sufferings. On the occasion of the establishment of the Third Republic in France, Arthur ad-dresses Will Noble's club. He calls for complete democracy, and points to the general strike as the means of establishing it. "Not content," he says, "with helping to keep our fellows alive, we must teach them their power!" But this is only a moment of boldness on his part and Gissing's, for in general Arthur, like his creator, seems to believe that the only hope lies in the awakening of the upper classes to their responsi-bility. The only well-to-do character in the book who accepts this responsibility, Helen Norman, Gresham's ward, estab-lishes a school for working girls in the slums.

The agnosticism of Helen Norman and Tollady's anticlericalism are perhaps the only qualities that distinguish Gissing's attitude, as he presents it in his first novel, from that of the Coleridge-Carlyle school. It is true, of course, that he was a Positivist, a Radical, and, in his own mind, a kind of Socialist, but in effect he scarcely went beyond Kingsley and Mrs. Gaskell. There is no recognition of the fact that the rich as well as the poor are what the social system has made them and only the vaguest intimations that the working class might profitably act for itself.

Gissing was a long way from Socialism in 1880, but he might have developed in that direction. If one wonders why he did not, there is an important clue in *Workers in the Dawn*. The hero of the novel marries a poor girl, whose taste for drink later ruins both of them. At the outset, while he is still in love with her, he tries to educate her. Gissing shrewdly says: "In his attempt to exalt her nature above the level on which it had hitherto moved, he, the democratic agitator, the ardent sympathizer with the most miserable of poverty's victims, waxed quite aristocratic in his conversation. In his heart he would rather have seen Carrie fall into the most complete snobbishness on the subject of riches and rank than continue at rest among the sympathies with vulgar life with which she had grown up." There is autobiography here. Unlike Morris, Gissing was very close to the poor, so close that his strongest passion was to escape from their disgusting way of life. He would change that way of life if he could, and at first that seemed the logical method of escape, but escape he must at all costs.

H. G. Wells tells us that, a few years after the writing of *Workers in the Dawn,* he and Gissing used to argue about education, Wells, of course, defending science and Gissing the classics. Wells suspects that Gissing regarded him as a barbarian, and he is probably right, for Gissing questioned the civilization of anyone, Charles Dickens included, who had not read ancient literature. On his side, Wells thought Gissing "horribly mis-educated," and their arguments confirmed his low opinion of the classical discipline.

Wells was wrong in believing that Gissing's education was directly responsible for the conservatism of the social theories he held in the latter part of his life, but he was right in his feeling that the classics had played an important part in shaping Gissing's mind. A poor boy from a lower-middle-class home, he saw in his fellowship at Owens College his opportunity to enter the world of dignity and refinement, and he regarded the knowledge of Latin and Greek he obtained there as a social as well as an intellectual distinction. Though his pleasure in the classics was genuine, even so late as *The Private Papers of Henry Ryecroft* there is a special quality of pride in his manner of speaking of the ancients. We can imagine him, then, as a man in his early twenties, actually in danger of being submerged in the mass of squalor and misery that he saw about him. Of course he clung to his classical education. That was what set him apart, made him know that he was different from these sordid masses and would never degenerate as they had done.

In the first two or three years of his poverty Gissing did not need reassurance so badly. He was confident of his ability to raise himself and to help raise the masses with him. But as poverty persisted, and the publication of *Workers in the Dawn* brought no relief, confidence weakened. Gissing points out that Dickens was subjected to poverty long enough to store his imagination but not long enough "to corrupt the natural sweetness of his mind." Gissing's own poverty lasted until whatever sweetness his mind may have had was thoroughly spoiled. The more he saw of the poor, the more he feared that he might sink to their level, and the more he clung to everything in himself that set him apart from them. The danger of being lost was in his mind far more than the hope of saving others, and gradually he convinced himself that there was no such hope. Indeed, he convinced himself that the poor did not deserve to be saved, and he began to look on them with contempt.

The transformation took place in three or four years. The letters he wrote to his family in 1880, the year of *Workers in the Dawn,* and in the next two years are full of enthusiasm for social reconstruction. Even when he describes the gruesome vulgarity of the masses on a bank holiday, he takes care to show why they are vulgar. But gradually he says less and less about the need for change, and in 1884 he confesses to his brother, "My own life is too sterile and miserable to allow my thinking much about the Race. When I am able to summon any enthusiasm at all, it is only for Art." A little later he speaks with horror of William Morris' arrest: "It is painful to me beyond expression. Why cannot he write poetry in the shade? He will inevitably coarsen himself in the company of ruffians. Keep apart, keep apart, and preserve one's soul alive —that is the teaching for the day. It is ill to have been born in these times, but one can make a world within a world."

His novels naturally followed the course of his changing opinions. In his second novel, *The Unclassed,* there are two literary men, both of them partly autobiographical. Julian Casti has Gissing's devotion to the classics, his love of Italy, and his unfortunate marriage. Waymark has his radical past and his literary aims. The latter says: "Let me get a little more experience, and I will write a novel such as no one has yet ventured to write, at all events in England. . . . The fact is, the novel of every-day life is getting worn out. We must dig deeper, get to untouched social strata. Dickens felt this, but he had not the courage to face his subjects; his monthly numbers had to lie on the family tea-table. Not virginibus puerisque will be my book, I assure you, but for men and women who like to look beneath the surface and who understand that only as artistic material has human life any significance." He goes on: "Life for its own sake?—no; I would drink a pint of laudanum tonight. But life as the source of splendid pictures, inexhaustible material for effects—*that* can reconcile me to existence, and that only."

Waymark, like Gissing, wants to write about the life of the poor, but he rejects the humanitarian reason for doing so. "When you begin to find your voice again," he tells Casti, "maybe you won't sing of the dead world any longer, but of the living and suffering. . . . Art, nowadays, must be the mouthpiece of misery, for misery is the key-note of modern life." He renounces the political views he once held: "I was not a conscious hypocrite in those days of violent radicalism, workingman's club lecturing, and the like; the fault was that I understood myself as yet so imperfectly. That zeal on behalf of the suffering masses was nothing more nor less than disguised zeal on behalf of my own starved passions. . . . I identified myself with the poor and ignorant; I did not make their cause my own, but my own cause theirs."

Waymark is Gissing's mouthpiece, and yet he is contrasted to his disadvantage with the philanthropic Ida. Gissing still is friendly towards the poor, critical of exploitation, appreciative of sincere efforts to relieve suffering. Ida, brought up in poverty, is one of the many Gissing characters to fall heir to a fortune, and she spends her money in trying to abolish the slums out of which her grandfather had made it. Waymark says to her: "You are too good for that; I should have liked to think of you as far apart from those vile scenes." She replies: "Can you, knowing me as no one else does or ever will, think that I could live here in peace, whilst those poor creatures stint and starve themselves to provide me with comforts?"

Isabel Clarendon, finished in 1885, was Gissing's first attempt to abandon the world to which he had pledged himself when he wrote *Workers in the Dawn*. Its snobbishness is manifest, particularly in the antipathy that Kingcote, the hero, feels towards his sister's landlady. "Aristocracy of race," Gissing explains, "cannot compare in pervasive intensity with aristocracy which comes only of the influence of intellect and temperament." The reader also is surprised by the idealization of country life, which Gissing had been given an opportunity to contemplate when he accompanied Frederic Harrison's sons to the Lake District the preceding summer. In the person of Kingcote he rejoices at "the absence of any hint of townish Radicalism," and is pleased to find the old order so undisturbed. "If only," he laments, "the schoolmaster could be kept away; if only progress would work its evil will on the children of the slums, and leave these worthy clodhoppers in their ancient peace!"

On the whole, *Isabel Clarendon* is a revelation of ignorance, as Meredith must have realized, for after reading it, he advised Gissing to keep to "the low-life scenes." Gissing took the advice, dealing in *A Life's Morning,* and often to good effect, with the poverty of a scholar such as himself. Then in *Demos* he returned to the slums. But in what a different spirit! *Demos,* he wrote his brother, "will be a rather savage attack on working-class aims and capacities." It was all of that. Gissing had obviously reached the point at which his abandonment of radicalism had to be justified, and *Demos* was the book in which he tried to defend himself. For plot it draws upon the old argument that, if a Socialist came into money, he would soon lose his Socialism. Richard Mutimer, who inherits his great-uncle's mines and attempts to run them on Socialist principles, not only loses his convictions but reveals extravagant depths of degradation.

The choice of such a plot is significant enough, but Gissing is by no means content to let the story speak for itself. At the outset he contrasts Richard Mutimer's grandfather with his great-uncle. The former was a Chartist, "a political enthusiast of insufficient ballast," who was killed in a riot. The brother worked hard, saved money, married a lady, and made a fortune. "The defects of his early education," Gissing points out, "could not of course be repaired, but it is never too late for a man to go to school to the virtues which civilize. Remaining the sturdiest of Conservatives, he bowed in sincere humility to those very claims which the Radical most angrily disallows: birth, hereditary station, recognized gentility."

This sets the tone for a novel that, even in an age of editorializing in fiction, is remarkable for the frequency and bitterness of its comments on the events it describes. Gissing says as much as usual about the brutality of the poor, but now has nothing to say about its causes. He decries popular education as vulgar, and regards his sincere upper-class idealists as ignorant. One of the characters says of another, obviously modeled on William Morris, "How has he fallen to this? His very style has abandoned him, his English smacks of the street corners, of Radical clubs. The man is ruined; it is next to impossible that he should ever again do good work, such as we used to have from him." Richard's Socialist schemes, even when they are in operation, do nothing but spoil the workers, and Gissing points out, with apparent approval, that no other employer would hire a man from the New Wanley mines.

Hubert Eldon, who is the rightful heir and who eventually receives the property, is Gissing's ideal and spokesman. He says to Wyvern, the vicar, "In the presence of these fellows I feel that I am facing enemies. It seems to me that I have nothing in common with them but the animal functions." Wyvern, who had once considered himself a Socialist, agrees. Eldon, when he owns the mines, decides to close them and let the grass and trees grow again. "The ruling motive in my life," he explains, "is the love of beautiful things: I fight against

ugliness because it is the only work in which I can engage
with all my heart. . . . Progress—the word is sufficient; you
have only to think what it has come to mean. It will be good
to have an example of reaction."

Adela, an aristocrat with a strong sense of noblesse oblige,
who married Richard out of sympathy with his professed aims,
learns how false her idealism is. Richard, she realizes, "was
not of her class, not of her world; only by violent wrenching
of the laws of nature had they come together. She had spent
years in trying to convince herself that there were no such
distinctions, that only an unworthy prejudice parted class
from class. One moment of true insight was worth more than
all her theorizing on abstract principles. To be her equal this
man must be born again, of other parents, in other conditions
of life." Of Richard's brother, Harry, Gissing says: "The
character of this young man was that of a distinct class, com-
prising the sons of mechanics who are ruined morally by being taught to consider themselves above manual labor. . . .
He pronounced the word 'clerk' as it is spelled; it made him
seem yet more ignoble."

Demos proved to be the bitterest of all Gissing's novels,
for, though he did not modify his opinions thereafter, he was
content to express them less violently. In the two novels he
subsequently wrote about the working class he chose characters of whom he could approve, and hence he could allow his
sympathies play without making concessions of which he was
afraid. In *Thyrza* there are two philanthropists: Walter Egremont, who proposes to raise the better members of the working class by giving them a cultural education, and Mrs. Or-
monde, who also is wise enough to bear class distinctions in
mind without ignoring individual virtues. Most of the workers
in the book are docile. Gilbert Grail, for example, spending
thirteen hours a day in a candle factory, hating his work and
longing for the chance to study, is nevertheless "not driven to

that kind of resentment which makes the revolutionary spirit." Luke Ackroyd, it is true, has something of that spirit, but he is cured through education.

By 1889, when he published *The Nether World,* Gissing was even more moderate. Indeed, he seems to feel the sufferings of the poor as he did when he wrote *Workers in the Dawn.* "Genuine respect for the law," he says at one point, "is the result of possessing something which the law exerts itself to guard." At moments the old passion against injustice creeps in, as in the exhortation that accompanies the description of a soup kitchen: "Have you still to learn what this nether world has been made by those who belong to the sphere above it? Gratitude, quotha? Nay, do *you* be grateful that these hapless, half-starved women do not turn and rend you. At present they satisfy themselves with insolence. Take it silently, you who at all events hold some count of their dire state; and endeavor to feed them without rousing their animosity."

Yet, if Gissing could once again view the poor without condemning them, he was as far from identifying himself with them as when he published *Demos.* In 1892 he wrote his sister: "I fear we shall live through great troubles yet, owing to the social revolution that is in progress. You will have understood, in part, my attitude to this revolution. We cannot resist it, but I throw in what weight I may have on the side of those who believe in an aristocracy of *brains,* as against the brute domination of the quarter-educated mob."

By this time Gissing had some reason, other than his ambitions, to rank himself with the aristocracy of brains, for the publication of *The New Grub Street* in 1891 had given him a name, and he could feel that he was no longer a mere pretender to intellectual eminence. In this famous account of writers' struggles Gissing's own hardships served, with the natural modifications of fiction, not only for the central character but for three or four minor figures as well. Biffen, Whelp-

dale, and Sykes are not to be identified with the author, as
Reardon is, but their experiences are drawn, as his are, from
a life of poverty and frustration too rich for a single character.
In every part of the story Gissing was dealing with the subject
that he knew best, and the novel has a kind of self-confident
authority that its predecessors lacked.

The radical opinions Gissing had once held play little part
in *The New Grub Street,* for his theme is the relationship between the writer and his middle-class public. "The chances
are," he tells the reader, "that you have neither understanding
nor sympathy for such men as Edwin Reardon and Harold
Biffen. They merely provoke you. They seem to you inert,
flabby, weakly envious, foolishly obstinate, impiously muti-
nous, and many other things. . . . Nothing is easier than to
condemn a type of character which is unequal to the coarse
demands of life as it suits the average man. These two were
richly endowed with the kindly and imaginative virtues; if
fate threw them amid incongruous circumstances, is their
endowment of less value? . . . The sum of their faults was
their inability to earn money; but, indeed, that inability does
not call for unmingled disdain." Gissing had learned that,
if it was difficult for him to ally himself with the poor, as he
had once tried to do, it was no easier for him to feel at home
with the successful men of the world.

Yet he was forced to deal more and more with the upper
classes in his novels, for there was nothing more for him to
say about the nether world, and he could not go on writing
about writers. In some of his later novels, such as *Eve's Ransom* and *The Town Traveller,* he showed a lightness of touch
of which he had not previously been capable, and all of the
novels of the nineties are put together with a certain crafts-
manlike precision. But on the whole nothing that he wrote
between *The New Grub Street* and *The Private Papers of
Henry Ryecroft* has much importance. He addressed himself,

rather pretentiously, to a series of middle-class problems. In *The Emancipated* he contrasts both evangelicalism and Bohemianism with what he regards as true classical restraint. *The Odd Women* is a study of marriage and feminism. *In the Year of Jubilee* exposes middle-class greed. *The Whirlpool* laments the absence of stable values in contemporary society. *Our Friend, the Charlatan* and *Denzil Quarrier* ridicule political ambitions.

Throughout all these novels Gissing expressed his distaste for industrial civilization. In *The Crown of Life* he wrote: "The brute force of money; the negation of the individual— these, the evils of our time, found their supreme expression in the City of London. Here was opulence at home and superb; here must poverty lurk and shrink, feeling itself alive only on sufferance; the din of highway and byway was a voice of blustering conquest, bidding the weaker to stand aside or be crushed. Here no man was a human being, but each merely a portion of an inconceivably complicated mechanism. . . . The smooth working of the huge machine made it only the more sinister; one had but to remember what cold tyranny, what elaborate fraud, were served by its manifold ingenuities, only to think of the cries of anguish stifled by its monotonous roar."

Yet Gissing, with an eagerness born of his poverty, wanted money and admired those who had it. On the process of making money, except when he chooses to satirize it, he is usually vague. The characters he likes have inherited a fortune or, like Spence in *The Emancipated,* made one in some obscure business from which they have retired. Best of all, of course, are those whose incomes derive from inherited estates. In *Henry Ryecroft* there is a pathetic echo of Coleridge, Carlyle, Disraeli, Kingsley, Ruskin: "Very significant," Ryecroft comments, "is the cordial alliance from old time between nobles and people; free, proud homage on one side answering to gallant championship on the other; both classes working together in the cause of liberty."

Neither his tastes nor his experiences fitted Gissing to write about the middle and upper classes, nor had he anything important to say about their problems. The problems, indeed, seldom seem to interest him deeply; they are simply available themes for marketable books. There is little of the passion that went into the early novels and less of the first-hand knowledge. Only in a reflective book such as *Henry Ryecroft* could he do anything with the talents that were left him. With the growing vogue of historical romance at the end of the century, he naturally saw a new opportunity, and it was on a novel of Rome under the Gothic kings that he was working when he died.

2. *Gissing as Realist.*

Gissing has seldom been ranked high among men of letters, but few students of English literature ignore him. He seems more important than any one of his books, in a sense more important than his whole literary achievement, for one feels that he almost gave British literature a new direction. Whatever he did grew out of the development of the novel in the nineteenth century. He might have come at his pioneering labors by the same path as Zola, since he, too, had read Spencer and Comte and Haeckel, but, though the influences of Positivism and Radicalism are not to be overlooked, he did not write *Workers in the Dawn* according to a preconceived theory, his own or another's. He began as a disciple of Dickens who, because of his particular experiences, knew there was something Dickens had failed to do and wanted to do it. The Victorian novel was his starting point, wherever he might go or fail to go.

In his *Charles Dickens* he describes the novelist as a representative member of a class "below the rank of capitalist but above the rank of proletarian." "He lived," Gissing says, "to become, in all externals, and to some extent in the tone of his mind, a characteristic member of this privileged society; but his criticism of its foibles, and of its grave shortcomings, never ceased. The landed proprietor of Gadshill could not forget (the great writer could never desire to forget) a miserable childhood imprisoned in the limbo of squalid London; his grudge against this memory was in essence a *class* feeling; to the end his personal triumphs gratified him, however unconsciously, as the vindication of a social claim."

Of Dickens' political views he writes: "He was a Radical. This meant, of course, one who was discontented with the slow course of legislation, moving decorously 'from precedent to precedent,' and with the aristocratic ideas underlying English life; one who desired radical changes, in the direction of giving liberty and voice to the majority of the people." Yet, Gissing insists, "he was never a democrat; in his heart he always held that *to be governed* was the people's good; only let the governors be rightly chosen." "He shows us poor men who suffer under tyranny, and who exclaim against the hardship of things; but never such a representative wage-earner as was then to be seen battling for bread and right." "Of noble discontent, Dickens cannot be said to give us any picture at all. . . . As for the rank and file of hungry creatures, they seem never to have heard that there is a movement in the land, that voices are raised on their behalf, and even to some purpose." "Dickens' remedy for the evils left behind by the bad old times was, for the most part, private benevolence."

This is sound analysis, not greatly colored by the fact that, at the time he wrote the book, Gissing was even less of a believer in democracy than Dickens. We can reconstruct from it what Gissing must have felt about Dickens in the late seventies. Then he would have quarreled with the lack of faith in

democracy and with the failure to portray "noble discontent."
But even in 1880, when he wrote *Workers in the Dawn,* Gissing was really no closer to the militant working-class movement than Dickens had been, and his attempt to describe it
offers but a slight improvement over *Hard Times.*

It was not in this way that Gissing could go beyond his
master, but there was a way in which he could and did. He
was not restrained by the "great heart" that, he felt, kept
Dickens from portraying the slum-dwellers as they really
were. Dickens had sentimentalized and softened, but Gissing,
like Crabbe setting out to describe the farmers' cottages of
the late eighteenth century, was determined to depict the
slum "as Truth will paint it and as bards will not." Fear and
loathing mingled with devotion to the truth, but he was trying to be a more truthful Dickens. The desire for reform
spurred him on, but perhaps the strongest motive was the
sense of a literary task that needed to be performed.

For this specific purpose Dickens' work offered the best
possible point of departure. In other respects, however, it
was a pity that Gissing accepted the conventions of the Victorian novel. Later he criticized Dickens for conformity, but
in his earlier work he too was a conformist, and perhaps had
no alternative. *The New Grub Street* attacked the institution
of the circulating library because it imposed the worst taste
of the genteel middle class and because it required the three-
volume novel. But Gissing was working in the Mudie era,
and he accepted Mudie standards.

Like Hardy, Gissing discovered at the outset of his career
that the middle class wanted plenty of action, but he could not
use the complicated plot for his purposes, as Hardy did, and
he had none of Dickens' offhand skill in manipulating incidents. In his hands the Dickensian device of a multiplicity of
sub-plots, depending on coincidence, violent death, and what

an earlier generation called divine intervention, constantly got in the way of the development of character and the portrayal of social conditions that were his real aims. It was not until *The New Grub Street* that he was willing to dispense with machinery of the Wilkie Collins type, and he re-introduced it in most of the subsequent novels.

He was equally troubled by contemporary standards of gentility, and his realism operated within recognizable limits. So far as lower-class characters are concerned, he permits himself to endow them with brutality of act and, within limits, of speech. He even describes, with stated disapproval, their subjection to sexual passion. He also refers to the vices of the rich. But he is frank only when he is dealing with what can be regarded as bestial. He is frank only when he can, at least by implication, condemn what he describes. There is no suggestion that sexual impulses play a part in the lives of ordinary, respectable men and women. Arthur Golding's marriage to Carrie in *Workers in the Dawn* seems motivated by a combination of pure benevolence and black magic, though the incident is so nearly autobiographical that Gissing must have understood it. *In the Year of Jubilee* contains a seduction, but, like all Victorian seductions, it is incredible, since the heroine is endowed with no emotion to which a seducer could appeal.

For temperamental reasons Gissing did not adopt the colloquial tone so popular from Fielding's time to his own, but he was no more objective, in the formal sense, than his predecessors. In the earlier novels he speaks in his own person, presents characters formally to the reader, and delivers homilies. As Taine had pointed out, the whole tradition of the British novel was moralistic, not merely in its inevitable representation of a point of view but in the direct preaching of the authors. There had been few British novelists who did not insist on buttonholing the reader and giving him a lecture.

And Gissing, though he avoided mere chattiness, was like his fellow-writers in not being able to resist the temptation to accompany presentation with commentary.

Gissing, then, was still a Victorian novelist. But within the limits of the Victorian novel he was doing something new. In *Workers in the Dawn* Mr. Tollady says to Arthur: "Paint a faithful picture of this crowd we have watched, be a successor of Hogarth, and give us the true image of *our* social dress, as he did of those of his own day. Paint them as you see them, and get your picture hung in the Academy. It would be a moral lesson to all who looked upon it, surpassing in value every sermon that fanaticism has ever concocted." [1] That was Gissing's program, as he first conceived it, moral purpose and all. Biffen's description of his aim in *The New Grub Street*— "absolute realism in the sphere of the ignobly decent"—might seem to fit Howells rather than Gissing, since decency is not the principal characteristic of the latter's slum-dwellers, but the conviction was strong in Gissing that literature could deal with the commonplace.

Frank Swinnerton in his rather patronizing little book on Gissing says: "It does very decidedly stand to Gissing's credit that at a time when most modern novelists, with the exception of Mr. Hardy and, in one novel, George Meredith, were finding inspiration in the middle and upper classes, he should have had the courage to strike below the pleasant surface of life." [2] This is understatement. Henry James, with that understanding of uncongenial authors that so often startles one, puts the case better: "The great thing is that his saturation is with elements that, presented to us in contemporary English

[1] Waymark in *The Unclassed* says the study of Hogarth "gave him a fresh impulse in the direction his literary projects were taking," and Alfred Gissing tells us that his father had admired Hogarth from boyhood.

[2] From *George Gissing,* by Frank Swinnerton, copyright 1923 by Doubleday, Doran and Company.

fiction, affect us as a product of extraordinary oddity and rarity: he reeks with the savors, he is bowed beneath the fruits, of contact with the lower, with the lowest middle-class, and that is sufficient to make him an authority—*the* authority in fact—on a region vast and unexplored." "We have recognized the humble," James continues, "the wretched, even the wicked; also we have recognized the 'smart.' But save under the immense pressure of Dickens we have never done anything so dreadful as to recognize the vulgar." Dickens' "pressure" consisted in making the vulgar funny or pathetic. Gissing resorts to no such device: "He has the strongest deepest sense of common humanity, of the general struggle and the general grey grim comedy. He loves the real, he renders it, and though he has a tendency to drift too much with his tide, he gives us, in the great welter of the savorless, an individual manly strain."

One has only to compare Gissing's earlier novels with Arthur Morrison's *Tales of Mean Streets* to see where the former's excellence lies. Morrison has a kind of technical skill that Gissing never acquired. Moreover, his attitude seems to be that at which Gissing arrived: loathing for the vulgarity of the poor, distrust of all attempts to raise them to a higher level, belief in the permanence of class distinctions. But Morrison manages to present himself as a mere observer, neither sympathetic nor profound, a seeker after a rather lurid kind of local color. In his tales, as in Stephen Crane's, but in greater degree, one feels a zeal for literary effects that is essentially insincere.[1] Though he probably held his reactionary views with full conviction, his attitude comes to seem, in the worst sense, literary. With Gissing, even in *Demos,* when he is guilty of mis-

---

[1] This is much less true of Morrison's *Child of the Jago* than it is of the better known collection of short stories. Morrison's account of the life and death of Dicky Parrott is sympathetic and often astute. Unfortunately, he thereafter devoted himself chiefly to detective stories and Japanese art.

representation for the sake of propaganda, there is the manly strain that James speaks of, a true seriousness that makes its impression.

No particular virtue attaches to novels about the poor, but surely, looking at the British novel in the nineteenth century, one is struck by the fact that nearly all the characters come from some ten or twenty percent of the population. Neither personal experience nor reasons of temperament can quite explain the devotion of most authors to the aristocracy and the upper middle class. When Mr. Swinnerton suggests that Gissing was striking below the pleasant surface of life when he dealt with the lower classes, he may be guilty of some confusion, but he quite correctly relates the Victorian pre-occupation with the well-fed to the general prudishness. Themes worthy of any artist were being neglected. Moreover, true realism was difficult in any field so long as novelists felt there were vast areas of British life with which they could not deal.

Despite all his weaknesses, Gissing does make the reader at home in the world of the impoverished masses. His descriptions are often set-pieces, but they are the work of a man who had lived in the slums, and in their totality they are moving as well as true. His characters, like Morrison's, are often chosen to exhibit the baseness of the poor, but even the most contemptible have a spark of life. Moreover, he has a succession of working-class characters—Tollady, Will Noble, Gilbert Grail, Thyrza Trent, Sidney Kirkwood—towards whom he feels and inspires sympathy and admiration. Others might portray the poor as all alike and brutishly simple in character, but Gissing, even while he hated them, knew their complexity.

Most critics agree that Gissing's earlier work was on the whole better than his later. Paul Elmer More speculates: "Possibly the long years of defeat began to shake his moral equilibrium; possibly the growing influence upon him of French and Russian fiction was to blame. Certainly the pride of English, what raises it, despite its deficiencies of form and ideas, to be the first of modern literatures, is the deep-rooted convention of moral responsibility." In the later novels, More continues, "in place of human nature battling with grim necessity, we now have a society of people contending against endless insinuations of tedium and vanity." And he goes on to speak of "sex-consciousness," "relaxing of moral fiber," and "the thrice-dreary theories of marriage."

If Gissing's moral fiber had been dangerously relaxed, he could scarcely have won Mr. More's approval with *The Private Papers of Henry Ryecroft*. What had happened was much simpler than that. Gissing was lost. When he abandoned the poor, he found himself compelled to write about a kind of life that he knew only superficially. Because he had turned his back on all proposals for social change, he had to concern himself with more or less trivial problems, in which he took only a slight interest and about which he had nothing significant to say. Finally, the withering of humanitarian feeling in the course of his struggle to save himself had robbed him of intellectual as well as emotional vitality. In his earlier novels one feels a mind at work—and this, as Virginia Woolf points out, is enough to distinguish him among British writers. But in the later fiction, though there are problems, there is little thought. Having himself surrendered intellectually, as the price he had to pay to escape a radicalism that he found unbearable in its implications, he could no longer create thinking human beings. Compare Tollady, Will Noble, Arthur, and Helen in *Workers in the Dawn* with Mallard in *The Emancipated,* Tarrant in *In the Year of Jubilee,* Harvey Rolfe in *The Whirlpool,* Mrs. Woolstan in *Our Friend, the Charlatan,* or Mr. Liversedge in *Denzil Quarrier*. These latter are all characters that Gissing seems to admire, and presumably they are to some extent his spokesmen. They are more artfully portrayed than the men and women in that amateurish first novel of his, but they do not show an advance in creative power.

In an essay that he wrote in 1895 Gissing deplored the limitation of the term "realism" to novels with unpleasant subjects. Only two qualities, he said, were important in fiction: sincerity and craftsmanship. "Realism, then, signifies nothing more than artistic sincerity in the portrayal of contemporary life; it merely contrasts with the habit of mind which assumes that a novel is written 'to please people,' that disagreeable facts must always be kept out of sight, that human nature must be systematically flattered, that the book must have a 'plot,' that the story should end on a cheerful note, and all the rest of it." For himself he recognized limits beyond which he would not care to go, but "at the same time I joyfully compare the novelist's freedom in England of today with his bondage of only ten or twelve years ago." "The great thing," he concluded, "is that public opinion no longer constrains a novelist to be false to himself. The world lies open before him, and it is purely a matter for his private decision whether he will write as the old law dictates or show life its image as he beholds it."

Freedom from constraint, however, could profit Gissing but little. Though he had gained in craftsmanship, he had lost in sincerity. Not that he was false to himself; he showed life its image as he beheld it, but he did not behold it as clearly as he once had. *The New Grub Street* was probably the last novel in which he set forth a vision of life that he confidently believed to be true and important. In trying to deal with problems of marriage, education, and politics as they presented themselves to well-bred ladies and gentlemen, he was handicapped by indifference as well as ignorance. There is a certain attempt to recommend the inner check, but even Mr. More recognizes the feebleness of the effort.

"My father," says Albert Gissing, "was growing weary of modern civilization with all its problems, and was inclined to

dwell more and more upon the thought of ancient Rome."
Whenever he was moderately prosperous, he hastened to
Italy. H. G. Wells, who was there with him in 1897, writes:
"He accepted and identified himself with all the pretensions
of Rome's triumphal arches. . . . At the back of his mind, a
splendid Olympus to our Roman excursions, stood noble sena-
tors in togas, marvellous matrons like Lucrece, gladiators
proud to die, Horatiuses ready to leap into gulfs pro patria,
the finest fruit of humanity, unjudged, accepted, speaking like
epitaphs and epics." Only the accident of having to cater to
a particular market led Gissing to postpone to the very end of
his life the historical novel he then began to write.

We come back to Gissing's achievement in *Workers in the
Dawn, The Unclassed, Thyrza, The Nether World,* and *The
New Grub Street,* which, though it was repeatedly marred by
defects of an uncommon grossness, was substantial. Gissing
contributed something, as Hardy and Butler and others were
doing, to the emancipation of literature. But far more important was the sense he gave of great possibilities in new
themes. Time has proven, in both England and America,
that even the clumsy craftsman, if he is immersed in the life
of which he is writing, and if he is serious and honest and
patient, can reach our imaginations. We have been forced,
almost in spite of ourselves, to respect saturation in the commonplace. Gissing, we now see, was showing the way, though
he himself did not follow it very long.

3. The Miracle of "Esther Waters."

Three years after George Gissing published *Workers in the
Dawn,* a young Irishman brought out his first novel. It was
not, however, his first book, for he had already written two
plays and a collection of poems. The latter was reviewed in
the *World* by Edmund Yates, who said that the book ought

to be burned and the author whipped. The review was entitled "A Bestial Bard."

George Moore's early life had nothing at all in common
with George Gissing's. He was born in Moore Hall, County
Mayo, Ireland, the son of a man who owned racing stables
and subsequently went to Parliament. After a fitful and not
very efficacious schooling, Moore went to Paris at the age of
twenty-one. With the snobbishness that he never overcame,
he wrote his mother, "I go into the frenchest of french society
now, houses where an Englishman never is heard of. I dine
twice a week generally at the Princess de la Tremoille and at
her most select dinners. . . . I was very pleased for a lady told
me that the princess said my manners were absolutely perfect." He studied painting and wrote the plays and poems that
preceded his first novel. At first opposed to both impressionism and naturalism, he was won over to the former by Manet
and to the latter by Zola. In 1881, after eight years in Paris,
he went to London, where he set himself up as one of Zola's
disciples.

Unlike Gissing, then, Moore opened his career as a novelist
with certain fixed convictions. The influence of Zola on *A
Modern Lover* is not easy to recognize, but, if one looks closely
and thinks of the state of the British novel in the eighties, the
source of Moore's inspiration is clear. His own impulse was
apparently to treat Lewis Seymour, whose three love affairs
are the theme of the book, as a kind of Don Juan, a romantic
figure, but this would never do in an avowed naturalist. His
romantic preferences are, therefore, kept in check, rather imperfectly, by a determination to exhibit Seymour as he thought
Zola would have done—that is, as the product of his environment. One of the sympathetic characters in the book says,
"The novel, if it be anything, is contemporary history, an exact
and complete reproduction of social surroundings: the novel
is, in a word, environment." To Zola himself Moore wrote,

"The fact that my novel has been successful may interest you; for, as I have already told you, I owe you everything."

Certainly *A Modern Lover* owes more to the French novelist than its emphasis on environment. Moore from the first liked to shock the public, but it was Zola who made him see that this might be a worthy as well as a pleasant occupation. "I invented adultery," he wrote many, many years later, "which didn't exist in the English novel till I began writing." He was not, of course, far wrong. Gissing's women, we have already observed, are incapable of passion. Moore, whether or not he had the profound insight into feminine psychology of which he boasted, at least was courageous enough to record certain elementary observations. There is not only adultery in *A Modern Lover;* there is sufficient passion to make the adultery plausible.

Moore had written Zola in 1882, "If it were only the public, I could destroy the inflexible prejudices which have caused the fall of the novel in England, but it is the question of libraries." When Smith's, one of the two great circulating libraries, banned *A Modern Lover,* Moore refused to be intimidated, and, careless of a reputation for immorality, protested the edict. In the same way he initiated the campaign against the three-decker that Gissing had desired. The publication of novels in three volumes not only led to a good deal of padding; it made books so expensive that they were far more commonly rented than bought. Seeing the advantage that this gave the circulating libraries, Moore persuaded Vizetelly, subsequently the translator and publisher of Zola, to issue novels in one volume.

The first one-volume novel that Vizetelly published was *A Mummer's Wife.* Here Moore dealt again with adultery but on a less literary level. Kate Ede, married to an asthmatic shopkeeper with a fanatically puritanical mother, runs away with an impecunious but romantic actor-manager. In a strange environment, and under the influence of poverty, she becomes a drunkard and eventually dies in alcoholic squalor. Moore states his theme frankly enough: "Kate Ede was the result of centuries of inherited customs and forms of thought, and when to this be added a touch of lightheadedness, so ordinary in character that, in the shop in Hanley, it had passed unperceived, it will be understood how little fitted she was to effect the psychological and even physical changes that her new life demanded. She was the woman that nature turns out of her workshop by the million, all of whom are capable of fulfilling the duties of life, provided the conditions in which they are placed, that have produced them, remain unaltered. . . . Not a whit worse was she than others of her kind, but one of those million chances of which our lives are made had drifted Mr. Lennox across her life." In other words, Bohemianism had destroyed the middle-class standards by which she had always lived, and since nothing took their place, she degenerated. Moore neither condemns nor justifies Bohemianism, and of middle-class standards he seems only to say, with a certain snobbishness, that they are all right for the middle class. He does his best, in short, to adhere to his theory and avoid the passing of judgment.

A Mummer's Wife not only comes closer to Zola's methods than *A Modern Lover;* it is in every way a better book. Moore, with his plan of "digging a dagger into the heart of the sentimental school" and "being in fact Zola's offshoot in England," set out, as Zola would have done, to gather material by making a study of the provincial theater. His observations were close and his reporting courageous. Moreover, he knew how to build on what he saw, using details to create an acceptable picture. Bad as the writing often is, it has substance and sincerity. And, though the book was condemned as disgusting by most critics except Frank Harris and William Archer, it went to three editions.

Moore's first two novels had a success that was denied the two that Gissing published in the same years. Gissing was awkwardly feeling his own way, whereas Moore had boldly chosen his master and learned from him. Gissing was struggling against poverty and could not afford to ignore Mudie's standards; Moore, though not rich, had some income. Gissing had been brought up in the lower middle class and clung in spite of himself to its standards, lest he succumb to what he regarded as the bestiality of the poor. Moore, born in a somewhat unconventional Irish family, had gone to Paris as a young man and known not only the books of the new school but its masters as well.

Yet Gissing had one advantage over Moore. Both of them wanted to write frankly and fully about kinds of life their predecessors had neglected. To do this knowledge of the world was as necessary as freedom from tabus. This Gissing had. Moore, when he wrote out of personal experience, had to deal, as he did in *A Modern Lover,* with artists and writers. When, as in *A Mummer's Wife,* he wanted to describe a tragedy of the lower middle class, he had to go out and get his material. Gissing had lived among the poor throughout his early manhood, and his familiarity with their lives was almost tragically complete.

And perhaps there was another advantage. Gissing was struggling against great handicaps to become a writer, and he wrote as he did because of strong beliefs. Even when his radicalism waned, there were emotional overtones that it took a decade to dispel. Such depth of purpose Moore lacked. He was open to all influences when he went to Paris, and Zola's happened to be the strongest, perhaps because Moore did not dislike the notoriety that was certain to accrue to any British disciple of a writer whose work was believed by the British public to be the baldest pornography.

If naturalism was merely a fad with Moore, one would

expect it to yield in time to some other fad, and in fact it did. In 1885 Moore read *Marius the Epicurean* and began to extol Pater, though at the same time, in a preface to *Piping-hot,* he referred to Zola as "one of the mighty monumental intelligences of all time" and the "Homer of modern life." By 1888, when he wrote *Confessions of a Young Man,* he was ready to repudiate Zola, and when, in 1893, Zola visited London and was received with praise, Moore made fun of him.

Yet Moore had not forgotten the lessons he learned from the master. Between 1888 and 1894 he wrote three novels, two books of essays, and a play, and he not only put himself on record as opposing Zola's theories but experimented with other literary methods. During all these years, however, he was thinking about and, with interruptions, working on a novel that was to prove his indebtedness to Zola. Moore, no doubt with a certain self-consciousness, called *Esther Waters* "as characteristically English as *Don Quixote* is Spanish," and he had reason to do so. But if it is in the tradition of Fielding, Smollett, and Dickens, it is also in the tradition of Balzac and Zola.

Esther Waters strikes the reader as a "modern" novel, as nothing of Gissing's does. The plot is simple and unforced, and there are no Victorian sermons or conversations with the reader. The method is rigorously objective, and yet there is neither real nor pretended indifference to the fate of the characters. It is unfair, perhaps, to compare it with *Tess of the D'Urbervilles,* for Hardy was writing high tragedy, but, if the comparison is made, *Esther Waters* seems the more nearly perfect achievement. If it never moves the reader as *Tess* does, it never irritates with incredibilities or irrelevances. It is realism in the best British tradition, but it is realism purged —thanks to Moore's discipline in the French school—of faults that had beset that tradition for a hundred years.

To one who has read Moore's books, both before and especially after *Esther Waters,* the novel seems miraculous. If, comparing it with other novels of the nineties, one is impressed by the absence of both squeamishness and moralizing, one is amazed, comparing it with Moore's other books, by the freedom from snobbishness and pose. Hardy would have felt called upon to defend Esther. Gissing would have attacked her and her William as vulgar, and would have denounced Barfield's wastrel habits. Moore accepts them all. And yet, for all its beautiful lucidity, the book is never cold. Moore, in defiance of all his theories, boasted that the novel, by its depiction of the evils of baby-farming, "had actually alleviated more material suffering than any novel of its generation." True or not, the boast suggests that more feeling for humanity went into *Esther Waters* than found its way into anything Moore wrote thereafter.

Moore had proven that the public would accept a truthful book about the lower classes. And he came very close to writing from within, rather than from without, those classes. Like any person in his situation, he knew something about servants, and the idea for the novel came from a magazine article on the difficulties of domestics that touched his imagination. More important, by making the racing world the background of Esther's story, he was able to draw on personal knowledge, and many of the characters are modeled on employees of his father's stables. Thus the natural sympathies of boyhood were permitted to illuminate his art, tempering his theories and giving life to the data of Zolaesque research.

Having domesticated naturalism by adopting from the French school those elements that could be profitably assimilated by the British tradition, Moore was immediately concerned with a different kind of achievement. *Esther Waters* was in his system and had to be written, but, even before it was finished, he was impatiently planning a new course. Insofar as it is a psychological study, *Esther Waters* had pointed the way, but *Evelyn Innes* is, to a strange extent, psychology for its own sake. Moore chose deliberately, out of his passion for the tour de force, to deal with a subject of which he knew nothing—music. To make his task even more difficult, he attempted, at a time when he was publicly avowing his Protestantism, to portray sympathetically the appeal of the Catholic Church. His success in concealing both his ignorance and his conviction is impressive, but less impressive than the dulness of the book.

The remainder of Moore's story does not belong in a study of the progress of realism in the British novel. One wonders, indeed, how much attention any literary history should pay to his later work. Certainly the unamiable poseur who reveals himself in *Memories of My Dead Life, Hail and Farewell,* and *Conversations in Ebury Street* does not seem to have much to say to any of us. It is a long way from *Esther Waters* to *The Lake, The Brook Kerith, A Story-Teller's Story, Héloïse and Abélard,* and *Aphrodite in Aulis,* and it is a way that only a few disciples, such as Charles Morgan, have cared to take.

If we did follow Moore through his Irish adventures, his disillusionment with Ireland, and his long years on Ebury Street, our principal concern would be with his style. Oscar Wilde once said that it took Moore seven years to discover grammar, that he then discovered the paragraph, and that he continued in this way, each time shouting his new discovery from the housetops. It is true that his earlier work showed an indifference to style, in his own later use of the term, that can only be paralleled in the writings of Theodore Dreiser. Then, in the early nineteen-hundreds, he began writing what Desmond Shawe-Taylor calls "fully conscious works of art," and he conceived what he himself described as "the only two prose epics in the English language." Yeats used to tell him, "Moore, if you ever get a style, it will ruin you. It is colored glass and you need a plate-glass window." Moore preferred the colored glass, and so have a few admirers, but most people regret the sentences like "ribbons of tooth-paste squeezed out of a tube."

One wonders if Gissing, who was actually five years younger than Moore and might have lived as long, would have followed a similar path. Would *The Private Papers of Henry Ryecroft* and *Veranilda* have pointed the way to other autobiographies that were more and more idealized and to historical romances that became exercises in style? Would his conservatism have become smugness and his independence of spirit the pose of eccentricity? It is possible, and even if his development had been different from Moore's, one doubts if it would have been more profitable. There is no reason to believe that he would have surpassed *The New Grub Street,* any more than Moore surpassed *Esther Waters.*

And Moore could not have bettered that novel or even have written other novels as good. So far as knowledge was concerned, he had already exhausted himself, and his tastes were not such as to make it easy for him to gather more.[1] Furthermore, he had not the slightest desire to continue in that vein. On the contrary, as we have seen, *Esther Waters* was itself the aftermath of a youthful enthusiasm, and for some years he had been eager to follow new gods. It was only a question of what course he would take, and when he discovered the existence of style, his fate was settled. *Esther Waters* remained admirable and unique.

4. *The Progress of Realism.*

The novel in 1880 was very much what it had been for the preceding fifty years. In view of the achievements of Victorian

---

[1] "He used to say that *Esther Waters* had done him evil by withdrawing him from poverty and from contact with the poor, yet he had a great love for his chairs, his Aubusson carpet, his pictures and his china." Joseph Hone, *The Life of George Moore,* 212.

novelists, it would be ridiculous to say that great literature could not be created within the limits established by Mudie's Library, but even the most Victorian writers lamented the restrictions imposed upon them. The later Victorians not only found the restrictions intolerable; they were in any case unwilling to follow in the familiar paths. Gissing's Waymark spoke for his creator and for many of his creator's contemporaries when he called the Victorian novel worn-out and announced his intention of digging deeper. The new generation felt, as new generations always do, that it should have and in fact did have something new to say, and it was not willing to sacrifice its freedom for the sake of protecting the alleged innocence of adolescence.

Across the channel, where, naturally, the history of literature had followed a somewhat different course, writers were already dealing with some of the problems that were just beginning to define themselves in England. In the late sixties Émile Zola, planning his Rougon-Macquart series, had begun to formulate a new literary method. In literature, he made clear, he owed most to Balzac and Stendhal, but he held that his greatest debt was to science. The novelist, he preached, must become a scientist, must be an experimenter, modeling himself after the man in the laboratory. He presents a milieu, created in accordance with observed facts. Into this milieu he introduces characters, whose actions he describes in the light of his knowledge of the laws of human conduct. He cannot attain perfect precision, but that must be his goal. His virtue is not the "imagination" on which the romanticists prided themselves but "the sense of the real." With moral standards he has nothing to do, and he is concerned neither to protect nor to shock the sensibilities of his readers. Reformers may use his discoveries, but he is not responsible for nor even interested in their application. Naturalism in literature is merely the extension of the scientific spirit.

So far as England was concerned, Zola's theories were less important than his practice, for of course there was a discrepancy between the two. He could pretend to be writing about "the human machine submitted to certain influences," but actually he knew that science had not defined the laws of human conduct. Naturalism in practice meant the avoidance of the arbitrary and the fanciful. It meant that description, instead of being used as ornamentation, should contribute to the understanding of the characters by showing their environment. It meant that elaborate plots should be avoided and that the novel should tend towards "simple studies, without sudden catastrophes and without climaxes, the analysis of a year of existence, the history of a passion, the biography of a person, notes taken on life and systematically classified." It meant that the novelist must be free to depict any kind of phenomenon, regardless of his readers' prejudices, so long as he told the truth.

If, as Zola so constantly lamented, French readers misunderstood naturalism, and insisted on regarding it as a matter of gross subjects and crude words, it cannot be surprising that in England the name of Zola symbolized nothing but obscenity. In 1884 Henry Vizetelly published a translation of *L'Assommoir,* and in the next three years issued a number of other translations. The novels appear to have sold well—probably, it must be admitted, for the wrong reasons. Then in 1887 W. T. Stead, fresh from his exposure of London vice, opened a campaign against what he called obscene literature, and was joined by the National Vigilance Association. Twice Vizetelly was put on trial, and the second time he was sent to prison for three months.

Nothing, of course, could have been better calculated to make the English aware of Zola and his work. The newspapers and periodicals began to discuss naturalism, and Tennyson denounced "Zolaism" in *Locksley Hall, Sixty Years After.*

Denunciation, as one would expect, was the rule, and ignorant denunciation at that. But the attack on what was thought to be naturalism served a useful purpose, for anything less dreadful than this obscene product of the degenerate French mind was increasingly likely to be regarded as harmless. Moreover, the excitement wore itself out, and Zola was well received when, in 1893, during the Dreyfus case, he took refuge in London.

Despite the widespread discussion of naturalism, Zola seems to have had little direct influence on English literature. Moore was, indeed, the only avowed disciple. Gissing refers to Zola in *The New Grub Street,* and it is almost certain that by 1890 he knew some of Zola's work, but there is no reason to believe that he had heard of naturalism when he wrote *Workers in the Dawn,* and if there is any influence on his later work, it is too slight to be recognized. Hardy, in an essay published in 1891, criticized Zola's theory of the scientific novel, and when *Jude* was called naturalistic said that the book seemed to him closer to Fielding than to Zola. Researchers have been able to find a few minor writers who considered themselves naturalists, but none of importance except Moore.

There were influences from across the channel at this time, but they seldom made themselves felt except in subtle ways. Through most of the nineteenth century, perhaps as a result of the Napoleonic wars, British intellectual life was peculiarly insular, and whatever was borrowed from Europe came from Germany. In the seventies and eighties, however, British authors began to be conscious of the traditions of French literature. They saw that, though their French colleagues were also attacked when they sinned against the code of the bourgeoisie, the attacks did not deter them, for they replied that they were concerned with revealing the truth, not with teaching morals. English novelists found that not merely Zola but Balzac, Stendhal, Flaubert, Daudet, and the Goncourts had done what they wanted to do. Short story writers followed the example of De Maupassant, and flourished as they had never done before. Poets were turning to Baudelaire and Mallarmé, and talking of symbolism. But there were few disciples; English writers for the most part took only what they needed to carry out their own purposes.

Not only the French but Ibsen and the Russians as well served to re-assure British authors. The grossness of the attack on Vizetelly in 1887 and the fury directed against Hardy in 1894, to say nothing of the passions roused by the Wilde trial in 1895, proved that the middle class was still strong, but its prestige had been irreparably damaged. By 1900 Maugham, Bennett, Galsworthy, Wells, and Conrad were beginning to build on the victories Hardy, Gissing, and Moore had won. Shaw had popularized Ibsen and written *Widowers' Houses* and *Mrs. Warren's Profession*. The poets, one after another, had declared their independence of the moralists. It still took courage for an author to defy the mores of the middle class, but he knew that he could count on support.

Much had been accomplished in twenty years, but less than many observers believed. Within considerably wider limits than before, novelists could show forth life as they saw it, but that did not guarantee that they would see it truly. Although the power of sexual passion could now be acknowledged, the nature of that passion was not necessarily any better understood than it had been in 1880 or, for that matter, 1800. The working class and the lower middle class were at last acknowledged to be fitting themes, but the forces that moved them were difficult to grasp. The novelist, except for some minor skirmishes that remained to be fought, had his freedom; the question was what he would do with it.

If the careers of Hardy, Gissing, and Moore taught anything, it was that the barest beginning had been made. All three of them, in the course of the nineties, forsook the realistic novel. Each had his own reasons, but back of all the reasons lay a sense of the difficulty of coming to terms with contemporary society. The very forces that had emancipated them from the restrictions of the Victorian era were by no means easy to reckon with, and the changes of which they and their works were part were mysterious and disturbing. It was no wonder that the three novelists turned to poetry and romance. Their abdication dramatized problems their successors would have to meet.

Chapter VI

OSCAR WILDE AND THE CULT OF ART

In spite of their various kinds of non-conformity, the great Victorians were accepted by the middle-class reading public as spokesmen rather than enemies, and some of them, notably Tennyson and Dickens, were not merely accepted but idolized. With the sixties and seventies, however, with Ruskin's attack on laissez-faire economics and with Swinburne's flouting of evangelical morality, writers and readers found themselves in opposing trenches. The warfare continued in the eighties, with Morris, Hardy, Gissing, Moore, and Butler rushing to the attack, each with his own particular weapons and his own particular battle-cry. And each was met with vituperation.

No one, however, was denounced so promptly and hysterically as Oscar Wilde. As soon as his first collection of verse appeared, the late Victorian reading public identified him as an intolerable threat to the home, the church, and the state. The scandal that Wilde's *Poems* created in 1881 was perhaps no greater than that which Swinburne's *Poems and Ballads* had aroused in 1867, but, thanks to Wilde's gifts for self-advertising, more persons were aware of the affront he had offered them. And the indignation was given no chance to die down, but steadily accumulated force from 1881 to 1895. At first the defenders of Victorianism satirized Wilde, masking their fury with an affectation of playfulness, but soon their viciousness was undisguised, and in the end they had a cruel revenge.

The kind of panic Wilde's work inspired was intensified by the appearance of a group of writers and artists who appeared to be his disciples. There was more and more talk in the eighties about estheticism, and in the nineties a disturbing word became current—decadence. The *Yellow Book* in 1894 and the *Savoy* in 1896 gave the word a certain content. Arthur Symons, Ernest Dowson, Max Beerbohm, and especially Aubrey Beardsley were held to be exponents of decay, with such writers as Lionel Johnson, John Davidson, Henry Harland, Richard Le Gallienne, and W. B. Yeats under suspicion. A certain number of self-constituted guardians of the British Empire and all its institutions found it easy to convince sections of the reading public that England's greatness was seriously threatened, and Victorianism fought back.

Though Wilde was not in fact the leader of the decadent cult, the public thought he was, and resentment concentrated on him, so that work for which he had no responsibility contributed to his downfall, which in turn affected writers who were in no sense his associates. The ostentatious worship of beauty in the eighties and nineties brought into action all the intolerance and meanness of the middle-class mind, and Wilde had the undeserved honor and pain of bearing the full brunt of this attack.

1. The Self-Made Symbol.

"I was a man," Wilde wrote in *De Profundis,* "who stood in symbolic relations to the art and culture of my age. I had realized this for myself at the very dawn of my manhood, and had forced my age to realize it afterwards. Few men hold such a position in their own lifetime, and have it so acknowledged. It is usually discerned, if discerned at all, by the historian, or the critic, long after both the man and his age have passed away. With me it was different. I felt it myself and made others feel it." What is most extraordinary about this statement is that, by and large, it is true. Wilde did, quite consciously, make himself a symbol, a symbol of the artistic mind in a Philistine civilization. That he was an adequate symbol may be doubted; that he compelled the acceptance of his symbolic quality is undeniable.

When he tells us that he realized his position at the dawn of manhood, we may understand him to refer to his years at Oxford, for there was little enough in his twenty years in Ireland to encourage that kind of self-confidence. Later he maintained that he had been famed as a conversationalist at Trinity College in Dublin, but his associates reported no such reputation to inquiring biographers. He did win some academic distinctions, and he did enjoy the friendship of the Rev. John Pentland Mahaffy, who acknowledged his pupil's assistance when he published his *Social Life in Greece from Homer to Menander*. He developed as any bright boy might, achieving some honor and acquiring a certain feeling for both Greek and English literature, and that is all that can be said.

Nor does it seem that his blossoming at Oxford was as sudden and as impressive as he liked to believe. The publication of poems in the *Dublin University Magazine,* the *Irish Monthly,* and *Kottabos* gave him some prestige, and the trip to Greece with Mahaffy fed his mind as Mahaffy's admiration fed his hopes. His first success at Oxford, the winning of the Newdigate prize, proved that his light need not be hid under a bushel. But most important of all was the discovery that, when he talked, people would listen. According to Frank Harris, Wilde said that on one occasion Walter Pater kissed his hand when he finished speaking. Almost certainly either Harris or Wilde lied, and it does not matter which. What does matter is that the many legends, of which this is merely the most highly colored, had a basis in truth.

England is always a challenge to an Irishman, and Wilde was not the first bright young man from Dublin to determine that he would force the British to look up to him. There was more than a little in his background to make him feel the full weight of the challenge. His father was a physician, highly regarded for his medical skill but held, not without evidence, some of it in court records, to be eccentric and immoral. His mother had won the love of Irish patriots by a dramatic gesture, but even her admirers knew that she was affected and unstable. It was a family that might well have produced a genius, but it was not one to impress the young men of Magdalen College, for it did not have even wealth to recommend it. When, in spite of these handicaps, Wilde did achieve recognition of a sort, his high opinion of his qualities was not unnaturally confirmed.

Certainly few young men can ever have left Oxford with more audacious plans. When he went to London in 1878, he described himself as "a Professor of Aesthetics and a Critic of Art," and what he proposed to do was simply to make himself felt as a personality. Though he was poor and had to make a doubtful living in journalism—a profession in which his brother Willie, more recently arrived from Ireland, surpassed him—he was undiscouraged. He aimed from the first at social success, and, if he failed to penetrate as far into the upper reaches of the nobility as his snobbishness desired, he found plenty of drawing-rooms in which to deliver his carefully rehearsed epigrams. His brother, on the *World,* contributed to his growing reputation, and Wilde was not slow to learn the advantages of publicity. Indeed, if Harris is to be believed, he frankly announced his intention of seizing every opportunity of advertising himself. Thus he adopted his "esthetic costume," appearing in knee breeches and silk stockings, with his hair long and with a cornflower or a lily in his buttonhole. If he had to be a buffoon to attract attention, he was prepared to make clownishness an art.

It is dangerous to speak of "the esthetic movement" without quotation marks, for it seems largely a creation of Wilde's ambition, but, in a vague sense, it did exist, and even had an historian. Walter Hamilton, who wrote about it as early as 1882, traced it to the Pre-Raphaelite Brotherhood. It had become talked about through various notorious quarrels, beginning with Whistler's suit against Ruskin. Ruskin, because of his championing of the Pre-Raphaelites and his insistence on the necessity of beauty, was one of the godfathers of the movement, but Whistler, who repudiated Ruskin's ethical preoccupations, was closer to the younger men. So far as the public was concerned, two brands of estheticism were at war, and the public learned that there were issues even if it did not try to understand them.

Robert Buchanan's attack on Rossetti in "The Fleshly School of Poetry," with the long controversy that followed, also helped to give estheticism notoriety. But chiefly it was *Punch* that, with Wilde's collaboration, created the esthetic movement out of flimsy materials. For nearly a generation sound men—readers of *Punch*—had been dismayed by all the talk about beauty. It was effeminate, absurd, and un-British. Everybody knew that Ruskin and Morris were crackpots, and Swinburne and Rossetti made no attempt to conceal their depravity. And yet there were Englishmen who took the esthetic movement seriously. People went to Grosvenor Gallery and pretended to be impressed by the Pre-Raphaelite paintings; women tried to look like Rossetti's tubercular models; homes were furnished in what was believed to be Morris' style; there was even a suburb for esthetes, the Bedford Park Estate, where esthetic wallpapers, tapestries, and painted tiles were as common as whatnots in the homes of *Punch's* readers.

Concerned to resist this subversive influence, *Punch* had been ridiculing the esthetes before Wilde left Oxford. Quite aware of the emotions that were troubling the editors of *Punch* and their right-minded fellow-citizens, Wilde made himself the symbol they were looking for. His costumes, his mannerisms, his flowers, his sayings, his ostentatious tributes to Lily Langtry, his sonnets to Ellen Terry, his rhapsodies on Sarah Bernhardt, all lent themselves, with a perfection that can only have been intentional, to the needs and the by no means subtle wit of the staff of *Punch*. *Punch* wanted a butt for its resentment, and Wilde wanted to be talked about. Both were satisfied.

What surprises one, looking at the cartoons and parodies that appeared, is the bitterness. There is, moreover, a kind of innuendo that would be inconceivable, given Great Britain's libel laws, in this day when knowledge of sexual abnormality is general. This was no mere foible that *Punch* was attacking, but a danger to the social system, and the dirtier the stick, the more effective the beating. Wilde might well have taken alarm if he had not been blindly self-confident and in his own way quite fearless.

For the moment the beneficent result of the onslaught was a sale for the *Poems,* which, privately published in June, 1881, was in its fifth edition within six months. Wilde, who did not have a low opinion of the merits of his poetry, knew well enough that it was the merits of his publicity that gave the volume its circulation. He also knew that the poems would add to the legend. The three longest and most pretentious, "The Garden of Eros," "The Burden of Itys," and "Charmides," were not quite what *Punch* called them, "Swinburne and water," but they had almost exactly the qualities that had shocked and titillated readers of *Poems and Ballads*. Almost any well-read person could see that the poems were imitative; the marks of Swinburne, Arnold, Tennyson, and, in at least one poem, Thomas Hood were unmistakable. More derivative even than most first volumes, *Poems* made it difficult to say where, in the mass of influences, the author was to be found. But the ideas were disturbing, even if they were somebody's else, and the rhetorical passages, Swinburnian though they were, satisfied a public that was looking for sensationalism.

The appearance of the volume naturally provoked *Punch* to new efforts, and the editor, F. C. Burnand, attempted to extend the scope of his ridicule by adapting a French farce, *Le Mari à la Campagne,* to his purposes. The resulting play, *The Colonel,* was vicious enough, but it was too clumsy to do Wilde much harm. *Patience,* which appeared in the same season, was a new victory in his campaign. Though Bunthorne's estheticism is interpreted, by Bunthorne himself in an aside, as an affectation, Gilbert was as good-natured as he was superficial, and the opera served chiefly to create curiosity about Wilde and his mission.

One immediate result was an invitation from Col. W. F. Morse, who was D'Oyly Carte's manager, to give a series of lectures in America. Since it is difficult to see how the already great success of *Patience* could have been enhanced by Wilde's presence, it is reasonable to suppose that Morse expected the play to make Wilde's appearances profitable. Wilde, for his part, needed money, and he saw new possibilities for the creation of fame. The decision was not without its heroic aspects, for he knew that he would be given a hearing because *Punch* and *Patience* had made his name ridiculous. He continued to play the clown on his arrival in America, but he delivered serious lectures to the best of his ability. With a kind of fortitude that scarcely fits the legend, he traveled across the continent and back, speaking day after day to audiences that were almost completely indifferent to what he had to say. His courage did not go unrewarded. The financial return was apparently not large, but he rose steadily in the esteem of the American people. At first the papers were even more violent, though less insinuating, than *Punch,* but Wilde could stand punishment, and appreciation of that virtue did much to lessen the objection to the man and his message.

But if from some points of view the American trip was a success, Wilde's campaign was not prospering as he had hoped. In Paris, whither he went soon after his return from the United States, he realized how distant he was from his goal. He had fame of a sort, but he began to realize the difficulty of transforming it into the kind of fame he wanted. In Paris he cut his hair and abandoned his breeches, but he adopted a new pose, appearing as a dandy of the days of Balzac. Paris was not impressed, for Parisian writers of an earlier generation had made such antics an old game. French society was indifferent to him, and authors he admired barely tolerated him. Meanwhile his two plays, *Vera* and *The Duchess of Padua,* had not found producers in England, and the former was a failure in New York.

Wilde had, then, little enough to show for himself when, on May 29, 1884, he married Constance Lloyd. He had lectured, with little success, in England and Scotland. He had had a failure in the theatre. He had come off second-best in an encounter of wits with Whistler. He had not impressed Paris. And he was still poor. The last problem was solved by his marriage. Some biographers have insisted that he was deeply in love with Miss Lloyd, others that the marriage served to mask his homosexual affairs, others that he was primarily interested in his wife's money. However that may be, the match did provide him with an income that he badly needed.

In the years immediately after the marriage Wilde settled down to work for the first time. He began doing book reviews more or less regularly for the *Pall Mall Gazette,* and now and then a story or essay appeared. Furthermore, in June, 1887, he surprised his friends by accepting the editorship of the *Woman's World*. As usual, public laughter did not deter him, and he did reasonably well a job that on every score he disliked. His literary comments were not what was expected of Oscar Wilde but what might be expected from the editor of the *Woman's World*. Wilde, who scorned banality, selected "Invictus" and "When I Was a King in Babylon" for praise when he reviewed a volume of Henley's poems. He wrote, "Mr. Bret Harte has never written anything finer than *Cressy*. It is one of his most brilliant and masterly productions." He found all sorts of books, forgotten these fifty years, subtle, poignant, powerful, clever, and charming. Of course his tongue was often in his cheek when he wrote for the *Woman's World,* but his reviews in the *Pall Mall Gazette,* though not so brashly undiscriminating, did not show a high level of critical insight.

At the same time, however, Wilde was doing work that could begin to justify his reputation. Seven years after *Poems* he published his second volume, *The Happy Prince,* and, though a collection of fairy stories was scarcely what had been anticipated, his admirers found in the tales proof that he was a master of prose. The following year, 1889, brought forth "The Decay of Lying," one of his more pretentious essays, and "The Portrait of Mr. W.H.," Shakespearean criticism in the form of fiction. 1890 was the year of *Dorian Gray,* which appeared in *Lippincott's Magazine,* and "The Critic as Artist." In 1891 came the publication in book form of *Dorian Gray, Lord Arthur Saville's Crime, Intentions,* and *A House of Pomegranates,* the magazine publication of *The Soul of Man Under Socialism,* and the sixth edition of *Poems.* The first performance of *Lady Windermere's Fan* was on February 20, 1892.

Here, then, were five fruitful years, culminating in the kind of success Wilde had longed for. After his youthful clowning he had remained unproductive just long enough to convince his enemies that he was wholly a fraud, and then had dazzled them with fairy tales, humorous short stories, critical essays, a novel, a sociological essay, and a play. Almost everything he wrote, moreover, was bizarre enough to add to his legend. What, for example, could the average Englishman make of "The Decay of Lying" and "Pen, Pencil and Poison" except to conclude that they were written in defense of crime? Why should an esthete write fairy tales if not to convey doctrines of a subtle immorality? Was not "The Portrait of Mr. W.H." an attack on the greatest of British authors, *The Soul of Man Under Socialism* an assault on the political and economic bases of national life, and *Dorian Gray* an affront to every decent Englishman?

Wilde believed in the policy of shocking people, and it had been so successful that he seldom considered the damage to himself. Yet certain passages in "The Portrait of Mr. W.H." and *Dorian Gray* indicated either ignorance on his part or a complete faith in the ignorance of his contemporaries. The age was ignorant; he was right about that. Though it has been said on good evidence that homosexuality was common, it was not understood. Mr. Justice Wills, for example, obviously believed that there were different levels of sensuality: a good man lived in matrimonial fidelity; a bad man had illicit relations with women; a worse man had illicit relations with men. In the course of human degradation, he apparently held, one form of sensuality led to another and lower form. This was the general belief, and consequently there was not only a good deal of injustice but also a curious kind of innocence. Much that would today seem evidence of homosexuality was then regarded as merely bizarre or effeminate.[1]

[1] See, for example, such a cartoon as "Maudle on the Choice of a Profession," in *Punch* for Feb. 12, 1881, which today would be regarded as a direct charge of homosexuality. Note also that, as late as 1925, when he wrote his *Autobiography,* Lord Alfred Douglas seemed to believe that he had cleared himself of the

If it had not been for this confusion, Wilde would not have been likely to write the passage in "The Portrait of Mr. W.H." in praise of the higher love between man and man, with its direct allusion to Plato's *Symposium,* nor would he have indicated quite so frankly the relationship between Dorian Gray and Basil Hallward and that between Gray and Lord Henry, who is so obviously Wilde himself. We cannot help assuming that Wilde did not want to flaunt his homosexuality as such, for he went to some pains to deny the charge even among friends. He had done much talking about secret and splendid sins, but it was not his intention to be too specific. The trouble was that it was easy to provide details from his own experience and to depend on the general ignorance. What he did not anticipate was that, though readers of *Dorian Gray* seldom knew exactly what was bothering them, they were troubled, and they did feel that Wilde had somehow betrayed himself. The critic in the *Saturday Review* failed, in the course of his long diatribe, to define his objections to the book, but the strength of his emotion was unmistakable and ominous. He seemed to feel, moreover, as did other critics, that Wilde was providing evidence that could eventually be used to destroy him.

In spite of the gathering opposition, Wilde was entering his period of triumph. It is worth noticing that three of his plays were problem-plays, and that in all three conventional morality is satisfied. *Lady Windermere's Fan* inquires whether, when lovely woman has stooped to folly, she should tell her daughter, and it reaches its climax in the redeeming self-sacrifice of the sinner. *An Ideal Husband* poses the problem of

charge of homosexuality when he said that he and Wilde did not commit sodomy, though he goes on to speak of "familiarities." Even Frank Harris, in chaps. xxii and xxiv of his *Oscar Wilde* (1930), puts forth a view of homosexuality that would be untenable today. For the general confusion on the subject of sexual abnormality, see one of Robert Ross's notes on Harris' book: "Your memory is at fault here. The charge against Horatio Lloyd was of a normal kind. It was for exposing himself to nursemaids in the gardens of the Temple." *Ibid.,* 461.

the early misdeeds of a successful man and the self-righteousness of his wife. *A Woman of No Importance* tells the old story of wronged innocence, and ends with the triumph of the victim over her betrayer. All three of them plead for tolerance for the sinner, but only within limits long established by literary convention.

What, it may be asked, was Oscar Wilde, the preacher of art for art's sake, doing with problem-plays? The best answer is probably that *A Doll's House* was produced in 1889 and *Ghosts* and *Hedda Gabler* in 1891. The British stage, after a drab century, was being brought to life by the problem-play, and, though it may be doubted whether Wilde was interested in the problems he dealt with, he was astute enough to know that the play-going public was. He did what he wanted to do in the conversations of Lord Goring, Lord Illingworth, and other persons of title, and gave the public its problems. The dialogue, needless to say, pleased audiences that had suffered from the stodgiest kind of dramatic writing, but it was not enough in itself to have given the plays their success.

His other two plays, usually listed by his admirers among his chief claims to greatness, were more purely characteristic. *Salome* owes much to Flaubert and Maeterlinck, but it has its original quality, a quality not calculated to reassure those who had been disturbed by *Dorian Gray. The Importance of Being Earnest* is not in that sense alarming, though, as Shaw has pointed out, it is hard and almost cruelly impersonal. What makes it uniquely Wilde's is that it is wholly composed of the brittle dialogue that figures in only a few scenes of the other plays, and that its artificiality, as more than one critic has pointed out, is perfectly sustained. Everyone talks like Oscar Wilde, including the governess and the clergyman, and, though there is sometimes a frantic grasping for witticisms, the talk is good. The once conventional comparison with Congreve has come in time to seem inept, and, perhaps because it has too frequently been performed by high school dramatic societies, the play is easy to dismiss as juvenile, but it is not impossible to understand why the nineties gaped.

An Ideal Husband was produced on January 2, 1895, and *The Importance of Being Earnest* on February 14. Four days later the Marquis of Queensberry, father of Lord Alfred Douglas, left for Wilde at the Albemarle Club a visiting card with an illiterate but libelous message. The resulting trial, which Wilde insisted on against the advice of most of his friends, was held in April, and Wilde's case collapsed in three days. Almost immediately he was arrested on charges of gross indecency. The first jury disagreed, but at a second trial he was found guilty, and on May 25 he was sentenced to two years' imprisonment at hard labor.

"The gods had given me almost everything," Wilde wrote in *De Profundis*. "I had genius, a distinguished name, high social position, brilliancy, intellectual daring; I made art a philosophy and philosophy an art; I altered the minds of men and the colors of things; there was nothing I said or did that did not make people wonder. I took the drama, the most objective form known to art, and made it as personal a mode of expression as the lyric or sonnet; at the same time I widened its range and enriched its characterization. Drama, novel, poem in prose, poem in rhyme, subtle or fantastic dialogue, whatever I touched, I made beautiful in a new mode of beauty: to truth itself I gave what is false no less than what is true as its rightful province, and showed that the false and the true are merely forms of intellectual existence. I treated art as the supreme reality and life as a mere mode of fiction. I awoke the imagination of my century so that it created myth and legend around me. I summed up all systems in a phrase and all existence in an epigram. . . ."

It does not matter how much of this is true. It is what Wilde, as he lay in Reading Gaol, wanted others to believe and must at moments have believed himself. It is easy to argue after the event that only catastrophe could have been a fitting climax for Wilde's life. Perhaps the argument is false, but how else could his life have ended? He had made himself, as he said, a symbol, and what he symbolized was hated by many men. That they would have their revenge no one but he could have doubted.

Quite possibly it was Wilde's habit of seizing every opportunity for publicity that prompted the fatal challenge to Queensberry. Having won the position he had planned for himself, he thought any kind of triumph easy, and a triumph over the Marquis of Queensberry would have been particularly dear. As it was, it was Queensberry who did the celebrating, after the stupid trial and the shocking sentence and the rejoicing in the streets. The forty gentlemen who honored the Marquis at dinner were sound citizens, who could understand a man's abusing his wife, as Queensberry was said to have done, and probably were tolerant of perversion in the sniggering way that men of the world often are. What they hated in Wilde was his insolent defiance of their whole carefully arranged scheme of life.

Wilde was a symbol, then, when he went to prison, and a symbol when he came out. He might have used his symbolic status to make a victory of his defeat, and "The Ballad of Reading Gaol" suggested that he was about to do this. He cast himself, as *De Profundis* [1] shows, in a new part. "Tired of being on the heights," he wrote, "I deliberately went to the depths in the search for new sensation. What the paradox was to me in the sphere of thought, perversity became to me in the sphere of passion. . . . I allowed pleasure to dominate

---

[1] *De Profundis* was published by Robert Ross in 1905. By eliminating from the letter the bitter and at moments hysterical attacks upon Alfred Douglas, Ross gave the impression of devout repentance. It was not until 1912, when Douglas sued Arthur Ransome for libel, that the less savory portions became known.

me. I ended in horrible disgrace. There is only one thing for me now, absolute humility."

In prison Wilde had seen for the first time something of the world that lay outside the narrow circle of London society and its hangers-on, and he had reached in "The Ballad of Reading Gaol" for a subject and a form that had wide appeal. Perhaps his humility would have been only one more pose, but it could have been a pose that would have rescued his reputation. What one realizes now, however, reading the suppressed passages of *De Profundis,* is that Wilde was no longer capable even of posing. The gross years of prosperity, the trial, and the prison term had broken the ambition that had pushed him so steadily onward. He made an effort immediately after his release, but he lapsed into self-indulgence and the miserable meannesses of his last years. The promise, such as it was, of "The Ballad of Reading Gaol" was illusory. Wilde's literary life had ended with the trial, and the only question was how long it would take for him to find his way to the grave.

2. *The Doctrine of Estheticism.*

Was Wilde an ambitious young man who adopted estheticism because it served his purposes, or was he, among other things, a sincere devotee of the cult of beauty? The question cannot be answered simply, and perhaps the answer does not matter, since his performances as a literary rebel are on record. His doctrine concerns us more than his motives for advocating it.

Wilde, it must be remembered, had no deep roots, for, as we have seen, the unusual character of his home helped to re-enforce the influence of his Irish birth. Moreover, possibly because of his homosexuality, he did not readily acquire loyalties to individuals or to groups. Hardy was rooted in Dorset.

Morris had family and business ties even before he was part of the Socialist movement. Wilde, like Samuel Butler and George Moore, went through life without patriotism, without political commitments, without binding personal obligations. He professed his devotion to the cause of art, and it is at least true that the cause had no important rivals.

Most of his contemporaries had their careers defined for them when they left Oxford; Wilde knew only that he must make his own position. Everything pointed to literature—his own tastes, the publication of his poems, his prizes. Moreover, talents could make a career in literature as almost nowhere else. Yeats said that Wilde ought to have been a man of action, and, so far as his character was concerned, the suggestion was not fantastic; but what kind of political life would have been open to him? In his later years he expressed his indignation at the easy successes of Lord Curzon, whom he called "a perfect example of plodding mediocrity." Wilde, to be sure, was never one to plod, but he had known that even a combination of brilliance and hard work would not do much for him in politics.

The kind of literature that would interest him was not the kind that would please the age, but that was no obstacle to Wilde, who had been nurtured in unconventionality and had learned at Oxford to scorn the opinions of the middle class. He was quite ready to attack the age, and not without sincerity. One doubts that he was ever deeply pained, as Ruskin and Morris often were, by the ugliness of the Victorian environment, but he was not to be described as insensitive. When he heard Ruskin lecture at Oxford, the words did not strike him, as they had struck Morris, with the force of divine revelation, but he saw in them important truth. Ruskin said that life was empty without beauty, and Wilde knew he was right. Although he subsequently told American audiences that he had worked for a time, with other Oxford students, in build-

ing a road under Ruskin's supervision, the social teachings of
the master did not impress him. Ruskin was for him simply
the apostle of beauty in literature and in life.

Wilde's rejection of Ruskin's social and ethical doctrines
was immediate and needed no conscious justification, but
it was strengthened by what he learned from another Oxford
lecturer, Walter Pater. Pater subsequently withdrew his preface to *The Renaissance,* with its famous words on success in
life, precisely because it had been applied by such men as
Wilde in ways that the timid don could not approve, but it
had already served its purpose. It justified Wilde's own
hedonism and made a perfect foundation for the body of
doctrine he was building up. Here was a gospel that he could
practice with pleasure and preach with the certainty of harass-
ing the middle class.

Wilde had borrowed what he wanted from both Ruskin
and Pater before he left Oxford, but his first essay, written for
the Chancellor's English Essay Prize at the University, shows
little evidence of the influence of either, probably because
Wilde did not care to endanger his chances for a prize that
he thought worth competing for. "The Rise of Historical
Criticism" is for the most part a parade of the kind of erudi-
tion he thought would impress the judges. Though it praises
the Greek historians who ruled out the supernatural in their
interpretations of history, it ends by commending Plutarch
for recognizing the divine behind the natural. Its tone is conservative, and there is a passage in which, speaking of France,
Wilde refers to "those divisions of caste and prejudice, of
landed aristocracy and moneyed interest, institutions in which
the vulgar see only barriers to Liberty," but which, in his
opinion, are "the only possible defenses" against tyranny. One
paragraph alone foreshadows the later Wilde: "History, no
doubt, has splendid lessons for our instruction, just as all good
art comes to us as the herald of the noblest truth. But to set

before either the painter or the historian, the inculcation of moral lessons as an aim to be consciously pursued, is to entirely miss the true motive and characteristic of art and history, which is in the one case the creation of beauty, in the other the discovery of the laws of the evolution of progress: 'Il ne faut demander de l'Art que l'Art, du passé que le passé.' " Shorn of its propitiatory qualifications, this was to become the heart of his doctrine.

It was ostensibly to call attention to the doctrine of beauty as its own justification that Wilde adopted the esthetic costume when he went to London. In his *Poems* he further elaborated the theme, especially in "The Garden of Eros," with its calendar of saints: Keats, Shelley, Byron, Swinburne, Morris, Rossetti. And what he had to tell America was that his beliefs were shared by the most important of the younger writers. For the content of his lectures he owed much to Ruskin and the Pre-Raphaelites, on whose work he drew when he wanted to illustrate what he meant by beauty. He was always careful, however, to explain how he differed from Ruskin, and in an introduction for Rennell Rodd's *Rose-leaf and Apple-leaf,* written at the time of his American expedition, he gave the clearest statement he had yet made of what he believed. "This increased sense of the absolutely satisfying value of beautiful workmanship," he wrote, "this recognition of the primary importance of the sensuous element in art, this love of art for art's sake, is the point in which we of the younger school have made a departure from the teaching of Mr. Ruskin—a departure definite and different and decisive. . . . The constancy of the artist cannot be to any definite rule or system of living, but to that principle of beauty only through which the inconstant shadows of his life are in their most fleeting moment arrested and made permanent."

This was, in one way or another, the theme of everything Wilde wrote, but he developed it most fully in the essays included in *Intentions.* "The only beautiful things, as somebody once said, are the things that do not concern us," he wrote in "The Decay of Lying." "As long as a thing is useful or necessary to us, or affects us in any way, either for pain or for pleasure, or appeals strongly to our sympathies, or is a vital part of the environment in which we live, it is outside the proper sphere of art. To art's subject-matter we should be more or less indifferent. We should at any rate, have no preferences, no prejudices, no particular feelings of any kind. . . . Art never expresses anything but itself. It has an independent life, just as Thought has, and develops purely on its own lines." As for criticism: "To the critic the work of art is simply a suggestion for a new work of his own, that need not necessarily bear any obvious resemblance to the thing it criticizes."

In "The Truth of Masks" Wilde wrote: "Not that I agree with everything that I have said in this essay. There is much with which I entirely disagree. The essay simply represents an artistic standpoint, and in esthetic criticism attitude is everything. For in art there is no such thing as a universal truth. A Truth in art is that whose contradictory is also true." After such a disclaimer, he is not to be reproached for inconsistency, and of course inconsistency is common. In "The Decay of Lying," for example, he attacks realism as such: "All bad art comes from returning to Life and Nature, and elevating them into ideals. . . . As a method, Realism is a complete failure, and the two things that every artist should avoid are modernity of form and modernity of subject-matter. To us, who live in the nineteenth century, any century is a suitable subject for art except our own." Yet in "The Critic as Artist" he argues merely that realism has become old-fashioned. Once it gave us "that *nouveau frisson* which it was its aim to produce," but in time it lost its ability to affect us, and its place was taken by impressionism. That too has been worn out. "Today the cry is for Romance, and already the leaves are tremulous in the valley and on the purple hill-tops walks Beauty with slim, gilded feet." The second indictment probably comes closer to Wilde's real views than the first, but in any case the important point is that he disliked realism and did not particularly care why.

A more significant inconsistency appears in his constant attempt to justify his theory by reference to principles that it denies. "All art is immoral," he says in "The Critic as Artist." "For emotion for the sake of emotion is the aim of art; and emotion for the sake of action is the aim of life, and of that practical organization of life that we call society." Yet he is not content to let the matter rest there, but goes on to argue that art can give us a higher morality, since it leads to the contemplative life, which "has for its aims not *doing* but *being,* and not *being* merely, but *becoming.*" He even suggests that art can save society: "We are trying at present to stave off the coming crisis, the coming revolution, as my friends the Fabianists call it, by means of doles and alms. Well, when the revolution or crisis arrives, we shall be powerless because we shall know nothing. . . . England will never be civilized until she has added Utopia to her dominions. There is more than one of her colonies that she might with advantage surrender for so fair a land. What we want are impractical people who see beyond the moment, and think beyond the day."

Wilde maintained that it did not matter what an author said so long as his manner of saying it was beautiful, and this dogma was his defense whenever the content of his work was criticized. Yet from the very first he was trying to say something. The poems have three themes. First, there is what may be called, conveniently if not accurately, paganism:

> Nay, let us walk from fire unto fire
> From passionate pain to deadlier delight,—
> I am too young to live without desire,
> Too young art thou to waste this summer night

Asking those idle questions which of old
Man sought of seer and oracle, and no reply was told.

Second, there is the humanitarianism of "To Milton," "Quantum Mutata," and "Sonnet to Liberty." [1] Finally, there is the Christian mysticism of "San Miniato," "Ave Maria Gratia Plena," and "Rome Unvisited." It is only fair to remember that these poems come from different years in the life of a very young poet. It must also be remembered that he did not prize sincerity highly and may have written the humanitarian poems in imitation of Swinburne and the religious poems as an appropriate exercise on a visit to Italy. But it will not do to dismiss these ideas as purely literary, for they recur, though less frequently than the paganism does, in his later work.

The search for new sensations was extolled in the essays, in passages in the plays, and in *Dorian Gray*. "The aim of life is self-development," Lord Henry Wotton tells Dorian. "To realize one's nature perfectly—that is what each of us is here for." "I believe," he continues, "that if one man were to live out his life fully and completely, were to give form to every feeling, expression to every thought, reality to every dream— I believe that the world would gain such a fresh impulse of joy that we would forget all the maladies of medievalism, and return to the Hellenic ideal—to something finer, richer, than the Hellenic ideal, it may be." "Ah! realize your youth while you have it," he urges. "Don't squander the gold of your days, listening to the tedious, trying to improve the hopeless failure, or giving away your life to the ignorant, the common, and the vulgar. These are the sickly aims, the false ideals, of our age. Live! Live the wonderful life that is in you! Let nothing be lost upon you. Be always searching for new

[1] The sonnet ends with these extraordinary lines:

These Christs that die upon the barricades,
God knows it I am with them, in some things.

sensations. Be afraid of nothing. A new Hedonism—that is what our century wants."

There is much more in the same vein, and it is all, of course, just what we associate with the name of Oscar Wilde. But we must set against this what he wrote in other moods. Though his first play, *Vera,* is ludicrous melodrama, he wrote it, he said, "to express within the limits of art that Titan cry of the people for liberty," and there is some suggestion of a similar aim in portions of *The Duchess of Padua.* It is in his fairy tales, however, that he clearly voices the humanitarian sympathies condemned by Lord Henry. "The Happy Prince," "The Selfish Giant," "The Young King," and "The Star-Child," all call attention to the sufferings of the poor. That the poor and those who take pity on them are divinely rewarded in these stories may be taken as a stroke of cynicism or, at best, as mere conformity with the tradition in which he was working, but the kind of warmth the tales have could not have been easily fabricated.

For all this, so adroit was Wilde in his poses, that we might continue to suspect his praise of generosity and humility and his satire of egotism and selfishness if we did not have *The Soul of Man Under Socialism.* It may be granted that there is little in the essay that Karl Marx would have recognized, and conceivably it was love of paradox that led Wilde to present his most eloquent plea for individualism in the guise of a Socialist tract. But he did have intelligence enough to see that capitalism made it impossible for the individual to realize himself, and his unexpected leap to Socialism, about which he had learned a little from Morris and Shaw,[1] was at least sig-

---

[1] In the letter to Frank Harris printed in his *Oscar Wilde,* Bernard Shaw tells the following story: "What first established a friendly feeling in me was, unexpectedly enough, the affair of the Chicago anarchists, whose Homer you constituted yourself by *The Bomb.* I tried to get some literary men in London, all heroic rebels and skeptics on paper, to sign a memorial asking for the reprieve of

nificant as criticism of contemporary society. In the actual establishment of Socialism or its practical problems of administration he had little interest, but he could go along with the Socialists in their attacks on capitalism, and he was willing to believe that they might have an effective substitute.

The essay proves that Wilde could not overlook the misery of the people of England so easily as he pretended to do. In spite of his professed hedonism, he tried to justify his selfishness and reconcile it with his sympathies by arguing that it is those persons who most fully develop their own capacities —he cites Darwin, Keats, Flaubert, and Renan—who do most to help the world. But the argument failed to satisfy him. He wanted, as so many others have wanted, to be allowed to do his own work without the consciousness of wide-spread misery, and he saw no reason why a system, which he chose to call Socialism, could not be devised to abolish misery and thus free him from irritating and illogical claims of conscience. "The only thing that one really knows about human nature," he writes in answer to the old argument, "is that it changes. . . . The systems that fail are those that rely on the permanency of human nature, and not on its growth and development."

Whatever his professions, Wilde sought for some sort of adjustment with society. Sometimes it seemed to him that Socialism, or what he thought to be Socialism, offered this adjustment by providing a program for a world in which he would be free because all men were free. At other times it was Christianity that attracted him. He was never, except when he was baptized into the Roman Catholic Church on his deathbed, a practicing Christian, but he was attracted to Catholicism at several periods in his life, and he had a per-

these unfortunate men. The only signature I got was Oscar's. It was a completely disinterested act on his part, and it secured my distinguished consideration for him for the rest of his life." P. 393.

sistent interest in the life and teachings of Jesus. In *The Soul of Man Under Socialism* he maintained that Jesus had shown the way to individualism through suffering and sorrow, but argued that the modern world, by abolishing poverty, could provide another path to the same goal. In *De Profundis,* on the other hand, he argues for Jesus' way. The avowal of agnosticism is candid, but Wilde nonetheless sets for himself the course of abnegation. "There was no pleasure I did not experience," he wrote. "I threw the pearl of my soul into a cup of wine. I went down the primrose path to the sound of flutes. I lived on honeycomb." But all the time he knew that there were other experiences in life, and he showed this in such works as "The Young King" and *The Soul of Man Under Socialism.* Then came his trial and his confinement in Reading Gaol: "I see a far more intimate and immediate connection between the true life of Christ and the true life of the artist." "Christ is the most supreme of individualists. Humility, like the artistic acceptance of all experiences, is merely a mode of manifestation." "His chief war was against the Philistines. That is the war every child of light has to wage." So Wilde went on, creating a Jesus to match his newfound ideals, Jesus the individualist, Jesus the romantic, Jesus the man who had suffered. "The Mystical in Art," he concluded, "the Mystical in Life, the Mystical in Nature—this is what I am looking for. It is absolutely necessary for me to find it somewhere."

He did not find it, nor did he long look for it. As other portions of the original letter to Douglas showed, Wilde was still the vindictive egotist, trying to thrust upon other shoulders the responsibility for his faults. The way of humility was much too hard for him, and, since it was the only way that was open, the only way, that is, that would provide a suitable role for him to assume, he soon lapsed into unproductiveness, and quickly found his way to death. Death completed his martyrdom and assured him of immortality, for he became an enduring symbol of the fate of the artist in a Philistine society. Scores of books have been written about him. Scores of his fellow-artists have paid tributes to his work, tributes really inspired, much of the time at least, by the fate of the man. "Most personalities have been obliged to be rebels," he wrote in *The Soul of Man Under Socialism*. "Half their strength has been wasted in friction." Wilde had been a rebel, and had been punished, men felt, for his boldness. In defending him they defended their own necessity for rebellion.

Art for art's sake! Nothing, actually, was farther from Wilde's mind. All his life he was preaching some sort of doctrine—his own version of paganism, or Socialism, or Christianity—and all his doctrines had at their core his dissatisfaction with the society of the eighties and nineties. That he never looked at the age closely enough to understand it, never discovered what was wrong with it or made more than sporadic gestures to offer a remedy, is obvious. His attacks were of the highly personal and melodramatic kind that one would expect. But he did have something that he wanted to say, and, in spite of all his pretenses, he said it. Unwilling to engage in lengthy debate with the Philistines, he sought to undercut their tedious arguments by his smashing announcement that everything they said was irrelevant. They could not apply their standards to him because he demanded judgment by his own standard, the standard of art. He did not, however, succeed in deceiving them, nor should we be deceived.

In saying that the artist must not choose as subject anything that is necessary or useful, or affects him deeply, or has immediate bearing on his life, Wilde was true to his professed beliefs, but he was disregarding the whole history of art, and he was limiting his own practice to an extent that, if he had been logical, would have proved intolerable. It is possible, under certain conditions and for certain special purposes, to look, not at what the writer is saying but at how the thing is said. Otherwise there could be no point in talking about artistic techniques. But, however important technical considerations may be, neither the author nor the reader is in practice indifferent to what is being expressed, and form and content are so closely linked that either can be understood only in its relation to the other. Wilde knew this as well as anyone. He represented a certain way of life, perhaps not admirable in itself but significant as criticism of the way of life then commonly followed. His attempt to conceal the fact only added to his symbolic quality.

3. *Writers of the Decadence.*

For the public Wilde symbolized a whole literary movement, but he was not in reality its leader. His disciples were men of rather slight talents: Lord Douglas, Robert Sherard, Robert Ross, and Reggie Turner. He knew, of course, all of his literary contemporaries, and was on friendly terms with many of them, but the more distinguished men were not in the circle closest to him, and several were a little scornful of both his personality and his work. They rallied, with some exceptions, to his defense when he was on trial, and they paid tribute to him after his death, but they never called him master.

The literary movement of the nineties, variously called esthetic and decadent and impressionistic, found its center in the *Yellow Book* and the *Savoy,* not in Oscar Wilde,[1] and, as Osbert Burdett has said, Aubrey Beardsley rather than Wilde was its representative figure. The *Yellow Book* grew out of the

---

[1] It is, however, obviously an accident that Wilde never contributed to either the *Yellow Book* or the *Savoy.* During the first year of the *Yellow Book's* existence he was busy with his plays, and then came the trial.

meeting of three men: Beardsley, Henry Harland, and John Lane. Lane, once a clerk in a railway office, became a bookseller and then a publisher, and by 1894, when the *Yellow Book* appeared, he had made the Bodley Head the publishing house of the young experimentalists. Harland, an American, had written a number of professedly realistic novels and tales about German Jews in New York City, and had then gone to Paris, where he had cultivated a new manner, first exhibited in *Mademoiselle Miss,* a collection of short stories published in 1893. Beardsley had turned to art after being employed in an insurance office, and his work for Lane had begun to establish his reputation as an illustrator.

In these three men were the forces that made the *Yellow Book* what it was. Lane was practical enough, in spite of his willingness to publish young poets. Harland was an increasingly popular practitioner of the romanticism that Wilde had hailed in "The Critic as Artist," and though one scarcely finds Beauty walking with slim, gilded feet in his tales, his preoccupation with style and his scorn for moral preaching made him acceptable to the other young men of his generation. Beardsley, however, was the only one of the trio to whom the label "decadent" could be applied with any meaning. It was the indefinable perversity of his drawings that impressed the purchasers of the *Yellow Book* and led them to see in the volume as a whole qualities that were not there.

For Beardsley did not set the tone of the quarterly. The leading contribution in the first number was Henry James's "The Death of the Lion," and James, who could be associated with the decadence only because the younger men united in admiring his craftsmanship, remained a frequent contributor. William Watson, Edmund Gosse, Arthur Waugh, and Richard Garnett gave respectability to the issue, and Leighton, Pennell, and Laurence Housman were among the illustrators. There was, it is true, a rather fleshly poem by Arthur Symons, and John Davidson, Max Beerbohm, and Hubert Crackanthorpe were included, but the advance-guard was in the minority.

As the *Yellow Book* had begun, so it continued, for Lane had achieved a formula that served his purpose. James continued to give distinction. Harland, Austin Dobson, Kenneth Grahame, Richard Le Gallienne, and various mediocrities provided charm and romance; Hubert Crackanthorpe, Ella D'Arcy, and others served up slices of life; Watson was often present for decorum's sake; Symons, Dowson, Lionel Johnson, Beerbohm, Davidson, Conder, and especially Beardsley furnished novelty and sometimes the sensationalism readers wanted. Four issues appeared edited according to this formula, and then, so the story goes, just at the time of the Wilde trial, Mrs. Humphry Ward persuaded William Watson to issue an ultimatum against Beardsley's drawings, and Lane capitulated. The *Yellow Book* continued for two years more, but it became less and less representative of anything except the taste for romantic fiction. Most issues opened with a story by Henry Harland and closed with one by Ella D'Arcy. Crackanthorpe and Miss D'Arcy and later Arnold Bennett were its realists, but Harland, Le Gallienne, Harold Frederic, Baron Corvo, and John Buchan brought down the scales on the romantic side. Many of the more distinguished authors and artists departed with Beardsley.

They were, most of them, contributing to the new magazine, the *Savoy*. After his break with Lane, Beardsley had found himself a new publisher in the somewhat disreputable figure of Leonard Smithers. Smithers launched the *Savoy* in January, 1896, with Arthur Symons as editor, and thus a new triumvirate was formed. The first issue of the *Savoy* was more impressive than the *Yellow Book* had ever been. Shaw, Beerbohm, Dowson, Yeats, and Havelock Ellis wrote for it, and C. H. Shannon, Charles Conder, and William Rothenstein

joined Beardsley as the magazine's artists. Beardsley contributed an amusing poem and the first installment of *Under
the Hill* as well as a dozen drawings. "We have no formulas,"
an editorial note ran, "and we desire no false unity of form
or matter. We have not invented a new point of view. We are
not Realists, or Romanticists, or Decadents. For us, all art is
good which is good art. . . . We could scarcely say more, and
we are content to think we can scarcely say less."

The second issue was as good and as successful as the first,
and with the third the *Savoy* became a monthly. This, as
Symons subsequently admitted, was a mistake. There were,
he pointed out, fewer persons than he had hoped who "really
cared for art, and really for art's sake," and he might have
added that there was not enough first-rate work to fill twelve
issues a year. Furthermore, a large bookseller, responding to
the general uneasiness, banned the magazine from his stores,
ostensibly because of a drawing by William Blake. The last
issue, published in December, 1896, was devoted entirely to
stories, poems, and essays by Symons and drawings by
Beardsley.

When the *Savoy* suspended publication, the movement it
had expressed was near its end. It was short-lived, but the remarkable thing is that, in a country in which writers have
been notably individualistic, there had been a movement. And
even more remarkable is the fact that the movement was made
up of men who wanted to raise individualism to a new pitch.
They had come together to defend their various individual-
isms against the assaults of an age of conformity. Most of
them either lived in London or frequently visited the city.
They went to music-halls and bars together, and the majority
belonged to the Rhymers' Club. Though they issued no mani-
festoes, they constituted a movement, and they had created
two magazines.

There is also a common pattern in their lives. Aubrey

Beardsley, even if he had not some claim to literary reputation because of his fragment of a rococo novel and his two poems, would have to be included in any discussion of the literary movement, since to most readers of the *Yellow Book* and the *Savoy* his drawings seemed to express what the movement was trying to say. Unwell from early childhood, he had begun to suffer from hemorrhages when he was seventeen. That was in 1889, when he was working in the insurance office. Encouraged by Burne-Jones and by Morris' disciple, Aymer Vallance, he studied art for a time in a night school, and then began his extraordinary career. As soon as John Lane had issued his edition of the *Morte d'Arthur,* he was offered many commissions. His style changed rapidly as he came under various influences, but, whatever models he chose, his work was always his. He was so persistently bawdy, in his drawings as in his speech, that Lane examined his work with a magnifying glass for hidden obscenities. But Beardsley did not have to be obscene in any ordinary sense to attract attention. His masculine women and feminine men, the expressions of malice or terror or secret knowledge that are on most of the faces he drew, the lines that are so pure in execution and so ambiguous in intent, these were sufficient to excite alarm as well as admiration.

He spared himself neither in his work nor in his diversions. He was often interrupted by hemorrhages, and in the last years he knew that the fatal attack might come at any time, but that did not lessen his exertions. In March, 1897, he became a Catholic, but, though his sincerity is not to be doubted, his work shows little change of attitude until his final, pitiful plea to Smithers to destroy his obscene drawings. The last year of his life was spent in France, where he died on March 16, 1898.

Ill health may have made him reckless, but his defiance went deeper than that. Whatever else his drawings contained, there was always contempt in them and disillusionment. He was seldom pornographic, except perhaps in privately published work, and if he was obscene, it was in ways not calculated to arouse desire. His respectable contemporaries pretended to be shocked, but actually they were bewildered and unnerved. He was even more hated than Wilde, who before his trial could be dismissed as a clown and afterwards as a pervert. Some passion of indignation burned within Beardsley, and there were many who feared the flames.

Ernest Dowson could never have upset the bourgeoisie as Beardsley did, for the bourgeoisie scarcely knew he existed. Unlike Beardsley, he was brought up in a family with literary interests, and he went to Oxford. Like Beardsley, he was ill from childhood, refused to consider his health, and died young. He was motivated by no intense hatred; his was a simpler relationship to a society he could not tolerate, a relationship based on shy indifference. In his life he sought the relief of drink and occasionally of drugs. In his poetry he celebrated the unhappy love affair in which, by some inner necessity, he was involved. When, Symons tells us, he had to leave the restaurant in which his inamorata worked, he would begin drinking and spend the night in some house of prostitution. Then, at a later stage there might be a sonnet or a villanelle—"for Adelaide."

Whatever it was that drove him to squalid excesses, it did not speak in his poetry. In that respect Dowson resembled another member of the Rhymers' Club, Lionel Johnson. Johnson did not indulge in sexual excesses—he was, according to Yeats, incapable of them—but he did drink heavily, and thus shortened his life. He, too, was an Oxford man, and had been under the influence of Pater and Symonds. Even earlier, while at Winchester, he had shown a serious interest in religion, and he had joined the Catholic Church in 1891. During the early nineties he wrote critical essays for London papers, erudite essays with an eighteenth century ponderousness. Excited by Yeats's Irish literary movement, he created an imaginary Irish ancestry for himself so that he might participate in it. He died in 1902.

There are, as Yeats points out, one or two poems in which Johnson symbolizes his inner struggle, but most of his poetry is that of a scholar and a Christian, just as Dowson's is that of a romanticist and a man of quiet melancholy. Dowson, with his echoes of Horace and the nice perfection of his lines, seems much of the time to be writing exquisite exercises upon themes assigned by some amiable schoolmaster. Johnson's poetry affects strength rather than delicacy, but it is unconvincing in the same way. Even without knowing the facts of his life, one would expect them to be somehow at variance with his verse. With both poets premature death is overshadowed by a greater tragedy.

John Davidson also belonged to the Rhymers' Club, but he was ten years older than most of the members, brought different experiences to his work, and found his way to a different—if parallel—conclusion. Born in Scotland, he went to work when he was thirteen. In 1890 he came to London, and for several years supported himself by hack work. He had rejected in youth the strict Calvinism in which he was brought up, but he was not tempted, as so many of his contemporaries were, by Catholicism. Instead he accepted the rigid materialism of the century, and in time he became a disciple of Nietzsche. While still in Scotland he had written a number of unactable verse plays that showed his ebullience and unconventionality and his admiration for the Elizabethans, but it was in *Fleet Street Eclogues* that he first spoke for himself. For a time his ballads had some success, but in the first years of the century he abandoned the form and wrote a series of philosophical poems he called testaments. He grew more and more bitter towards society, and in 1909 he committed suicide.

If it were not ridiculous to suggest that writers of this or any other period can be classified, the question might legitimately be raised whether Davidson belongs with the writers of the decadence or with the school of energetic manliness and imperialism. He believed in the superman, opposed social reform, emphasized the will, and was unafraid of violence in his verse. He was a member of the Rhymers' Club, but he damned his fellow-members as lacking "blood and guts." Though he objected as strongly as they did to the accepted Victorian authors, he resisted the influence of the French symbolists and sought a new basis for poetry. He did not follow Beardsley, Johnson, and Harland into the Catholic Church, nor had he any sympathy with Yeats's kind of mysticism.[1] Yet one can see why he was a member of the Rhymers' Club, and certainly "The Ballad of a Nun" was not out of place in the *Yellow Book*. If he quarreled with the symbolists and decadents, he fought side by side with them against the prevailing convictions of the middle class, and by his suicide he accepted the pattern that belongs to the group.

Hubert Crackanthorpe also committed suicide, as did Francis Adams and Laurence Hope. Beardsley died in his twenties, Dowson and Johnson in their thirties, Charles Conder, Henry Harland, Oscar Wilde, and Francis Thompson in their forties. The death of each, except possibly Harland, might have been postponed. It is no wonder that some critics have talked of a death-will and associated it with the literary aims and conceptions of the movement.

Richard Le Gallienne, Arthur Symons, Max Beerbohm, and W. B. Yeats were the principal survivors. Le Gallienne quickly

---

[1] Perhaps, however, he had his own kind of mysticism. "Davidson is in his scientific ideas primarily a poet and not a scientist or philosopher. He argues indeed in favor of his hypotheses, but more often he enunciates things on the basis of his own authority. Things cannot be known scientifically, he announces several times; they can be apprehended by poetic powers only." Hayim Fineman, *John Davidson*, 29–30.

proved himself to have been nothing but a romantic hanger-on, a self-made man of letters with the face and manners of a poet. Beerbohm continued as he had begun, but the more he wrote and the more he drew, the clearer it became that his association with the group was accidental. Symons lived on, but his mind was periodically clouded, and he did little important work after the appearance of *Images of Good and Evil* in 1899. Yeats continued to grow and change, until finally he took his place in the front rank of living poets.

Yeats's career, more strikingly than Beerbohm's, helps us to understand why it is so comparatively easy and so approximately just to give definite boundaries to the literary movement of the nineties. We do not think of Yeats as representative of that movement because he means so much more than that. But the majority of the writers died before they could mean more. Perhaps they never would have done anything better or anything very different, just as Symons never did. That we cannot know. But it is clear that, in the history of British literature, the movement was a passing phase, sharply marked because so many of the writers passed with it.

4. The Break with the Bourgeoisie.

"I was born," Arthur Symons wrote,[1] " 'like a fiend hid in a cloud,' cruel, nervous, excitable, passionate, restless, never quite human, never quite normal, and, from the fact that I have never known what it was to have a home, as most children know it, my life has been in many ways a wonderful, in certain ways a tragic one: an existence, indeed, so inexplicable even to myself, that I cannot fathom it. If I have been a vagabond, and have never been able to root myself in any one place in the world, it is because I have no early memories of any one sky or soil. It has freed me from many prejudices in

[1] From *Dramatis Personae*, by Arthur Symons. Copyright date, November 7, 1923. Reprinted by special permission of the publishers, The Bobbs-Merrill Company.

giving me its own unresting kind of freedom, but it has cut me off from whatever is stable, of long growth in the world."

Wilde could have said somewhat the same thing. Dowson, who in his youth had drifted about the Continent with his family, divided his later years between France and England, and his *nostalgia de boue,* so eminently in the decadent tradition, grew out of his homelessness. Davidson, Harland, and Yeats were all expatriates, and Yeats was the only one who thought of rooting his poetry in his homeland. Lionel Johnson pathetically envied Yeats his country, and tried to make himself an Irish poet. Max Beerbohm came from a solid enough British family, but nothing about him so impressed his contemporaries at Oxford as his utter detachment. As for Beardsley, he seemed to friends a changeling, quite unrelated to the mother and sister with whom he lived.

There is perhaps nothing unusual in this, for the artist often has few obvious ties to contemporary society. Yet most writers do become spokesmen for groups that are bound together by more than merely literary tastes. That is true of all the major Victorians and of William Morris. It is true in a sense of Hardy and Butler and for a time of George Gissing. It is true of the writers of the nineties only to the extent that restlessness and disillusionment were not rare in the decade. What they had in common with each other and with a certain number of their contemporaries was a centrifugal impulse.

Few of them succeeded in coming to terms with society— even the kind of terms that are represented by a consistent opposition. One can see, for example, that Lionel Johnson conceived of himself as a Catholic gentleman and scholar, not as a chronic alcoholic. Dowson would have chosen to live not in the mud but on a high romantic level. Yeats did in some measure achieve his desired identification with Ireland, but, instead of becoming a bard for the masses, became one of the most abstruse and difficult poets of his generation. Beardsley could not restrain his pen from blasphemy, the while he sincerely professed Catholicism. Symons, it is true, seemed to be what he wanted to be, but a psychologist would point to the mental crises of his middle years as proof of conflict. Davidson remained wholeheartedly a rebel, but he broke under the strain.

It does not distinguish these writers to say they were in revolt against the age in which they lived; so were Morris and Hardy and Butler and Gissing; so were Shaw and Wells and a score of the younger authors. Yeats admits this in *The Trembling of the Veil.* "As time passed," he writes, "Ibsen became in my eyes the chosen author of very clever young journalists, who, condemned to their treadmill of abstraction, hated music and style; and yet neither I nor my generation could escape him because, though we and he had not the same friends, we had the same enemies." Again, he says of Shaw: "He could hit my enemies and the enemies of all I loved, as I could never hit, as no living author that was dear to me could ever hit." Yeats and his friends hated greed and hypocrisy as much as Shaw did. Yeats even, for a time, accepted Morris' Socialism because he shared so completely his distaste for contemporary ugliness. If Socialism would bring what he wanted, then Yeats felt, just as Wilde did when he wrote *The Soul of Man,* that he was for Socialism.

But the more obvious way was to leave the bourgeoisie to its ugliness and to go about the creation of beauty. The writers of the nineties might feel their hopes rise when there was a strong popular movement against capitalism, but they could not believe that it was their duty to initiate or nourish such a revolt. They were, for the most part, men of unusual sensitivity, men who shuddered at the turmoil and the rawness of industrial and commercial life. When one remembers how many of them were weakened by disease, one cannot wonder that they were incapable of offering any direct resistance to the evils they were so conscious of. They were readily convinced of the impregnability of ugliness and greed, and they sought what they wanted wherever they could, even if fleetingly, find it.

Here, then, were a dozen men coming from all parts of the British Isles to London, though they felt no particular loyalty to the city. They had none of the faith of the early romantics in nature, and little of their faith in man. They hated the social order of which they were part, but they were powerless to change it and ready to believe that it could not be changed. If their sensitiveness might be called abnormal, they could say with some reason that normality was no virtue in an age such as theirs. They had no respect for Victorian morality and, except for Davidson, no confidence in Victorian science. They believed in beauty as artists of all ages have done, but they believed in it more intensely, for it was all they believed in.

Naturally they turned, as writers have always done, to those of their predecessors and older contemporaries who had seen life somewhat as they saw it. With the majority of the Victorian spokesmen they had no sympathy. Yeats has told how Huxley, Tyndall, Carolus Duran, and Bastien-Lepage represented for him the unimaginativeness he hated. What they set forth as reality was to him an illusion. His friends agreed, and they also condemned, even more vigorously, every writer who could be suspected of supporting Victorian morality. That left, in England, the Pre-Raphaelites and Pater. The Pre-Raphaelites had refused to regard art as a branch of pedagogy, and, while insisting on precision in detail, had tried to give the imagination freedom. Pater had done more, and he remained a force in the literature of the nineties after the Pre-Raphaelites were accorded only appreciative sympathy. The famous preface to *The Renaissance,* with its emphasis on the isolated sensation, made the younger men understand what life and poetry and art meant to them. They understood, as Yeats put it, "that Swinburne in one way, Browning in another, and Tennyson in a third, had filled their work with what I called 'impurities,' curiosities about politics, about science, about history, about religion; and that we must create once more the pure work."

They turned to France, where "pure work" was being created. They had no difficulty in doing so, for Paris was as much their home as London, and they were more at ease with French than with British contemporaries. Insular British literature, as we have seen, was once more reaching out to the literature of a foreign land. Certain French writers had already traveled or were traveling the path that the young men of England and Ireland saw stretching before them: Baudelaire, Verlaine, Barbey d'Aurevilly, Huysmans, Villiers de l'Isle-Adam, and others.

It is no surprise that both George Moore and Oscar Wilde paid tribute to Huysmans' *Against the Grain* and imitated it, for it was the perfect bible of the decadence. Soberer and perhaps more significant authors might, even on first contact with its glamor, sense its defects, finding in it the tawdriness that was so obvious in the imitations, but it remained for many a "wonderful" and "poisoned" book, and its central theme, the superiority of the neurotic personality, was a powerful consolation. Its autobiographical hero, Des Esseintes, did not merely feel himself set apart from his times; that isolation was made his claim to greatness. He could not endure works of literature, art, and music that had "the approbation of the general voice," and his quest for the esoteric sent him to decadent Latin authors and the least appreciated of his contemporaries. The shudder that he felt at all contact with the public and that led him to take refuge in "a refined Thebaid," was proof to him that he was of a higher race. He could not find pleasure where others found it: sexual indulgence had to have some element of perversion, and the artificial was always preferable to the natural. "Nature has had her day," Huysmans wrote, in phrases Wilde was to copy; "she has definitely and finally tired out by the sickening monotony of her landscapes and skyscapes the patience of refined temperaments." Des Esseintes cared only for "the distillation of overwrought and subtle brains." He abandoned real for artificial flowers, and then wanted "natural flowers imitating the false." The search for the unique, the confusion of the senses, the breaking down of all barriers between the imaginary world and the real—the qualities, in short, of symbolism —were given an intensely melodramatic form.

For us *Against the Grain* is important less because of its direct influence, which was considerable, than because of its revelation of the animus of the decadence. Huysmans' hatred for mankind reduced itself, again and again, to a hatred for the bourgeoisie. "Nobility was utterly decayed, dead; aristocracy had fallen into idiocy or filthy pleasures! . . . The least scrupulous, the least dull-witted, threw all shame to the winds; they mixed in low plots, stirred up the filth of base finance. . . . After the aristocracy of birth, it was now the turn of the aristocracy of money; it was the Caliphate of the counting-house, the despotism of the Rue du Sentier, the tyranny of commerce with its narrow-minded, venal ideas, its ostentatious and rascally instincts. . . . More nefarious, more vile than the nobility it had plundered and the clergy it had overthrown, the bourgeoisie borrowed their frivolous love of show, their decrepit boastfulness, which it vulgarized by its lack of good manners, stole their defects which it aggravated into hypocritical vices. Obstinate and sly, base and cowardly, it shot down ruthlessly its eternal and inevitable dupe, the populace, which it had itself unmuzzled and set on to spring at the throat of the old castes. Now the victory was won. Its task once completed, the plebs had been for its health's sake bled to the last drop, while the bourgeois, secure in his triumphs, throned it jovially by dint of his money and the contagion of his folly. The result of his rise to power had been the destruction of all intelligence, the negation of all honesty, the death of all art; in fact, the artists and men of letters, in their degradation, had fallen to their knees and were devouring with ardent kisses the unwashed feet of the high-placed horse-jockeys and low-bred satraps on whose alms they lived."

Would Beardsley or Dowson or Johnson or Davidson or Symons or Yeats have quarreled with this statement? It was the bourgeoisie that they hated and either openly attacked or harried with flamboyant proclamations of their own dissidence. Baudelaire's hostility to the bourgeoisie had sent him to the barricades in forty-eight, though his sympathies with the proletariat had not survived their defeat. In the eighties and nineties the bourgeoisie, both in France and in England, seemed more firmly entrenched than ever. The signs of a break in bourgeois power that Morris could see were scarcely visible to the London and Paris poets, and insofar as they were recognized at all, they were regarded as evidences of bourgeois misrule, proof of bourgeois stupidity and not of bourgeois weakness. The only thing to do was to secede. Art must be taken away from the bourgeoisie and from the artists who kissed the unwashed bourgeois foot. And if that meant the rejection of much that had once seemed to be art but now was irremediably sullied by the admiration of the uncritical, then the decadents were prepared to limit themselves to the esoteric. Art, by their theory, true art, could appeal only to the chosen few, and to prove their membership in the elect they rejected as "a thing polluted, commonplace, almost repulsive" any work that the middle class liked.

Against the Grain defined the new attitude. Romanticism had earlier been part of a great expansive movement of the human mind. The decadents were romantic in their scorn of the conventional and their preference for the indefinite, but romanticism was now a movement of contraction. Politics, science, history, religion, Yeats said, did not properly belong to art. "No preferences, no prejudices, no particular feelings of any kind," said Wilde. The decadents did not—perhaps could not—practice all that they preached, but the limitations they did accept would never have been tolerated by the first generation of romantics.

Against the Grain also exhibited, in however exaggerated a form, the personality of the decadent artist. Des Esseintes could stand, *mutatis mutandis,* for Baudelaire, Verlaine, and Mallarmé, as well as for Huysmans himself. He could stand, too, for Dowson, Symons, Johnson, Beardsley, Wilde, Conder. It may be that all the conflicts that grew out of the creation of an industrial civilization had increased the number of neurotic personalities. But whether that is true or not, the conditions under which an artist worked in the eighties and nineties could only intensify any antecedent instability of character. Yeats, more firmly rooted than most of his contemporaries, nevertheless had a long struggle to achieve stability, and his success was almost unique. The notion not unnaturally flourished that sanity was a bourgeois trait and therefore to be condemned. Unable to overcome their vices, the decadents made virtues of them, dramatizing in their works the tragic consequences exhibited in their lives.

In political life anarchism is the refuge of the hopeless, and the decadence was anarchistic. Yet its writers had a deep passion for order. In Huysmans this was shown by the attraction, to which he eventually yielded, that Catholicism had for him. *Against the Grain* shows Huysmans haunted by the dread that none of his acts has any significance, and wondering what in that case becomes of his vaunted superiority over the masses of mankind. Even his sins are merely the whims of unstrung nerves and a depleted digestion if there is no absolute standard by which they can be judged. That is the attraction, for him as for Barbey d'Aurevilly, of demonolatry, and it is no wonder that d'Aurevilly said of *Against the Grain,* "After such a book, it only remains for the author to choose between the muzzle of a pistol or the foot of the cross."

Huysmans chose the cross, and so did many of his contemporaries in England. Both Lionel Johnson and Francis Thompson turned to Catholicism and made themselves Catholic poets. Beardsley was converted to the faith, in part by the persuasions of John Gray, a delicate if imitative symbolist poet, himself a convert. Robert Ross became a Catholic and was presumably responsible for the presence of the priest at Wilde's deathbed, and two other disciples of Wilde, Sherard and Lord Alfred Douglas, subsequently adopted that faith. And, to complete the list of converts, there were Henry Harland and Ernest Dowson.

One cannot help suspecting that the doctrine of art for art's sake was not enough in itself to support these men. In their rebellion against contemporary society they needed some sort of bulwark. The church, of course, did not sanction their way of life or even their doctrine of art, but underneath both lay their distrust of contemporary society, and it was precisely at that point that the church could sustain them. For, especially in England, where its position was always difficult, the church stood apart from the progress of capitalism. Not only was it the one organization that could look back to a pre-capitalist past; not only did it set its values against the values of a competitive world; it was relatively unpolluted by the vulgarity that had overcome the representative churches of the British middle class. Yeats and Davidson felt the same need for support as did the converts, but Yeats found his mysticism adequate to sustain him, and Davidson told himself he was a superman and committed suicide when he could no longer believe it.

"No poem," said Baudelaire, "can be so grand, so noble, so truly worthy of the name of poem as that which is written solely for the pleasure of writing a poem." And again: "I say that, if the poet has pursued a moral end, he has diminished his poetic force, and it is not rash to predict that his work will be bad. Poetry cannot, under pain of death or decay, be assimilated to science or morality. It does not have truth for its object, but only itself." A dozen British writers would at one time or another have subscribed to that doctrine, but not one was consistent in adherence. All of them felt the need of relating their art to a philosophy of life.

Indeed, their work had always rested on a non-literary principle, that is, on hatred of the bourgeoisie. As Wilde's career has already made plain to us, the doctrine of art for art's sake was a protest against contemporary standards and a way of escaping from bourgeois controls. It was an attempt to fight the old battle on a new front, one on which the artists had at least a momentary advantage. But if there were strategic gains, there were creative losses, and the position had to be abandoned.

The mortality rate was so high that a literary generation simply vanished. Moreover, it left few disciples and had little enduring influence. In the general battle to free British writers from the demands of an outworn and therefore stultifying moral code, the esthetes played a part, but otherwise it is hard to see how they have affected the course of English literature. Later writers learned much from the symbolists, but learned it direct from the French, not from their English disciples and inferiors. Wilde's reputation persisted because he was a symbol. Other reputations, with the exception of Beardsley's, quickly dwindled. Yeats's prestige continued to grow, but after his Irish experiments and his pre-occupation with the

"Great Wheel," it became increasingly difficult to remember what he had stood for—or had been thought to stand for—in the nineties.

The Wilde incident and the episode of the *Yellow Book* and the *Savoy* are almost unique in English literary history, and it is impossible to understand them apart from the tensions of the closing decade of the century. Slight as their literary results seem to have been, their effect upon the public was incalculable. If the esthetes thought to escape bourgeois criticism by repudiating bourgeois standards, they were mistaken, for Wilde and Beardsley, and to a lesser extent their associates, were attacked with unprecedented virulence. But it was precisely the feverishness of the attack that gave the decadents their measure of victory, since it resulted in a closer scrutiny of prevailing standards than had been effected by any of the more direct critics. The writers were ill-equipped for survival in the struggle, and few of them survived, but they had their revenge, for Victorianism was dying too. It took a longer time to die than the delicate poets of the eighties and nineties, but its doom was just as sure.

Chapter VII

THE CODE OF THE EMPIRE BUILDERS

THE late Victorian mind had been almost incessantly buffeted about. It was true that the violence of the thirties and forties had yielded to the prosperity of the Manchester era, but an army of heretics plagued the complacent. The attack on the Manchester theories, Darwinism, the undermining of evangelical morality—were there any certainties left? There was one—trade. And when the depression of the eighties followed that of the seventies, the last bulwark of Victorian optimism was gone.

Whatever happened, Victorianism was doomed. If the economic system collapsed, as Morris was predicting, the change would be drastic and perhaps catastrophic. The whole system of middle-class control would be destroyed. But even if prosperity could be restored, that would not preserve the way of life that the middle class had imposed upon the nineteenth century. Either the growth or the decay of capitalism would serve to dispose of Victorianism. Naturally the middle class wanted to see capitalism expand, no matter what the consequences, and it was frightened by the signs of economic decline as it could be frightened by nothing else, but the whole process of change was disturbing.

Most of the late Victorian writers contributed to disintegration, and that is why they were met with anger. If the questions they asked were alarming, the answers they gave or implied were even more so. The middle-class public longed for books that would be re-assuring. Of course there was plenty of pious claptrap, as there always is, but it failed to carry conviction. Where was the author who could make them feel the old confidence, who could say the simple, old-fashioned things so that they would be believed? Such a writer, dealing in old certainties and new hopes, would not have to seek a public; his public was looking for him.

It was Stevenson who first persuaded late Victorian readers that they were being troubled unnecessarily by the doubts and fears that figured so largely in contemporary literature, and he had his reward. But Kipling did even better. He showed the old virtues at work in new ways, ways that seemed to more and more persons to be the hope of salvation. Kipling might have been popular if there had been no growing sentiment for imperialism, but, his qualities being what they were, that sentiment made his apotheosis inevitable. England rode into the twentieth century on the tide of imperialism, and Kipling so perfectly expressed the imperialist mood of the nineties that superficial observers believed he had created it.

1. The Romantic Gospel.

Preacher of virility and adventure, of reckless defiance and high honor, Robert Louis Stevenson was an invalid. The two things one must always remember in thinking about him are his father and his lungs. Adolescence and young manhood were spent in breaking away from the family pattern, but the remainder of his life was occupied in a curious kind of retracing of that pattern. What made the dual process tense and dramatic was the imminence of death.

The Stevensons were a middle-class Scottish family, originally with Whig tendencies. They had become Tories, however, as they rose in wealth and prestige, and Thomas Stevenson, who built lighthouses and improved harbors and rivers, as his father had done before him, and as his two brothers were doing, could no more conceive of a Stevenson being a Liberal than he could conceive of one not being a Presbyterian. If Robert Louis Stevenson had been a normal, healthy child, his father probably would have succeeded in imposing upon him the Stevenson stamp. "Old Mr. Naseby," wrote Stevenson in *The Story of a Lie,* "had the sturdy, untutored nature of the upper middle class. The universe seemed plain to him. 'The thing's right,' he would say, or 'the thing's wrong'; and there was an end of it. There was a contained, prophetic energy in his utterances, even on the slightest affairs; he *saw* the damned thing; if you did not, it must be from perversity of will; and this sent the blood to his head." Thomas Stevenson had a richer, fuller nature than Mr. Naseby, but he had the same capacity for knowing right from wrong.

He took it for granted that his son would become a civil engineer, and for three and a half years the boy studied at the University of Edinburgh, spending parts of the summers in practical work. The years of ill health, however, the years when Louis had been coddled, when he had spent much of his time in reading, had made him realize that there were other worlds than his father's. He accepted neither his father's religious and political views nor his choice of a profession. Thomas Stevenson proved, as his wife recorded in her diary, "wonderfully resigned," but he insisted that his son should study law, so that, if literature failed, he would at least be trained for a profession.

Stevenson meanwhile was scribbling away, playing the sedulous ape, as he later wrote in a famous essay, to every new master of style he discovered, and he neglected law for literature, as he had neglected engineering. At the same time he began to venture into other fields. In full revolt against Presbyterian dogma, he proclaimed himself an agnostic in arguments with his fellows, and of course word of his heresy eventually reached his parents. Thomas Stevenson, who had written tracts in defense of Presbyterian Christianity, was deeply hurt as well as angry, and Louis suffered over his father's suffering.[1] The Commissioner of Northern Lights suffered even more when he realized that his son had also broken with Presbyterian morality. Despite the attempt of certain friends to conceal the facts, diligent researchers such as John Steuart and George Hellman have been able to discover that the young law student frequented low resorts and had affairs with "Highland lassies." Stern discipline and financial strictness were his father's response.

For at least a time the revolt was many-sided. Stevenson went to Edinburgh a convinced Tory, joined the Conservative Club, and made speeches denouncing the Liberals. By the time, however, that he was reading law, he had so far departed from his father's principles as to help found a secret society, mysteriously called the L.J.R., which was devoted to "red republicanism." That particular phase did not last long. Only five years later he could write of it: "I am no more abashed at having been a red-hot Socialist with a panacea of my own than at having been a sucking infant. I look back to the time when I was a Socialist with something like regret. I have convinced myself (for the moment) that we had better leave these great changes to what we call great blind forces: their blindness being so much more perspicacious than the little, peering, partial eyesight of men. . . . Now I know that

---

[1] On February 2, 1873, Stevenson wrote Charles Baxter: "The thunderbolt has fallen with a vengeance now. On Friday night after leaving you, in the course of conversation, my father put me one or two questions as to beliefs, which I candidly answered. . . . If I had foreseen the hell of everything since, I think I should have lied, as I have done so often before. I so far thought of my father, but I had forgotten my mother. And now! they are both ill, both silent, both as down in the mouth as if— I can find no simile. . . . They don't see either that my game is not the light-hearted scoffer; that I am not (as they call me) a careless infidel. . . . I reserve (as I told them) many points until I acquire fuller information, and do not think I am thus justly to be called 'horrible atheist.' . . . If all that I hold true and most desire to spread is to be such death, and worse than death, in the eyes of my father and mother, what the devil am I to do?" *Letters*, I, 45–6.

in thus turning Conservative with years, I am going through the normal cycle of change and traveling in the common orbit of men's opinions . . . but I do not greatly pride myself on having outlived my belief in the fairy tales of Socialism." He was twenty-eight when he wrote this.

As a matter of fact, no phase of revolt was of long duration. If he always remained in some sense an agnostic, he learned to curb the expression of his skepticism, and, though never a conformist in behavior, he ceased to flaunt his unconventionalities to the world. What remained constant during these years of rapid change was his desire to be an author, and towards that end he showed a diligence that would have surprised his father and his professors. He has written frankly about his apprenticeship, and we know how faithfully he carried his notebook and wrote in it, how persistently he studied and marked and imitated the authors he admired. "No one," he once said, "ever had such pains to learn a trade as I had, but I slogged at it day in, day out, and I frankly believe (thanks to my dire industry) I have done more with smaller gifts than almost any other man of letters in the world." It is not a bad judgment. Stevenson wanted to be a writer before he had any idea what he wanted to write, and, having challenged his father's will and thus pledged himself in his own mind to success, he spared no pains.

We can understand why he worked so hard; it is less easy to understand why he worked the way he did. "I lived with words," he wrote, and it is true. Montaigne, Hazlitt, Lamb, Sir Thomas Browne, Defoe, Hawthorne, and Wordsworth— he studied them all, and not only studied but practiced till he could achieve their effects. "There is," he said, "only one merit worth considering in a man of letters—that he should write well; and only one damning fault—that he should write ill." Good writing, he obviously believed, was something that existed in the abstract. It never occurred to him that words are tools and that the styles that had served Montaigne or Hawthorne might not serve him. He never realized that, in apprenticing himself to a man's prose, he was making himself the servant of the man's mind. He never saw that he was preventing the writer in whom he was most interested—one Robert Louis Stevenson—from coming into existence.[1]

His first published essay, "On Roads," appeared in the *Portfolio* for December, 1873. Other descriptive essays followed, and his first books were *An Inland Voyage,* published in 1878, and *Travels with a Donkey,* published the next year. He had tried his hand, meanwhile, at other kinds of essays, at reviews, and at stories. Yet while it appeared that anything would serve his purpose so long as it gave him a chance to write, he was gradually showing that he was, above all else, a moralist. The first part of "Virginibus Puerisque" was printed in 1876, "On Falling in Love" and "An Apology for Idlers" in 1877, "Crabbed Age and Youth" and "Aes Triplex" in 1878. In 1879 he started work on "Lay Morals," which he never finished. His father, who had written "A Layman's Sermon," was probably too distressed by the heterodoxy of his son's ethics to recognize his own handiwork.

It is strange to think that Walt Whitman, who was so completely a democrat and whose style was so far from fastidious, helped Stevenson to realize what he wanted to preach. There were other forces, to be sure. Stevenson's revolt was pretty well spent by the mid-seventies. He was beginning to find congenial friends, and the taverns of Edinburgh seemed less inviting. One of his professors, Fleeming Jenkin, had shown him that a man could be serious without being pious and dogmatic. Ill health had sobered him. And with all this

---

[1] John A. Steuart, not a hostile critic, says: "There is scarcely a piece of his writing, from the early paper on 'Roads' to the late *St. Ives,* which is not in essense a conscious and self-conscious exercise in style in the various manners of his various masters. Not till he reached *Weir of Hermiston* did he show a real understanding of the art of arts for the creative writer." *Robert Louis Stevenson,* I, 99.

came the reading of Whitman, who justified Stevenson's impatience with convention and at the same time gave him a positive gospel to preach. Stevenson was still too close to his own "red-hot Socialism" to be totally indifferent to Whitman's democratic faith, but he found it easy to ignore its personal implications. Whitman's self-confidence, his fearlessness, and above all his optimism—these were the qualities Stevenson admired. Whitman went his way, indifferent to public opinion, saying what he thought, doing what he believed needed to be done, never once doubting that the universe was on his side. The kind of transcendentalism that underlay Whitman's attitude meant nothing to Stevenson; it was the attitude itself he sought to imitate. Whitman had none of the calculating prudence that distressed Stevenson as it appeared in his own family circle and in the writings of such men as Franklin and, on quite a different level, Thoreau. He was as optimistic as Browning, whom Stevenson also admired, but his optimism was much more rugged and focused more truly on the modern world.

It was nothing very substantial that Stevenson borrowed from Whitman. Few moralists have launched themselves upon the world with a more meager equipment, and a higher polish has seldom been applied to platitudes. What saves Stevenson's moral teachings from complete banality is, of course, the personal courage that he exemplified, the indifference to consequences that he showed in his own life, the hope that he clung to so persistently. If it had not been for his rotted lung, one could scarcely forgive his willingness to condemn those whom life has beaten. As it is, though one cannot help seeing how much of the optimism is forced, the will that forces it is worthy of respect. When Stevenson preaches indifference to death, as he does so eloquently in "Aes Triplex," we not only have to tender him our personal homage; we have to admit that the platitudes have been given new force.

Stevenson would not have been distressed at being told he was dealing in platitudes. What he was trying to do, one judges from the fragment of "Lay Morals," was to give the old platitudes new life. To his surprise he found in the New Testament, once he had lost his Presbyterian blinders, something of the recklessness he admired in *Leaves of Grass*. He disregarded Jesus' theological assumptions, as he had disregarded Whitman's, and fastened upon attitudes he admired. Thus armed with brave rules of conduct, he did not deny the agnostic's conception of the universe; he defied it. "We inhabit a dead ember swimming wide in the blank of space," he wrote, "dizzily spinning as it swims, and lighted up from several million miles away by a more horrible hell-fire than was ever conceived by the theological imagination." And yet there is in man "something which is apart from desire and fear, to which all the kingdoms of the world and the immediate death of the body are alike indifferent." "It may be the love of God; or it may be an inherited (and certainly well-concealed) instinct to preserve self and propagate the race; I am not, for the moment, averse to either theory; but it will save time to call it righteousness." To keep the old morality but rid it of asceticism, to defy the new despair, to disparage the gospel of respectability and success—that was Stevenson's aim. At moments it led him close to Pater's theory of the hard, gem-like flame; at others it brought him back to his Presbyterian ancestors. At no time did it lead him to say anything new about conduct. But it satisfied the preacher in him, the Presbyterian who had to have a moral code, the victim of tuberculosis who had to find a rationale of life and death.

So long as Stevenson was merely the moralizing essayist, he found only the smallest of publics, though subsequently, when he had won popularity, many were to pore over his essays with affection and gratitude. He moved slowly from the essay to fiction, encouraged by W. E. Henley, another invalid who was preaching the strenuous life. In 1878 Henley published the *New Arabian Nights* in his *London Magazine,* but the tales attracted little attention. They were, however, fairly popular when they appeared in book form in 1882. Late the next year came *Treasure Island,* again a failure as a serial but an instant success as a book. *Prince Otto* and *More New Arabian Nights* in 1885 did only moderately well, but 1886 was a year of indubitable success. *Dr. Jekyll and Mr. Hyde* owed its popularity as much to its moral lesson as to its bizarre theme. Critics compared it with the tales of Poe and Hawthorne, and ministers preached sermons on it. A few months later *Kidnapped* brought the praise of the *Times,* the *Literary World,* and most of the other critical journals. America was even more enthusiastic over both *Dr. Jekyll* and *Kidnapped* than England, and when Stevenson reached New York in 1887 he found that he was a public figure, with reporters seeking interviews and editors urging contracts upon him.

Being what he was, Stevenson had to have a theory of romance, and he had been elaborating one in "A Gossip on Romance," which was written in 1882 and was followed by "A Note on Realism," "A Humble Remonstrance," and similar essays. Style, in his sense of the word, he naturally placed first, calling it "the one quality" in which the apprentice author "may improve himself at will." Next came the choice of the proper circumstances: "One thing in life calls for another; there is a fitness in events and places. . . . This is one of the natural appetites with which any lively literature has to count. The desire for knowledge, I had almost added the desire for meat, is not more deeply seated than this demand for fit and striking incident." It is the incidents, he insists, that create illusion for the reader; he cannot, as a matter of fact, identify himself with characters, but he can be swept off his feet by events. Realism in the ordinary sense does not matter. The author is better off if he does not clutter up his pages with lems would take care of themselves. Persons who are doing fairly well in the world as it is are likely to trust in "the great blind forces," and to feel that the exhibition of personal courage is more important than—and in some way incompatible with—the exercising of social intelligence.

To politics as such Stevenson paid comparatively little attention, but at moments his interest became feverish. In 1881, when Gladstone, whom Stevenson detested, was in power, the Liberal government was faced with a problem inherited from its predecessors. The Boers and the British fought at Majuba Hill, and the eventual outcome was the granting of independence to the Transvaal. When he heard of the battle, Stevenson wrote an indignant article, which he was somehow persuaded not to publish. "A man . . . may have been a Jingo," he said, "from a sense, perhaps mistaken, of the obligations, the greatness, and the danger of his native land, and not from any brutal greed of aggrandizement or cheap love of drums and regimental columns. . . . I was not ashamed to be the countryman of Jingoes; but I am beginning to grow ashamed of being the kin of those who are now fighting; I should rather say, who are sending men to fight in this unmanly Transvaal War. . . . We are in the wrong, or all that we profess is false; blood has been shed, glory lost, and, I fear, honor also."

These are brave words, and it is perhaps impertinent to wonder whether they would have been spoken had the Tories been in power. What Stevenson particularly hated was the inept and curiously dishonest way in which the Liberals defended the Empire. In theory they disapproved of expansion, but they were never quite able to take a decisive stand, and the result was that they acted for imperialist ends, but acted stupidly and ineffectually. The half-hearted Soudan campaign, resulting in the death of General Gordon, particularly enraged Stevenson. Gordon was his kind of hero, and his abandonment was almost a personal affront. "I fear England is dead of Burgessry," he wrote Sidney Colvin, "and only walks about galvanized. I do not love to think of my countrymen these days; nor to remember myself." "Why should I blame Gladstone," he asked J. A. Symonds, "when I too am a Bourgeois? when I have held my peace? Why did I hold my peace? Because I am a skeptic: i. e., a Bourgeois. We believe in nothing, Symonds; you don't, and I don't; and these are two reasons, out of a handful of millions, why England stands before the world dripping with blood and daubed with dishonor."

Much can be told from the causes of a man's wrath. Nothing in public life ever roused Stevenson as did Gordon's death. He was, however, nearly as much moved by the terrorism that attended the Irish campaign for freedom. His biographers insist that he had always been conscious of Ireland's wrongs, but certainly he was not moved to protest against these wrongs as he protested against certain attempts to right them. In the early eighties bombings in London inspired the satirical passages in *The Dynamiters,* passages in which Stevenson not only attacked the methods but scurrilously defamed the motives of the terrorists. In 1886 a farmer named Curtin was killed in Ireland, and it was reported that his family was being persecuted. Stevenson seriously proposed to go and live on the derelict farm, as a form of protest, and was only dissuaded by the fatal illness of his father.

How his mind was working can be surmised from an essay he wrote in 1887 for the *Contemporary Review,* "The Day After Tomorrow." "We are all becoming Socialists without knowing it," he said. "There is every chance that our grandchildren will see the day and taste the pleasures of existence in something far liker an ant-heap than any previous human polity." The result, he prophesied, would be slavery. The further result would be boredom: "Our race has not been strained venson seem as simple, brave, honorable, and full of faith as his own David Balfour, and almost as stupid. Perhaps it was legitimate, by his own standards, for the figure of their creation did belong in a world blended of day-dreams and Tory morality.

2. *The Amazing Young Man.*

In August, 1890, Stevenson wrote to Henry James: "Kipling is too clever to live. . . . He is a Beast, but not human, and, to be frank, not very interesting." The next December he partly amended his judgment: "Kipling is by far the most promising young man who has appeared since—ahem—I appeared. He amazes me by his precocity and various endowment. But he alarms me by his copiousness and haste. . . . At this rate his works will soon fill the habitable globe; and surely he was armed for better conflicts than these succinct sketches and flying leaves of verse. I look on, I admire, I rejoice for myself; but in a kind of ambition we all have for our tongue and literature I am wounded. If I had this man's fertility and courage, it seems to me I could heave a pyramid."

Kipling at this time was not quite twenty-five. The world as a whole felt all of Stevenson's wonder, and with none of his reservations. On his side Kipling often praised Stevenson's stories and is said to have called him master. Though he probably owed more to Edgar Allan Poe and Bret Harte, he was right in feeling that he belonged to Stevenson's school: he, too, was a moralist, bringing men back to the simple virtues; he, too, carried excitement into the lives of routine-driven clerks. He had, however, great advantages over Stevenson: he was apparently untroubled by the doubts against which Stevenson had to struggle; he was, even at twenty-five, a man of experience and action; he was spokesman for an increasingly popular cause.

There can never have been a career quite like Kipling's.

Born in India, the son of the talented curator of the Lahore Museum, he went to England when he was seven, and for six years lived a cruel life in Southsea, with an old woman who talked constantly of hellfire and was a mistress of torture. He matured rapidly under this treatment, and seemed more than thirteen when he went to the United Services College at Westward Ho! on the Devon Coast. This was in 1878. The school had been founded a few years earlier by a group of army officers who wanted to provide an economical education for their sons. Seventy-five percent of the boys had been born outside of England, and most of them expected to enter the army. Kipling himself would presumably have chosen that career if his eyesight had permitted.

The picture of the United Services College in *Stalky & Co.* is in some respects an idealized one, but Kipling was under no temptation to conceal the brutality of the school, for he regarded it as a virtue. In his autobiography he admits that he was miserable during his first year and a half, when he was bullied by the older boys, but after he got his growth he had little trouble. General Dunsterville, Kipling's Stalky, also says that the bullying was excessive, but both he and Kipling seem to feel that they have provided an adequate defense when they say it was a clean school. What Kipling himself regarded as its chief educational value he made clear in "A School Song":

> This we learned from famous men
>   Teaching in our borders,
> Who declaréd it was best,
> Safest, easiest, and best,
> Expeditious, wise, and best—
>   To obey your orders.

Yet it is apparent that Kipling learned something more than military discipline. The head master, Cormell Price, was not wholly without imagination, and when he saw that this boy, who was unfit for military service, had literary talent, he encouraged him. Kipling became editor of the school paper, the *Chronicle,* and Price gave him the run of his study. The boy read Tennyson and Browning and Swinburne, and he began to write poetry. The verse of his schooldays is, as one would expect, imitative, but the imitations aim high. This is no "sedulous ape," studiously acquiring a style; it is a precocious youth, trying to say something of his own. The poems are youthful, but many are on adult themes, and few smack of the United Services College, at least as portrayed in *Stalky & Co.*

One of the Stalky stories, "The Flag of Their Country," deals with the embarrassment of the boys at the flag-waving, self-conscious patriotism of a visiting Member of Parliament. Love of the Empire, Kipling says, was too deep and real to be a subject of public addresses or casual conversation. Consequently it is not surprising to find that only one of the schoolboy lyrics attempts an expression of the loyalty that, above all else, the school sought to foster. "Ave Imperatrix," written in 1882, on the occasion of an attempt on Victoria's life, offers the greeting of the school—

> Such greeting as should come from those
> Whose fathers faced the Sepoy hordes,
> Or served You in the Russian snows,
> And, dying, left their sons their swords.

Of himself and his schoolmates he writes:

> And all are bred to do Your will
> By land and sea—wherever flies
> The Flag to fight and follow still
> And work Your Empire's destinies.

> Once more we greet You, though unseen
> Our greeting be, and coming slow.
> Trust us if need arise, O Queen;
> We shall not tarry with the blow!

Imperialism was something to be taken for granted, but the Empire was then as always first in Kipling's mind. His earliest memories were of the British in India, and the school was made up of boys who came from the Empire and were destined for the Empire. If England was and always would be home for them, they did not and never could think as boys did whose lives had been lived, and their fathers' before them, within the boundaries of the island.

Loyalty to the Empire had long been deeply implanted in Kipling when, not quite seventeen, he went to India to take a place on the *Civil and Military Gazette* that Price had secured for him. It was hard work, ten to fifteen hours a day. "From the modern point of view," he wrote in *Something of Myself*, "I suppose the life was not fit for a dog, but my world was filled with boys, but a few years older than I, who lived utterly alone, and died from typhoid mostly at the regulation age of twenty-two." His associates were, naturally, young men in the army and civil service, and perhaps the thought that he ought to be doing what they were doing helped to reconcile him to his job. Moreover, he was learning a great deal. In the Punjab Club every man was an expert in one field or another, and, as Kipling demonstrated his ability as a journalist, he was sent over half of India to cover floods, celebrations, riots, receptions, trials. Alert, curious, with a quick understanding and an extraordinary memory, he quickly achieved the appearance of omniscience.

By the time he was twenty-one Kipling was holding up a highly polished mirror before the British in India. In 1885 he began publishing verses and stories in the *Gazette* as space permitted, and in 1886 he brought out a book of verse, *Departmental Ditties*. In 1887 he was transferred to the sister-paper of the *Gazette,* the influential *Pioneer* of Allahabad. In addition to his regular work he edited a weekly supplement, for which he wrote many short stories. So rapidly did these stories accumulate that by the end of 1888 there was material for seven small volumes. The first of these was *Plain Tales from the Hills*. After it came the six paper-covered books in A. H. Wheeler's Indian Railway Library: *Soldiers Three, The Phantom Rickshaw, The Story of the Gadsbys, In Black and White, Under the Deodars,* and *Wee Willie Winkie*. He had also written series of articles on travels through India, subsequently published under such titles as *Letters of Marque* and *The City of Dreadful Night*. What he had written before his twenty-fourth birthday occupies several thousand pages in his collected works.

What bowled people over was his knowledge. In his early twenties, he wrote with equal authority about civilians and military men, officers and privates, white men and natives, adults and children. With a sophistication in which the occasional false note was not at all easy to detect, he wrote about flirtations and jiltings and scandals of every sort in Simla. Quick in defense of the private soldiers, he portrayed them as foul-mouthed and violent, and showed them in the maddest exploits, in both peace and war. He hinted at fabulous scandals in the affairs of the British government, and spoke openly about inefficiency and stupidity, but his loyalty was beyond question, and he made it clear that he knew far worse things about the native states. The supernatural came within his range, and he could be as circumstantial about ghosts as he was about Simla tea-parties and military maneuvers.

The knowledge poured out of him, and there was force behind it. That, of course, was why Stevenson at first felt him something of a beast. He had seen young men die—"mostly at the regulation age of twenty-two"—and he knew that India did not put a high value on life. He had to seem to have hardened himself, making his stories tough-fibered and strong. Certainly he was not insensitive, but he knew how to keep his emotions in check, disciplining them as a British officer would have to do. He was not averse to shocking his readers, feeling that it was good for them to see what he had seen, but he was careful to hide his own shock. There was agony, for example, in such a story as "Thrown Away," but it made itself felt through the brittle, cynical sentences, the tight, harsh observations, the gruesome details. In the framework of "With the Main Guard" men are suffering in the heat, both fearing and hoping for death, thinking irresistibly of suicide. And to distract them from their misery, Mulvaney tells the story of a peculiarly bloody engagement. Death is everywhere in these early tales of Kipling's, death by disease and in battle, sometimes heroic, sometimes ugly, but always a fact to be reckoned with, a fact to be thrown in the faces of quiet, comfortable people who ended their lives without drama. It is no wonder that the famous author in "A Conference of the Powers" is overwhelmed by the experiences of the very young officers he encounters. He was wrong, Kipling says, in blaspheming his own work as of no importance compared with theirs, but it was an understandable temptation.

India, Kipling took pains to point out, had a way of knocking the nonsense out of a man's head. There was, for instance, the case of Aurelian McGoggin, who had read Comte and Spencer. ("There was no order against his reading them, but his Mamma should have smacked him.") He became convinced that "men had no souls, and there was no God and no hereafter, and that you must worry along somehow for the good of Humanity." "I do not say a word against this creed," Kipling comments. "It was made up in Town where there is nothing but machinery and asphalt and building—all shut in by the fog. Naturally, a man grows to think there is no one higher than himself, and that the Metropolitan Board of Works made everything. But in India, where you really see humanity—raw, brown, naked humanity—with nothing between it and the blazing sky, and only the used-up, overhandled earth underfoot, the notion somehow dies away, and most folk come back to simpler theories. Life, in India, is not long enough to waste in proving that there is no one in particular at the head of affairs."

This was a good deal like Stevenson's creed, but Stevenson had no India to hurl at the heads of recalcitrant readers. That intimate knowledge of India was what made Kipling so persuasive. He did not have to talk about the Empire as a theory: he showed the servants of the Empire in action. Towards the natives his attitude was not one of superciliousness or contempt, and he often accorded a measure of respect, not only to the personal courage of some of them but also to their customs and their ancient wisdom. "Lisbeth" and the later "Without Benefit of Clergy" are sympathetic enough, and there are many incidental tributes in other stories. Kipling was convinced, however, that the natives could not govern themselves. If the British withdrew, chaos would result, and the cruel exploitation of native rulers would take the place of the just, if severe, administration of the conquerors. Therefore British rule must be preserved, and whatever means served that end were good. "Never forget," he wrote in "His Chance in Life," "that unless the outward and visible signs of Our Authority are always before a native he is as incapable as a child of understanding what authority means, or where is the danger of disobeying it." The natives in *In Black and White* are by no means contemptible, but they have their own codes of revenge and their own conceptions of truth, and they have to be kept in order by a strong hand. One of the earliest stories, "The Strange Ride of Morrowbie Jukes," shows what happens to the half-educated native when he is free from authority. Kipling can understand easily enough Gunga Dass's passion for revenge, but that does not make it less dangerous. Jukes is surprised when he finds himself calmly contemplating murder. So, Kipling implies, the British are likely to be shocked at the methods they must use to preserve their authority, but their lives and the Empire and civilization itself demand that it be preserved.

The virtues he admires are those that serve the Empire, not as an abstract, patriotic idea, but as the living force of British administration in India. Strickland, who appears in several stories, is one of the greatest of his heroes, for he adds subtlety and wisdom to absolute courage and devotion. But courage and devotion will do, as is shown by "Only a Subaltern," whose hero, Bobby Wick, is simply Wee Willie Winkie grown up. There are many of these fine young officers, and Kipling greatly admires them, but he reserves his affection for the more colorful private soldiers, notably Mulvaney, Learoyd, and Ortheris. "I do not think," he wrote, "that my friends concerned themselves much with the social or political aspects of the East," but they were the salt of the earth and the ultimate bulwark of the Empire. That soldiers should be treated with contempt, as they often were, enraged him, and he protested in prose and verse. He found more than a little pathos and a great deal of humor in their lives, as well as the finest courage and unshakeable loyalty.

The British in India provided Kipling not only with his first themes but also with his first audience, and they welcomed his work with all the enthusiasm of a not very literary people for the bard who somehow enriches life by giving them a chance to stand off at a little distance and look at it. But impressive as his work was in India, it was even more impressive in England. There it was revelation and romance. Many of the stories were trivial, it is true; they were, after all, the incidental efforts of a phenomenally busy journalist. Some of his tricks were obvious: the slick patter of native terms, the sprinkling of hard little facts, the affectation of cynicism, the mannered introduction of such trade-mark phrases as "But that is another story." Second thought, moreover, might hint that his knowledge of human nature was a great deal less profound than the first reading of his self-confident sentences suggested. But there it all was, a fine, furious onsurge of life, a great crowded stage created, as many a critic remarked, out of the most fertile imagination since Dickens'.

While his tales were traveling westward to England, Kipling was moving eastward to the same goal. In 1886 he had happened upon a book by Walter Besant, called *All in a Garden Fair,* and this had inspired him with the belief that he could make a living as a writer. Finding his work on the *Pioneer* less pleasant than that on the *Gazette,* he sold for £200 the stories that made up the six little volumes of the Railway Library, and set off for England by way of Japan and the United States, writing his impressions for the *Pioneer.*

He did not like the United States. He did not like the way Americans talked or their habits of eating and drinking. He found the young women charming but brash, and he objected to female domination. He was oppressed by "the ghastly vulgarity, the oozing, rampant Bessemer-steel self-sufficiency and ignorance," and shocked by the Chicago minister who talked confidentially about the way God did business. He found the Negroes incompetent and stupid, and criticized their enfranchisement. In general the conduct of government seemed to him unsound, and widespread corruption proved to him the undesirability of democracy.

Yet he found many Americans likeable, and he praised their hospitality. When other Britishers attacked them, he came to their defense: "Let there be no misunderstanding about the matter. I love this People, and if any contemptuous criticism has to be done, I will do it myself. . . . They are bleeding-raw at the edges, almost more conceited than the English, vulgar with a massive vulgarity which is as though the Pyramids were coated with Christmas-cake sugar-works. Cocksure they are, lawless, and as casual as they are cocksure; but I love them and I realized it when I met an Englishman who laughed at them." In particular he was impressed with their potentialities, the greatness that would some day be the nation's, and he broadened his dream of the Empire so that it embraced the Anglo-Saxon race: "There must be born a poet who shall give the English *the* song of their own, own country —which is to say, of about half the world. Remains then only to compose the greatest song of all—The Saga of the Anglo-Saxon all round the earth. . . . Will any one take the contract?"

Kipling was a likely enough candidate, but he was not quite ready for the job. He arrived in England in the fall of 1889, and found that some measure of fame had preceded him. Editors were interested in stories and articles, and the *National Observer* began publishing the *Barrack Room Ballads.* Its editor was William Ernest Henley, Stevenson's friend, who had, as Kipling afterwards said, "an organic loathing of Mr. Gladstone and Liberalism," and who shared Kipling's enthusiasm for the Empire. He had already written some verse in praise of "the glory of battled adventure" and "the sacred quality of patriotism," and was destined to equal Kipling in imperialist fervor if not in eloquence and popularity. He, Walter Besant, and Rider Haggard were among the young man's new-found friends.

Kipling had brought back with him both stories and memories, and out of this store he began contributing to the magazines. Some of the best of the "Soldiers Three" stories were published in *Macmillan's Magazine* in 1890, as well as "Without Benefit of Clergy." India was still vivid in Kipling's mind, and he was far from having exhausted his knowledge. But many of the stories that he wrote in 1890, most of which appeared the next year in *Life's Handicap,* were rather more portentous than anything he had written earlier. In "The Mutiny of the Mavericks" he satirized conspirators, more in bitterness than in humor, as Stevenson had done before him and Conrad was to do after him. "The Man Who Was" sounded a warning, often repeated, against Russia, and preached the futility of democratic reform in India. "At the End of the Passage," dramatic enough in itself, had a prologue to refute Radicals who called India "the pet preserve of the aristocracy of England." And "The Head of the District" demonstrated the folly of giving administrative office to natives, even if they had been educated at Oxford.

Most didactic of all was "The Enlightenments of Pagett, M.P.," which appeared in the *Contemporary Review* for September, 1890. Poor Pagett was a Radical—which automatically made him the object of Kipling's contempt—but he had wisdom enough to go to India, and there he learned as much as a Radical brain was capable of absorbing. He believed in self-government when he arrived, and was interested in the plans for a National Congress. Orde, a classmate who had become "a cog-wheel in the machinery of the great Indian Government," introduced him to a variety of Hindus and Mohammedans to prove that only a handful of mis-educated natives, eager for soft jobs, favored the scheme. Even an old acquaintance of Pagett's, a mechanic who had been a Radical in England, tells him that "things are different out here." "There's precious little," he insists, "one can find to say against the Government, which was the main of our talk at home, and them that do say things are not the sort o' people a man who respects himself would like to be mixed up with. There are no politics in a manner of speaking in India. It's all work." The only advocate of the Congress Pagett can find is a graduate of a mission college, vague and ill-informed and incompetent, to whom he takes an instant and un-Radical dislike.

There is no doubt about it; Kipling was becoming more self-conscious about the Empire. For the first twenty-three or twenty-four years of his life he had taken it for granted, living as he did among imperial servants. He knew, of course, that there was opposition, but it seemed too irrational and remote to be worth bothering with. His travels in America and his return to England taught him the contrary, taught him how few people realized the greatness of the Empire and its importance to civilization. He became aware that he had a mission, and he turned both prose and verse to his new purpose. When a government commission exonerated certain Irish patriots, charged with complicity in murder, Kipling wrote "Cleared," and Henley published it. From epithet to epithet it rose to the climax:

If black is black or white is white, in black and white it's down,
You're only traitors to the Queen and rebels to the Crown.
If print is print or words are words, the learned court perpends:—
We are not ruled by murderers, but only—by their friends.

And in "The English Flag" he tried to render "the whole sweep and meaning of things and effort and origins throughout the Empire." "What," he asked in the key-line, "should they know of England who only England know?" He was taking up his own challenge and becoming the poet of the English and their Empire.

Henry James, writing on Kipling in 1891, gave an incomparable list of his qualities, as they impressed this diligent student of the craft of writing: "his prodigious facility, which is only less remarkable than his stiff selection; his unabashed temperament, his flexible talent, his smoking-room manner, his familiar friendship with India—established so rapidly, and so completely under his control; his delight in battle, his 'cheek' about women—and indeed about men and about everything; his determination not to be duped, his 'imperial' fiber, his love of the inside view, the private soldier and the primitive man." "People," he commented, "who know how peaceful they are themselves and have no bloodshed to reproach themselves with needn't scruple to mention the glamor that Mr. Kipling's intense militarism has for them." It was not merely the militarism; a whole new way of life, colorful and heroic, revealed itself to Kipling's readers. Morris' Socialism and Hardy's pessimism proved as unreal in the searing light of India's plains as the Comtean philosophy of Aurelian McGoggin. Both personal and national gloom vanished before the new vision of England's power. It cannot be denied that, despite what James justly called his "active, disinterested sense of the real," Kipling was offering his readers a way of escape, but it was also, as he saw it and made them see it, a way of salvation.

3. *The Discovery of the Empire.*

Kipling probably never thought of asking why, at the outset of his career, the English people were only beginning to be interested in the Empire and still needed his sermons. He simply saw that they had fallen from grace, and did his best to show them the light. If he had bothered to explore the history of imperialist sentiment, he would have learned that, after two flourishing centuries, it had begun to decline at the end of the eighteenth century. After the Americans won their independence, many people in England believed that the other colonies would sooner or later follow their example. And why not, it was asked. Adam Smith and Jeremy Bentham, attacking the old mercantile theories, insisted that colonies cost far more than they were worth. The Manchester School accepted their contentions, and, through the first half and more of the nineteenth century, urged that the colonies be cast off. Cobden said in 1836: "The colonies, army, navy, and church are, with the Corn Laws, merely accessories to our aristocratic government. John Bull has his work cut out for the next fifty years to purge his house of those impurities." The rebellion in Canada in 1837 strengthened the case for separation, and when, after being given fiscal autonomy, the colonies adopted protective tariffs, the advocates of free trade could not be rid of them quickly enough. Colonies, John Bright argued, not only were an expense but offered a constant threat of war. Britain's experience with the United States showed that trade could grow without colonial ties, and emigration was just as feasible after as before separation. In 1863, in *The Empire,* Goldwin Smith stated the whole case for independence, maintaining, with the cold logic of the utilitarian school, that it was equally desirable from the point of view of the colonies and from the point of view of the mother country.

England was the workshop of the world, and during the first three-quarters of the nineteenth century it did not have to worry about markets for its goods. But it was not England alone that was indifferent to colonies. Statesmen of other countries, hoping to achieve England's prosperity, were quite willing to follow the path it had taken. In 1868 Bismarck said: "All the advantages claimed for the mother country are for the most part illusions. England is abandoning her colonial policy; she finds it too expensive." France, too, was impressed by the logic of the Manchester School. After the Franco-Prussian War the French offered Germany Cochin China and other colonies in lieu of Alsace-Lorraine, but Bismarck, though a few influential merchants urged him to accept, was still true to laissez-faire principles.

As might have been expected, the opposition to the breaking up of the British Empire came from those who had no sympathy with utilitarian assumptions. Coleridge had written: "Colonization is not only a manifest expedient, but an imperative duty on Great Britain. God seems to hold out his finger to us over the sea." Carlyle's hero-worship, his identification of might and right, and his contempt for "niggers," all made him sympathetic to imperialism, and he, too, felt that God had reserved for the English the task of civilizing the world. Whenever the Malthusians talked of over-population, Carlyle pointed to the colonies. There men unwanted in England could save themselves from the moral deterioration that seemed to him so characteristic of the nineteenth century, and could at the same time strengthen the mother country and extend its beneficent influence. He called for the organization of more emigration societies, so that every honest workman could go to the new world, "there to be a real blessing, raising new corn for us, purchasing new webs and hatchets from us; leaving us at least in peace; instead of staying here to be a Physical-Force Chartist, unblessed and no blessing."

In spite of Coleridge and Carlyle and their disciples, the movement for separation grew, and even Disraeli, prior to 1872, granted its inevitability. Little territory was annexed between 1815 and 1875. There were long delays before Natal and New Zealand were made parts of the Empire, and the chief of the Fiji Islands had to offer his kingdom to Britain thrice before it was accepted. The Transvaal was given independence in 1852 and the Orange Free State in 1854.

With the majority of the Liberal Party solid in favor of separation, and with no effective opposition from the Tories, the disintegration of the Empire seemed certain when Gladstone came to power in 1868. His intentions were immediately put to the test. The British in New Zealand appealed to the government to aid them in putting down the Maoris. Gladstone refused. The *Times* supported him, but many newspapers were critical. Opposition seemed to spring up from nowhere, opposition whose existence had never been guessed. Apparently it was one thing to talk about the dismemberment of the Empire, but quite another to let it happen. Having forced Gladstone to reverse his policy, the imperialists pressed their advantage. In 1869 the Colonial Society, later the Royal Colonial Institute, was formed with Viscount Bury as president. In 1870 opponents of separation secured the signatures of 104,000 workmen to a petition stating that the colonies "were won for Your Majesty and settled by the valor and enterprise and treasure of the English people," and "ought not to be surrendered, but transmitted to Your Majesty's successors whole and entire, as they were received by Your Majesty." In that year and the next J. A. Froude published a series of articles in *Fraser's Magazine,* arguing that England's greatness was inseparable from the possession of its colonies. In 1871 the Westminster Conference, with the Duke of Manchester and the Earl of Shaftesbury among the participants, recommended imperial federation as a means of conciliating separatist opinion in the colonies while keeping the Empire intact. On June 24, 1872, Disraeli, speaking at the Crystal Palace, committed the Conservative Party to imperialism.

The discovery that separation was likely to become a reality undoubtedly had the effect of destroying indifference and unifying the opposition, but the reaction was strengthened by practical considerations. Froude wrote in 1870: "There are symptoms which suggest, if not fear, yet at least misgiving as to the permanency of English industrial supremacy." To the Liberals his alarm seemed excessive, and they were inclined to charge that he was parading these misgivings in order to strengthen the case for imperialism. Between 1850 and 1870 there had been only three years in which exports had failed to increase. The American panic of 1857 had spread to England, but with no very disastrous effects, and, though the American Civil War had paralyzed the cotton factories, other industries had prospered. What, however, Froude could legitimately point out was that France, Germany, and the United States were rapidly catching up with England and would soon be dangerous rivals. To Froude the danger of foreign competition was one of the least important reasons for maintaining the Empire, but the argument had a powerful appeal in many sections of the public. Certainly 104,000

workmen could not have been persuaded to petition Queen
Victoria if unemployment had not been widespread in London at the moment.

Events rapidly justified alarm over England's industrial
leadership. In November, 1873, there was a crisis on the stock
exchange, and prices, employment, and exports all declined.
For four years the depression, though not comparable to that
in the United States, was severe. Exports, reaching their lowest
point in 1878, began to rise again in the next year, but they
had not equaled the high point of 1872 when, in 1883, a new
depression began.

The depression of the seventies and eighties reshaped
British thought. One consequence, as we have seen, was the
revival of radicalism in the labor movement. A second was
the growing pressure for the abandonment of free trade,
marked by the formation in 1881 of Randolph Churchill's
Fair Trade League. A third was the strengthening of imperialism. Disraeli had already set the pace after he came to
power in 1874. In 1875 he secured control of the Suez Canal.
In 1876 he annexed the Transvaal, made Baluchistan a pro-
tectorate, and had Victoria proclaimed Empress of India. The
new imperialism involved England in armed struggle against
the Zulus in the Transvaal and against the natives of Afghanistan. It came near to involving the country in the war between
Turkey and Russia, and in the Treaty of Berlin Disraeli received Cyprus as a reward for his belligerence. This was the
jingoism that Morris denounced, and it distressed many even
of those who advocated the strengthening of the Empire.
They insisted that they favored only the preservation of ties
with the existing colonies, and they charged Disraeli with
taking more interest in his own political future than in the
future of the British people. But the Tory voters made no such
subtle distinctions; Disraeli had dramatized the Empire for

them, as he had sought to do, and had thus contributed to the triumphant growth of imperialist sentiment.

Meanwhile Jules Ferry was telling the French that they would always be a fourth-rate people if they did not have an empire, and in the early eighties France took Tunis and Tonkin. In Germany both merchants and missionaries were repeating the arguments of Friedrich List, who had long since stated the case for colonies, and Bismarck was cautiously abandoning his predilection for free trade. The growth of other empires and the general growth of nationalism on the Continent furnished added arguments for English imperialists. Many Liberals were converted outright to imperialism, and the party formally renounced any intention of separating the existing colonies from the mother country. It still opposed expansion, but that did not save it from the Soudan venture, and its half-hearted policies, dramatized in Gordon's death, were infuriating to others besides Stevenson.

The literature of imperialism grew. In 1883 John Robert Seeley, whose *Ecce Homo* had been sensational in 1865, published *The Expansion of England,* in which he maintained that the colonies offered the key to Britain's history and explained its greatness. In 1886 Froude published *Oceana, or England and Her Colonies,* repeating Carlyle's contention that the colonies could be the salvation of British manhood, threatened by industrialism at home. Eighty thousand copies were sold of Seeley's book, and about the same number of Froude's.

Both Seeley and Froude, with their distaste for the Manchester School, offered moral rather than mercenary arguments for imperialism, but those who had mercenary interests in the colonies did not hesitate to avail themselves of the moral support. The exporters, especially the exporters of cotton and iron, wanted a sure outlet for their goods. The importers, especially the importers of rubber and other tropical products, wanted control over the sources of their material. The military men talked in terms of raw materials, naval bases, and lines of communication. Missionaries wanted a chance to spread the gospel, and colonial officials thought of their jobs. But the group that was most concerned was made up of investors. Statistics demonstrated that colonies were of relatively small importance to exporters and importers, but the safety of investments was a different matter. As a result of the prosperity England had been enjoying, there were vast sums of capital seeking investment, and money invested in backward areas brought a much greater return than money invested at home. As Henry N. Brailsford pointed out, the absence of the ten commandments may have lured the British soldiery east of Suez, but it was the absence of the Factory Acts that tempted British capital. Between 1862 and 1872 the amount of British capital invested abroad more than quadrupled, and in the next decade, despite the depression, it rose by nearly fifty percent. Between 1872 and 1893 foreign and colonial investments grew at the rate of seventy-seven percent a year. The national income of Great Britain approximately doubled between 1865 and 1898, and in the same period the income from foreign investments increased nine-fold.

John Hays Hammond, the American engineer associated with Cecil Rhodes in South Africa, gave the most cogent explanation of the interest of investors in imperialism. In the Transvaal, he said, good government would mean a saving of six shillings a ton on the cost of producing gold ore, and this would figure up to an increase of $12,000,000 a year in profits. This was the mathematics of the imperialism of investment. The investor demanded security, and in practice he felt secure only when he was under the British flag with the British army and navy back of him. By the end of the nineteenth century some five billion dollars of British money were invested in India. In the sixties four thousand square miles were brought under direct British control at the expense of the native and border states; in the seventies, fifteen thousand; in the eighties, ninety thousand; in the nineties, one hundred and thirty-three thousand.

Not only Carlyle's disciples but the early imperialist societies had paid little attention to the native colonies, being chiefly concerned with areas inhabited by Englishmen. But the needs of capitalism picked up the arguments invented for one kind of imperialism and used them for another kind. Not only was India brought more closely under British control; not only was the British grip on Egypt and the Soudan tightened; new territory was rapidly added. In East Africa Harry Johnston and Captain Lugard spent the later eighties in negotiating treaties, to the detriment of the natives and in direct rivalry with the Germans, and in the nineties protectorates were established over Uganda and British East Africa. In South Africa Bechuanaland was essential to British plans for a Cape-to-Cairo railroad, and it was taken over in 1885. In 1888 Lobengula, king of the Matabeles and Mashonas, was persuaded by a missionary to exchange his birthright for a few baubles, a little cash, and some rifles. By this time gold had been discovered in the Transvaal, and the fate of the Boers was settled.

In 1886, the year that gold was found on the Witwatersrand, Kipling published *Departmental Ditties* and Joseph Chamberlain resigned from Gladstone's cabinet. Born of a middle-class London family, son of three generations of master cordwainers, Chamberlain entered his father's business in 1852, at the age of sixteen, and two years later went to Birmingham to represent his father's interests in a wood screw firm operated by his cousin. By efficiency and the elimination of competitors, he built up a considerable fortune, but his heart was in politics. In 1869 he was elected to the Birmingham Town Council, and in 1873 became mayor. A year later he retired from business, and in 1876 he was elected to Parliament. A Radical, believed to have republican sympathies, he stood for trade unions, aid to the farmers, free and undenominational schools, and the disestablishment of the Church of England. After his election he said to his constituents: "No man can sit for Birmingham who does not represent the working classes, which form four-fifths of this great constituency. I therefore refuse altogether to consider myself, in any sense, a representative of middle-class interests."

In Parliament he surprised his associates by his gentlemanly manners, but he stood consistently with the Radical wing of the Liberal Party. He denounced Disraeli's jingoism in the Anglo-Russian crisis of 1878 and deplored British fighting in Afghanistan. More than that, he voted against the annexation of the Transvaal in 1877, and four years later, paying tribute to the Boers, he asked for emancipation: "A great nation can afford to be generous. What is the use of being great and powerful if we are afraid to admit an error when we are conscious of it?" "Our possessions," he said on one occasion, "are sufficiently ample, our duties and responsibilities too onerous and complicated."

In 1885, speaking at Birmingham, he said: "Society is banded together in order to protect itself against the instincts of men who would make very short work of private ownership if they were left alone. That is all very well, but I maintain that society owes to these men something more than mere toleration in return for the restrictions it places upon their liberty of action. I think in the future we shall hear a great deal about the obligations of property, and we shall not hear quite so much about its rights." At Inverness the same summer he declared: "Squalid homes, unhealthy dwellings, overcrowding: these are the causes—the fruitful causes—of the crime and immorality of great cities. They are the direct result of a system which postpones the good of the community to the interest of individuals."

A few months later Gladstone again took office, and Chamberlain, who had previously served as President of the Board of Trade, was asked to become President of the Local Administration Board. In March he resigned from the cabinet in protest against Gladstone's Home Rule policy. He had many times lamented the sufferings of the Irish, and he called himself a Home Ruler, but he objected to Gladstone's plan of land purchase because it would put too great a burden on the taxpayer, and he criticized the proposed Irish legislative assembly on the ground that it would weaken the Empire. Campaigning as a National Unionist, he said: "I have cared for the honor, and the influence, and the integrity of the Empire, and it is because I believe these things are now in danger that I have felt myself called upon to make the greatest sacrifice that any public man can make." "Will you," he asked the voters, "be so poor-spirited as to break up your ancient constitution, to destroy your venerable Parliament, and to surrender your well-earned supremacy to the vile and ignoble forces of anarchy and disorder?"

The Radical Unionists succeeded in defeating Home Rule, and, after nine years of opposition to his old party, in 1895 Chamberlain found himself in a Tory-Unionist cabinet as Secretary of State for the Colonies. By this time he was completely at home with his Tory associates, and, though many of them were still distrustful of some of his proposals for domestic reform, one Tory was astute enough to say, "No one more truly represents the profound statesmanship of Lord Beaconsfield." By the nineties Chamberlain certainly belonged in the Disraeli tradition of Tory democracy, and perhaps he always had. In his famous "ransom" speech of 1885 he had frankly argued for concessions to the working class on the ground that these constituted the surest protection for private property. Imperialism, he fully realized, made the concessions relatively painless. He became more and more outspoken. "I think I may congratulate you," he said in 1890, "that within the present year, without striking a blow, we have added a vast empire to the dominions of the Queen in Africa." In 1895 he declared: "We are not afraid to take upon ourselves the burden and responsibility which attach to a great governing race." And in 1900 he could rejoice: "We have at last abandoned the craven fears of being great, which were the disgrace of a previous age." The task of colonization, he told the students, when he was elected Rector of Glasgow, had been imposed by God upon the British people. "I have faith in our race and our nation," he assured them. "I believe that, with all the force and enthusiasm of which Democracy alone is capable, they will complete and maintain that splendid edifice of our greatness, which, commenced under aristocratic auspices, has received in these later times its greatest extension."

It was Cecil Rhodes who said what Chamberlain and many others were thinking. "I was in the East End of London yesterday," he told W. T. Stead, "and attended a meeting of the unemployed. I listened to the wild speeches, which were just a cry for 'bread,' 'bread,' 'bread,' and on my way home I pondered over the scene, and I became more than ever convinced of the importance of imperialism. . . . My cherished idea is a solution for the social problem, i. e., in order to save the 40,000,000 inhabitants of the United Kingdom from a bloody civil war, we colonial statesmen must acquire new lands for settling the surplus population, to provide new markets for the goods produced in the factories and mines. The Empire, as I have always said, is a bread and butter question. If you want to avoid civil war, you must become imperialists."

For Rhodes, of course, this was only one of many reasons for building the Empire, but it was nonetheless a reason. One of twelve children of a vicar, he went to South Africa originally for his health. He was eighteen when he followed an older brother to Kimberley, where he pumped water from mines, sold ice cream, and bought up claims. His commercial ability quickly demonstrated itself, and he was clearing £100 a week and was the owner of valuable holdings when he decided to go to Oxford. Here he heard Ruskin say in a lecture: "Will you youths of England make your country again a royal throne of kings, a sceptred isle, for all the world a source of light, a centre of peace? . . . This is what England must do or perish. She must found colonies as fast and as far as she is able, formed of the most energetic and worthiest of men; seizing any piece of fruitful waste ground she can set her foot on, and there teaching her colonists that their chief virtue is to be fidelity to their country, and that their first aim is to be to advance the power of England by land and sea."

"I have tried to combine the commercial with the imaginative," Rhodes said later in his life. By the time he heard Ruskin lecture in 1877, he had already shown his commercial talents, and those eloquent words of Ruskin's, so reminiscent of Coleridge and Carlyle, served to release his imagination. He reasoned, he told Stead, that if there was a God, He would want man to do what He was doing. Darwin had shown that God was perfecting the race through the survival of the fittest. Observation clearly demonstrated that the English-speaking peoples were the best of the species. Therefore God's purpose must be the unification and the triumph of the English-speaking race. In a will that he drew up at this time Rhodes proposed the establishment of a secret society that would lead to the universal reign of the British and the achievement of Utopia. This was the first of six wills in which his creed took expression, the last being that which established the Rhodes scholarships.

His imagination was never inactive, but neither was his commercial sense. He maintained his interests in South Africa even while he was an Oxford undergraduate, and he never forgot that this was the area in which he personally was to carry out God's will. By 1886 he was master of the DeBeers Mining Company, which paid twenty-five percent dividends on a capital of two million pounds, and by 1890, having forced Barney Barnato into an amalgamation, had a monopoly of South African diamonds and controlled nine-tenths of the world's supply. He also established the Consolidated Gold Fields of South Africa, which often paid fifty percent dividends, and created the British South Africa Company to exploit Lobengula's lost kingdom.

Business and politics went hand in hand. Rhodes was Prime Minister of the Cape from 1890 to 1896, but his influence was not dependent on office. It was at his suggestion that Bechuanaland was annexed, and it was his machinations that led to the Matabele War. The profits of his companies grew, and so did his prestige. Lord Rosebery compared him to Sir Walter Raleigh and the other great Elizabethan adventurers. The Duke of Abercorn, presiding at a meeting of stockholders of the British South Africa Company, said: "It would have been a crime against justice and humanity if, on the refusal of Lobengula to put an end to his raiding and interference with the Mashonas, hostilities had not been commenced, and the cruel military system of the Matabele, so destructive to civilization, broken." In the eyes of those who profited from his activities, Rhodes could do no wrong.

It was not only the beneficiaries of imperialism who grew excited about the Empire. As Rhodes had said, the profits of Empire could be used to appease the hungry masses. 1886 not only saw the beginning of Kipling's career as an author and Chamberlain's career as an imperialist; it was not only the year of the discovery of gold in the Transvaal; it was also the year of the riotous march of the unemployed down Pall Mall. William Morris was not the only one who was thinking of revolution in that year, nor was Rhodes alone in seeing the Empire as the solution of the social problem.

The Empire had a double value: it made possible concessions to the masses, and it was a cause that could compete for public attention with revolutionary programs. In the late eighties and nineties imperialism rapidly became a great popular movement. There was a favorite song in the music halls:

> Off with your hat when the flag goes by
> And let the heart have its say!
> You're man enough for a tear in your eye
> That you will not wipe away.

The old attitude of disdain towards the army, which Kipling had so often deplored, was being changed. As one song said, "A little British army goes a long, long, way." A disciple of Kipling's sang:

> Oh Tommy, Tommy Atkins, you're a good 'un heart and hand,
> You're a credit to your calling and to all your native land.

"Soldiers of the Queen," one of the most popular songs of the decade, told what would happen to England's enemies. Imperialism had its folk-songs as well as its heroes and its prophets.

4. *The Great Man.*

Kipling's gifts would have attracted attention, no doubt, in any age, but it was the growth of imperialist sentiment that made him a great man. For a time he was not a mere author but a public figure, as Scott and Dickens and Tennyson had been before him. Just at the moment when people were becoming interested in the Empire, he made it real to them, doing almost by accident what today the radio and movies are consciously used to accomplish. He both expressed and intensified emotions that people were just beginning to feel. He made the esthetes seem trivial and the pessimists ridiculous. The greatness of the Empire stood behind him as he re-affirmed the old values.

Of the first three books he published after his return to England, two served to enhance his reputation, and one did not. If today *Life's Handicap* indicates a growing self-consciousness, it seemed to contemporary readers merely more evidence of Kipling's prodigious talents. *Barrack Room Ballads,* with its dogmatic political verses, its vivid tributes to the private soldier, its sharp, brutal pictures of life in India, contained poems that became part of the folk-speech—"Gunga Din," "Mandalay," "The Ballad of East and West." Kipling's first novel, on the other hand, *The Light That Failed,* was a disappointment to all but the idolators. In the short story Kipling knew precisely how to make the most of his knowledge and insight and how to conceal his deficiencies. The novel permitted no such manipulation. *The Light That Failed* is full of good scenes, but nothing could be more flatly amateurish than the development of the relationship between Maisie and Dick. Critics said that Kipling could not portray women or that he could not depict romantic passion. They might better have said that he could not portray any human relationship that was many-sided and changing.

Kipling was shrewd enough to recognize his limitations, and he knew that he must limit himself to tales and ballads. He was shrewd in many ways. Finding that he was going stale after some eighteen months in London, he decided to travel. In Italy he met Lord Dufferin, who talked to him about the Empire. He went to Cape Town, Australia, New Zealand, and India. In January, 1892, he was married to an American, sister of Wolcott Balestier, his collaborator in the writing of *The Naulahka*. He and his bride crossed Canada and visited Yokohama, thereafter settling down near the Balestier home in Vermont. There he spent four years, writing both *Jungle Books, Captains Courageous,* and most of the stories in *The Day's Work.* After his return to England, he wrote *Stalky & Co.* and started work on *Kim.*

More and more Kipling was deliberately assuming the prophetic function, offering himself as the poet of England, the Empire, and the Anglo-Saxon race he had called for in his letter from America. The verse of the nineties is one long sermon on a single text. "A Song of the English" hails the chosen people, for whom God "hath smote a pathway to the ends of all the Earth." "Hold ye the Faith," he exhorts, "whoring not with visions." "Keep ye the Law—be swift in all obedience." "England's Answer" and "The Houses" praise the idea of the Commonwealth. "A Song of the White Men" hails the day "when the White Men join to prove their faith again." [1] "The White Man's Burden" welcomes the United States to the rank of the mature, imperialist nations.

It should be quite clear that the Empire was never to Kipling merely or primarily a means of maintaining the interest rate. Commercialism in its grosser forms he hated, and he was contemptuous of pecuniary standards. He had, it is true, no patience with the romantic, pseudo-artistic fear of industrial enterprise. He recognized that business was business, a necessary part of life. But to make business the whole of life was abhorrent to him, and to regard the Empire as a business affair was blasphemy. Kipling believed that the civilizing of the world was a task God had imposed on the white race, and, since, when one came down to brass tacks, only the Anglo-Saxons were quite reliable, and since, moreover, the Anglo-Saxons across the Atlantic were a lawless crew, that meant in effect that the British must do the job. This was no business

[1] This was in 1899. In 1902, when Germany proposed that England should help her in a naval demonstration to collect debts from Venezuela, he wrote "The Rowers" to protest against the idea of an alliance with "the Goth and the shameless Hun."

of exploitation; it was a matter of duty, a burden, a daily routine of patience and heart-breaking sacrifice. The young officers and civilians who died at twenty-two did not die for the profits of London financiers, but for the glory of the Empire, which was the hand of God.

The Empire became, then, essentially a moral problem, and Kipling, who had once tried to conceal his evangelistic nature under a mask of cynicism, was more and more the open preacher of imperialist morals. In his autobiography he tells how "there came to me the idea of beginning some tracts or parables on the education of the young." Thus *Stalky & Co.* was written. At first some readers were dismayed at the picture it gave of school life, and there were protests that Kipling found it hard to understand. On the whole, however, it was accepted, and is still read, as an hilarious account of schoolboy exploits. Kipling could permit himself to be humorous only when he dealt with private soldiers and adolescents, only, that is, when he could make it quite clear that lapses from high moral seriousness were incidental to, or in preparation for, the important affairs of life. As the second part of "Slaves of the Lamp" says quite explicitly, the curious pride and devilish ingenuity of Stalky and his associates is the stuff that, properly disciplined, makes empire-builders. Education is simply the development of moral fiber—a growth that, as these stories, as well as *Captains Courageous,* are meant to prove, may often be stimulated in unorthodox fashions.

If the lesson of *Stalky & Co.* was not immediately apparent, perhaps being all the more effective for that reason, the lesson of the *Jungle Books* could not escape even the juvenile eye. "The law of the jungle," of which "the head and the hoof and the haunch and the hump is—Obey!" may not be known to the naturalists, but it was perfectly real to Kipling. "Kaa's Hunting" teaches that disobedience must be punished, "Tiger, Tiger" that only the law-abiding are free. Mowgli may have been brought up by wolves, but he is blood-brother to Stalky and a dozen other heroes. The mongoose in "Rikki-Tikki-Tavi" has the virtues of a British officer, and the mules and horses in "Her Majesty's Servants" learn the lessons a British private must learn. "The King's Ankus" is a sermon against greed, and "Red Dog" teaches the old lesson of loyalty.

It was not only in the *Jungle Books* that Kipling used animals for his pedagogical purposes. The *Just-So Stories* are intended to instruct as well as to amuse, and of course there is "The Maltese Cat," this time with a polo pony cast in the role of British gentleman. Animals serve the purposes of political satire in "The Walking Delegate," with a Kansas horse mouthing the ineffable follies of Populism and the other horses proving him a traitor to his race and punishing him accordingly. Even machinery is personalized in ".007" and "The Ship That Found Herself" to teach the value of discipline and team-work.

But Kipling did not limit himself to fables. He continued to show the heroism of the British in India, in "William the Conqueror" and the most famous of his romances, "The Brushwood Boy." The gods themselves paid tribute to British enterprise in "The Bridge Builders," and "Judson and the Empire" showed the workings of the imperial mind and the futilities of democracy. Lest any of this should be obscure, Kipling wrote "One View of the Question," in the form of a letter from one native of India to another. Shafiz Ullah Khan, visiting England in the service of Rao Sahib, tells what he has seen. There are, he says, many poor and miserable people in England, and these have votes. The members of Parliament they elect divide into parties, lying to their followers and abusing each other, so that there can be no respect for law. In Ireland lawlessness is rampant and unchecked. In England workingmen are permitted to form unions and obstruct their employers. ("They have made the servant greater than the master, for that he is the servant; not reckoning that each is equal under God to the appointed task.") There are countless un-employed, who should be put into military service, but are not because the army is deliberately kept weak. Women enter politics instead of having babies. Shafiz Ullah Khan, after recounting all these horrors, says, "If this people be purged and bled out by battle, their sickness may go and their eyes be cleared to the necessities of things. But they are now far gone in rottenness." The incompetents in Parliament are already talking of relaxing the imperial grip on India, and when that happens, he points out, chaos will come, and there will be great opportunities for plunder.

If this was what he saw, it is no wonder that Kipling was troubled. "At the back of my head," he says in *Something of Myself,* "there was an uneasiness based on things that men were telling me about affairs outside England." It was in this mood that he wrote "Recessional," at the time of the Jubilee, calling upon the God of the British Empire to see to it that His people did not forget Him, as they seemed likely to do. Soon afterward he went to South Africa to see for himself what was happening. Only a little earlier the famous Jameson Raid had taken place. The Boers were interfering with profits in the gold fields of the Transvaal, and Rhodes determined to take care of that obstacle as he had taken care of so many others. His friend Dr. Jameson proved a willing, if impatient and perhaps not very wise, agent. Their scheme of overthrow-ing Kruger's regime miscarried. Jameson had to surrender to the Boers; Rhodes resigned as Prime Minister; and Cham-berlain himself, charged with complicity, was under fire.

Kipling soon met both Jameson and Rhodes, and it was Jameson he had in mind when he wrote "If." Rhodes became one of his few close friends. Kipling apparently never saw him as a multi-millionaire, a shrewd and ruthless and some-times very cynical business man. He saw him, as Rhodes saw himself, as an empire-builder. "What is your dream?" Rhodes asked him. There was no need of the question. Kipling and Rhodes were dreaming the same dream—of a world ruled, for its own good, by the British, or more correctly, by a handful of Englishmen, as much like Cecil Rhodes as possible.

The failure of the raid merely postponed the fulfillment of Rhodes' particular dream for the Transvaal. Chamberlain, after some slight embarrassment, continued to call for expansion: "The Providence that shapes our ends intended us to be a great governing power—conquering, yes, conquering, but conquering only in order to civilize, to administer and to develop vast places on the world's surface, primarily for their advantage, but no doubt for our advantage as well." A few months later hostilities began in South Africa, and Mr. Chamberlain, speaking at a fishmongers' banquet in January, 1900, could well say, "We are all imperialists now." "A seat lost to the Government is a seat sold to the Boers," he told the voters in the "khaki election" of that autumn, and a majority of the voters believed him.

The outbreak of the war helped Kipling to escape from the sense of futility that troubled him whenever he was being merely a man of letters. He wrote "The Absent-Minded Beggar," and the *Daily Mail* used it to raise money for the troops. He helped edit a paper for the soldiers, and did a little nursing now and then. And of course he wrote poetry. There were other imperialist poets now, among them the venerable Swinburne, W. E. Henley, and the poet laureate, Alfred Austin. But Kipling had the advantage of being on the spot, and a good many other advantages as well. He was perhaps not so successful in catching the moods of the private soldier as he had been when he wrote *Barrack Room Ballads,* but there was something of the old life in his verse. Like the fighting men, he respected the Boers, and could write "Piet" in their praise as he once wrote "Fuzzy-Wuzzy" in tribute to the natives of the Soudan. Not all his verse, however, was of military life. The occasion was too good to miss, and he found a dozen ways of saying, "I told you so." He called upon the British to admit, "as a business people should," that "we have had no end of a lesson: it will do us no end of good." Or, as he put it at the end of his poem, "We have had an Imperial lesson; it may make us an Empire yet!" In "The Islanders" he spoke more bitterly, attacking his self-centered, ease-loving fellow-countrymen, attacking even "the flanneled fools at the wicket or the muddied oafs at the goal," calling for less attention to games and more to military training. "The Reformers" and "The Old Men" offered the same instruction. The British people, grown too prosperous, had forgotten the old truths, neglected the old disciplines, and in the Boer War they had paid a sorry price for the resulting inefficiency. Kipling spoke as the Hebrew prophets had spoken, summoning his people to repentance.

As a matter of fact, the prophetic function was rapidly superseding any merely literary aim. Kipling was discovering that the fount of inspiration could run dry. The nineties were as rich in honor for him as the fabulous first five years of his career, but they had not seen the fulfillment of that promise of which critics had talked so much. He had found some new themes. In "The Record of Badalia Herodsfoot," for example, he had beaten his friend Arthur Morrison at the game the latter had played in *Tales of Mean Streets,* but England could never give him the rich material that India had lavished so profusely on his youth. He had boldness of a sort, and whenever he wrote about animals or about machinery, men hailed him as a literary pioneer. But that he simply was not. He had one theme, the Empire, and one source of material, India. Canada, Vermont, South Africa, England—he extracted some nourishment from each, but none could sustain him as India had done.

India gave him his last characteristic book. There is a touch of nostalgia in *Kim*. India is not taken for granted as it was in the early tales, but thought about, dwelt upon, recollected in the tranquility of a great reputation. There is no denying, however, that *Kim* brings India to life. Kipling made no demands, as he had done when he wrote *The Light That Failed,* on talents that he did not have. Frankly picaresque in form, *Kim* lets him sweep India, from north to south and from east to west. All his knowledge is poured into it, all the color that his eye had caught, all the sounds his ear had registered. The enormous diversity of India, its emphatic differences from western civilization, its sudden violence, its romantic adventure—all these he put on paper. His hero, son of a sergeant of the Maverick regiment, raised in India, is as honorable and courageous as any young British officer, but at the same time he is as unconventional as Mulvaney and as ingenious as Stalky. He is engaged, like Strickland—and, as a matter of fact, with Strickland—in "the Great Game," the work of the British secret service, which always inspired Kipling's eloquence. If *Kim* lacks the hard immediacy and brutal self-assurance of *Soldiers Three* and *Plain Tales from the Hills,* it has the perfection that comes only when an author has found the right way of saying what he most wants to say.

Kim, on which Kipling had been working for several years, was published in 1901. Thereafter he wrote nothing that could add to his reputation with the discriminating. He was still at all his old tricks. *Puck of Pook's Hill* and its sequel were fables wrought out of English history, "meant for grownups," though written for children, and intended to be "a sort of balance to, as well as a seal upon, some aspects of my 'Imperialistic' output in the past." There were stories—re-workings of Indian themes, fragments from British experience, new ventures with machinery—all teaching the old lessons. And of course there was a constant outpouring of didactic verse.

Kipling was not well pleased with the way the twentieth century was beginning. England had not learned the lesson of the Boer War. In 1903 he wrote "The Peace of Dives" to denounce the financiers and munitions makers. Men were still worshiping money and being corrupted by the ease that money brought. Looking about for an enemy, so that he might raise England's ancient pride, he first attacked Russia, which, as an Englishman in India, he had long distrusted. But, after the formation of the Triple Entente, he was too diplomatic to quarrel with an ally, and Germany had to bear the brunt of his fury. When, therefore, the World War began, he could again stand forth as a prophet. In a journalistic way his reputation once more rose, but even as invective his denunciations of the Huns had lost the old subtlety and fire. Shrieking of atrocities, belaboring the United States before it entered the war, howling at Russia after the revolution, he sounded more and more like an apoplectic old man holding forth to the fellow-members of his club.

He had ridden hard and fast, and gone very far while he was still young. Luck had been with him, and there was little he could do after it left him. He wrote nothing that hinted, as *Weir of Hermiston* did, at a new kind of maturity. As a matter of fact, he never surpassed the work he had done before he was twenty-five. He did gain technical skill, though to be sure he had begun with a good deal, but no amount of professional competence could equal in effectiveness the utter self-assurance of his early work. Maturity, which might have built upon those amazing gifts of his youth, he never achieved. Not only was his philosophy of life adolescent; he was completely impervious to whole ranges of experience that seem close to the essence of civilization. It may be an advantage for an officer in India to retain a certain kind of intellectual innocence; he may do his job more effectively if his thoughts and feelings are sharply circumscribed; but that is not an ideal state of mind for a man of letters.

Prolific during the war, he was largely silent thereafter, and became almost a legendary figure, so that, when he died, people were surprised at his having been so recently alive. He had often written for young people and aimed at their elders. He ended by finding his audience, even for the grown-up books, among youth. It must be true of Kipling, as of Stevenson, that those who come upon his work too late in their own lives can only wonder at the excitement of the eighties and nineties.

5. *Fruits of Empire.*

Rudyard Kipling may not have been concerned with the effect of expansion on the opportunities for exporting capital, but it was the imperialism of finance capital that he served. There had been a whole generation of talk about the Commonwealth and the Anglo-Saxon race and the civilizing of the world, and the upshot of it all appeared to be that investors were a great deal better off than they had been. England was no longer the workshop of the world, but rather, as Allen Hutt suggests, its pawnshop. "England," a German economist wrote, "is gradually being transformed from an industrial state into a creditor state." Business men were concerned less and less with production and more and more with financial manipulations. There could be no denying, however, that the country appeared to be prosperous, and the upper classes were well satisfied.

There was no talk of revolution now. The decline of militant Socialism that had begun in the nineties continued. There was still misery on a wide scale, but the Fabians and the labor leaders explained that it would be eliminated, gradually, no doubt, but inevitably. Certain sections of the working class were gaining ground, winning concessions that their employers could well afford to make, and they had no desire to overthrow the system that was benefiting them. The Labor Party was pressing for moderate reforms, and the Liberals, led by Lloyd George, matched the Laborites in attractive promises.

If such a situation destroyed any possibility of the immediate fulfillment of Morris' dream, it was no less fatal to Kipling's hopes for England. The rugged virtues were disappearing, even those that found expression in hard work, close calculation, and bitter competition. The capitalist class in England was becoming parasitic, and turning more and more to luxury. "Now, at last," Esmé Wingfield-Stratford writes, "Dives was free to enjoy, to an extent scarcely equaled even in the days of imperial Rome, the good time that science and the social system ensured to those whose bank balances enabled them to levy the necessary toll on the labor of all who toiled for hire or salary from China to Peru." As Kipling must have seen it, the rich were being spoiled by luxury and the poor by coddling. Presumably it never occurred to him that he had a share of responsibility for the conditions he deplored.

One thing was sure: Victorianism was dead. The growth of monopoly had killed laissez-faire economics, though its ghost lived on in the textbooks. State regulation and control grew constantly greater, with Liberals and Tories alike contributing to the multiplication of government bureaus. The colonial policy of the Manchester School had long since been forsaken, and there was a growing pressure to abandon free trade. The era of industrial capitalism had ended, and the men of enterprise promptly discarded dogmas that no longer served their purpose.

Evangelicalism fared no better. Science had done much to undermine its theology, and economic change had altered the habits and attitudes of the middle class. The old discipline had had meaning in an age in which thrift, hard work, and practical knowledge laid the foundation for success. The entrepreneurs of the early nineteenth century made stern demands on themselves, as well as on others, and it was not surprising that they thought their virtue responsible for their prosperity. In an age of gambling, however, the mechanics of success were laid bare, and no one could pretend that the evangelical life was the best preparation for the manipulation of options or the floating of an issue of foreign bonds. The elastic, matter-of-fact, slightly cynical morality of Samuel Butler suited the new age. Of course, millions of people continued to go to church, and doubtless many of them believed in the old doctrines and did their best to live up to the moral codes of their fathers, but piety had become unfashionable, and what was beginning to be talked of as the new morality would have seemed to the Victorians no morality at all.

Victorianism was dead, but no one knew what was to take its place. The majority of people, however, faced the future without undue alarm. To the late Victorians it had seemed that any change was revolutionary, and in the eighties revolution itself was not impossible. With the disappearance of that threat, the mood of the middle class became more tolerant. Experience taught it that, if capitalism could be preserved, changes of other kinds need not be feared. It no longer felt the need of a conspiracy to ignore the problems of society, for it was confident of its ability to find solutions that would prove beneficial to itself.

It was in this pleasant atmosphere that discussions went on, with no great sense of urgency. No one could accuse the post-Victorians of indifference to social issues. On the upper economic levels great numbers of highly articulate people were quite conscious of the existence of problems and quite willing to discuss at any length their solution. It was exactly the kind of talk Kipling most disliked, feverish, unending, and not very close to reality.

It must not be assumed that nobody saw harsher possibilities for the future, but not many people did. There were, of course, many Cassandras among the Tories, who looked with distress on every Liberal reform, but not one in a thousand of them really believed for a moment that the Empire was in any serious danger. In the same way, the affectation of pessimism was common among the intellectuals, and Hardy's prestige rose as Kipling's declined, but they betrayed by word and deed how far they were from the despair Hardy had felt. The upper classes and certain sections of the lower class were doing rather well, no matter how much they might pretend the contrary.

One thing had been accomplished: literature had been emancipated from Victorian restrictions. We know well enough, of course, that in its own day Victorianism had not been incompatible with great literary creation, but it is true that, in the years of Victorian decline, the restrictions had been insupportable. Now, though they might be enforced from time to time, they need give no serious writer much concern. Authors could and did write about all sorts of people that the Victorians regarded as disreputable, and, though perhaps there was a new kind of snobbishness, the old gentility had almost vanished. As for sexual conduct, though greater freedom of treatment was to be won after the World War, it was already true that most authors could say anything they wanted to say.

Victorianism rested on the foundation of industrial expansion. In time industrialism had expanded so much that it led to the substitution of monopoly for competition, produced severe crises, and eventually found its way of salvation in imperialism. Such drastic changes in the way the upper classes functioned naturally brought about changes in their habits and attitudes. Men of letters had long been dissatisfied with the way of life that rested on industrial capitalism, and had bitterly criticized it. As, therefore, decay began, they rapidly pressed their advantage, and the authors of a new generation —such men as we have been considering—witnessed, and of course contributed to, the destruction of the old attitudes.

At first that seemed a considerable accomplishment, but the Victorian interventionists could have told the emancipated Edwardians that the most urgent problems still remained. Finance capitalism was not a better basis than industrial capitalism on which to build a culture; the growth and the effects of parasitism proved the contrary. Morris would have gone even further, and told the Edwardians that finance capitalism could not last. He might also have predicted that they could never be more than post-Victorians, an aftermath, not a beginning. They, too, were figures of transition.

BIBLIOGRAPHY

Chapter I

General economic and political history of the nineteeenth century: Paul Mantoux, *The Industrial Revolution in the Eighteenth Century* (London, 1928); R. H. Gretton, *The English Middle Class* (London, 1917); Sidney and Beatrice Webb, *The History of Trade Unionism* (London, 1894); Friedrich Engels, *The Condition of the Working-Class in England in 1844* (London, 1892); M. Beer, *A History of British Socialism* (London, 1919–20); Allen Hutt, *This Final Crisis* (New York, 1936); J. L. and Barbara Hammond, *The Village Laborer, 1760–1832* (London, 1912), *The Skilled Laborer, 1760–1832* (London, 1919), *Lord Shaftesbury* (London, 1925), *The Rise of Modern Industry* (New York, 1926), *The Age of the Chartists* (London, 1930); Élie Halévy, *A History of the English People, 1830–1841* (London, 1927); W. Lyon Blease, *A Short History of English Liberalism* (New York, 1913). Also: George Unwin, *Industrial Organization in the Sixteenth and Seventeenth Centuries* (Oxford, 1904); George Townsend Warner, *Landmarks in English Industrial History* (London, 1930); J. F. Rees, *A Social and Industrial History of England, 1815–1918* (New York, 1920); F. S. Marvin, *The Century of Hope* (Oxford, 1919); W. H. R. Curtler, *A Short History of British Agriculture* (Oxford, 1909); O. F. Christie, *The Transition from Aristocracy, 1832–1867* (New York, 1928).

History of thought: Crane Brinton, *English Political Thought in the Nineteenth Century* (London, 1933); A. V. Dicey, *Law and Public Opinion in England* (London, 1926); Élie Halévy, *The Growth of Philosophic Radicalism* (New York, 1928); Leslie Stephen, *The English Utilitarians* (New York, 1902); Harold Laski, *Political Thought in England from Locke to Bentham* (New York, 1920), *The Rise of Liberalism* (New York, 1936); D. C. Somervell, *English Thought in the Nineteenth Century* (New York, 1929); Benjamin E. Lippincott, *Victorian Critics of Democracy* (Minneapolis, 1938); S. Maccoby, *English Radicalism, 1832–1852* (London, 1935).

On life in the Victorian period: G. M. Young, ed., *Early Victorian England, 1830–1865* (London, 1934); Arthur L. Hayward, *The Days of Dickens* (London, 1926); Ralph Nevill, *The Gay Victorians* (London, 1930); R. P. Utter and G. B. Needham, *Pamela's Daughters* (New York, 1936); Esmé Wingfield-Stratford, *The Victorian Tragedy* (London, 1930).

Literary history: Louis Cazamian, *Le Roman Social en Angleterre* (Paris, 1903); Vida Scudder, *Social Ideals in English Letters* (Boston, 1898); H. A. Taine, *History of English Literature* (New York, 1908); John Drinkwater, ed., *The Eighteen-Sixties* (New York, 1932); Harley Granville-Barker, ed., *The Eighteen-Seventies* (New York, 1929); Walter de la Mare, ed., *The Eighteen-Eighties* (New York, 1930).

On individual writers: John H. Muirhead, *Coleridge as Philosopher* (New York, 1930); Emery Neff, *Carlyle and Mill* (New York, 1924); Louis Cazamian, *Carlyle* (New York, 1932); D. C. Somervell, *Disraeli and Gladstone* (New York, 1926); George Gissing, *Charles Dickens* (New York, 1898); W. Walter Crotch, *Charles Dickens, Social Reformer* (London, 1913); T. A. Jackson, *Charles Dickens, The Progress of a Radical* (New York, 1938); G. O. Trevelyan, *The Life and Letters of Lord Macaulay* (New York, 1875); J. Cotter Morison, *Macaulay* (London, 1909); Harriet Martineau, *Autobiography* (Boston, 1877); John Stuart Mill, *Autobiography* (Oxford, 1924); Anthony Trollope, *Thackeray* (London, 1906); Frederic Harrison, *John Ruskin* (New York, 1910); Amabel Williams-Ellis, *The Exquisite Tragedy* (New York, 1929); Leslie Stephen, *George Eliot* (New York, 1909); Anthony Trollope, *An Autobiography* (New York, 1912); George Meredith, *Letters* (New York, 1912); Edmund Gosse, *The Life of Algernon Charles Swinburne* (London, 1917); Harold Nicolson, *Swinburne* (New York, 1926); Frances Winwar, *Poor Splendid Wings* (Boston, 1933).

On the Eyre case: J. B. Atlay, "The Case of Governor Eyre," *Cornhill Magazine,* Feb., 1902; article on Eyre in *Dictionary of National Biography,* second supplement; Henry Bleby, *The Reign of Terror* (London, 1868); W. F. Finlason, *The History of the Jamaica Case* (London, 1869). See also biographies and autobiographies of the various men of letters and science involved.

On the rise of science: W. C. D. Dampier-Whetham, *A History of Science* (New York, 1929); J. G. Crowther, *Men of Science* (New York, 1936); Julian Huxley, *Science and Social Needs* (New York, 1935).

Chapter II

On Morris: J. W. Mackail, *The Life of William Morris* (New York, 1911); May Morris, *William Morris, Artist, Writer, Socialist* (Oxford, 1936), introductions to volumes of *Collected Works* (London, 1910–1915); J. Bruce Glasier, *William Morris and the Early Days of the Socialist Movement* (London, 1921); Anna A. von Helmholtz-Phelan, *The Social Philosophy of William Morris* (Durham, N.C., 1927); Wilfrid Scawen Blunt, *My Diaries,* Part I (New York, 1922); Madeleine L. Cazamian, *Le Roman et les Idées en Angleterre,* Vol. II (Paris, 1935).

Socialism and Socialists: M. Beer, *op. cit.;* Allen Hutt, *op. cit.;* Karl Marx and Friedrich Engels, *Selected Correspondence* (New York, 1935); Edward R. Pease, *A History of the Fabian Society* (London, 1916); John Strachey, *What Are We to Do?* (New York, 1938); Beatrice Webb, *My Apprenticeship* (New York, 1926); Edward Carpenter, *My Days and Dreams* (New York, 1926); Henry M. Hyndman, *The Record of an Adventurous Life* (New York, 1911), *Further Reminiscences* (London, 1912); Herbert F. West, *Robert Bontine Cunninghame Graham* (London, 1932); A. F. Tschiffeley, *Don Roberto* (London, 1937); Richard Whiteing, *My Harvest* (New York, 1915); H. G. Wells, *Experiment in Autobiography* (New York, 1934).

Chapter III

Florence Emily Hardy, *The Early Life of Thomas Hardy* (New York, 1928), *The Later Years of Thomas Hardy* (New York, 1930); Ernest Brennecke, Jr., *The Life of Thomas Hardy* (New York, 1925); Lionel Johnson, *The Art of Thomas Hardy* (London, 1895); Mary Ellen Chase, *Thomas Hardy from Serial to Novel* (Minneapolis, 1927); Harvey Curtis Webster, *The Development of Thomas Hardy's Philosophic Thinking* (University of Michigan Dissertation, 1935, unpublished); John Morley, *Recollections* (New York, 1917); Frederic Harrison, *Autobiographic Memoirs* (London, 1911); F. W. Maitland, *The Life and Letters of Leslie Stephen* (London, 1906).

Chapter IV

Henry Festing Jones, *Samuel Butler* (London, 1919); C. E. M. Joad, *Samuel Butler* (London, 1924); Mrs. R. S. Garnett, *Samuel*

Butler and His Family Relations (London, 1926); Clara Gruening Stillman, *Samuel Butler, A Mid-Victorian Modern* (New York, 1932); Malcolm Muggeridge, *The Earnest Atheist* (New York, 1937).

Chapter V

On Gissing: Algernon and Ellen Gissing, ed., *Letters of George Gissing to Members of His Family* (Boston, 1927); Morley Roberts, *The Private Life of Henry Maitland* (New York, 1912); Frank Swinnerton, *George Gissing, a Critical Study* (New York, 1923); Ruth C. McKay, *George Gissing and His Critic Frank Swinnerton* (Philadelphia, 1933); H. G. Wells, *Experiment in Autobiography* (New York, 1934). Also some essays: Alfred C. Gissing, "George Gissing—Some Aspects of His Life and Work," *National Review,* Aug., 1920; Ellen Gissing, "Some Personal Recollections of George Gissing," *Blackwood's Magazine,* May, 1929; Austin Harrison, "George Gissing," *The Nineteenth Century and After,* Sept., 1906; Paul Elmer More, in *Shelburne Essays,* Fifth Series (New York, 1908); Henry James, in *Notes on Novelists* (New York, 1914); Robert Shafer, introduction to *Workers in the Dawn* (New York, 1935); Virginia Woolf, introduction to *Selections Autobiographical and Imaginative from the Works of George Gissing* (London, 1929).

On Moore: Joseph Hone, *The Life of George Moore* (New York, 1936); Charles Morgan, *Epitaph on George Moore* (New York, 1935); W. B. Yeats, *Autobiography* (New York, 1938).

On naturalism: Émile Zola, *Le Roman Expérimental* (Paris, 1902); Ernest A. Vizetelly, *Émile Zola* (London, 1904); William C. Frierson, *L'influence du Naturalisme Français sur les Romanciers Anglais de 1885 à 1900* (Paris, 1925); Madeleine L. Cazamian, *Le Roman et les Idées en Angleterre,* Vols. I and II (Paris, 1923 and 1935).

Chapter VI

On Wilde: Robert H. Sherard, *Oscar Wilde, the Story of an Unhappy Friendship* (London, 1902), *The Life of Oscar Wilde* (New York, 1911); Alfred Douglas, *Oscar Wilde and Myself* (New York, 1914); Frank Harris, *Oscar Wilde, His Life and Confessions* (New York, 1930); Vincent O'Sullivan, *Aspects of Wilde* (New York, 1936); Lloyd Lewis and Henry Justin Smith, *Oscar Wilde Discovers America* (New York, 1936); G. J. Renier, *Oscar Wilde* (New York,

1933); Arthur Ransome, *Oscar Wilde* (London, 1913); Boris Brasol, *Oscar Wilde, the Man, the Artist, the Martyr* (New York, 1938).

On estheticism and decadence: Walter Hamilton, *The Aesthetic Movement in England* (London, 1882); Holbrook Jackson, *The Eighteen Nineties* (London, 1913); Osbert Burdett, *The Beardsley Period* (London, 1925); Richard Le Gallienne, *The Romantic Nineties* (New York, 1925); Harold Williams, *Modern English Writers* (London, 1925); William Archer, *Poets of the Younger Generation* (London, 1902); J. M. Kennedy, *English Literature, 1880–1905* (London, 1922).

On individuals: R. A. Walker, ed., *Letters from Aubrey Beardsley to Leonard Smithers* (London, 1937); Robert Ross, *Aubrey Beardsley* (London, 1909); A. W. King, *An Aubrey Beardsley Lecture* (London, 1924); Bohun Lynch, *Max Beerbohm in Perspective* (London, 1921); Hayim Fineman, *John Davidson* (Philadelphia, 1916); Lionel Johnson, *Some Winchester Letters* (London, 1919); W. B. Yeats, *Autobiography* (New York, 1938); William Rothenstein, *Men and Memories* (New York, 1931–32).

Chapter VII

On Stevenson: Graham Balfour, *The Life of Robert Louis Stevenson* (New York, 1901); Sidney Colvin, ed., *The Letters of Robert Louis Stevenson* (New York, 1899); John A. Steuart, *Robert Louis Stevenson, a Critical Biography* (Boston, 1924); George S. Hellman, *The True Stevenson* (Boston, 1925); Jean Marie Carré, *The Frail Warrior* (New York, 1930).

On Kipling: Rudyard Kipling, *Something of Myself* (New York, 1937); G. F. Monkshood, *Rudyard Kipling: An Attempt at Appreciation* (London, 1899); Cyril Falls, *Rudyard Kipling, a Critical Study* (London, 1915); André Chevrillon, *Three Studies in English Literature* (New York, 1923); Arley Munson, *Kipling's India* (New York, 1915); L. C. Dunsterville, *Stalky's Reminiscences* (London, 1928).

On imperialism and economic conditions: C. A. Bodelsen, *Studies in Mid-Victorian Imperialism* (New York, 1925); Victor Bérard, *L'Angleterre et l'Impérialisme* (Paris, 1900); Parker T. Moon, *Imperialism and World Politics* (New York, 1926); V. I. Lenin, *Imperialism, the Highest Stage of Capitalism* (New York, 1923); J. A. Hobson, *Imperialism* (London, 1938); H. N. Brailsford, *The War of Steel and Gold* (London, 1914); G. H. Perris, *The Industrial History of Modern*

322   *Bibliography*

England (New York, 1914); J. H. Clapham, *An Economic History of Modern Britain,* Vol. II (Cambridge, 1932); R. C. K. Ensor, *England, 1870–1914* (Oxford, 1936); Allen Hutt, *This Final Conflict* (New York, 1936); Wilhelm Dibelius, *England* (New York, 1930); L. G. Chiozza Money, *Riches and Poverty* (London, 1911); Raymond Postgate and Aymer Vallance, *England Goes to Press* (Indianapolis, 1937); N. Murrell Marris, *The Right Honorable Joseph Chamberlain* (London, 1900); Alexander Mackintosh, *Joseph Chamberlain, an Honest Biography* (London, 1906); Sarah G. Millin, *Rhodes* (London, 1933); William Plomer, *Cecil Rhodes* (New York, 1933); Esme Howard, *Theatre of Life, 1863–1905* (Boston, 1935); Esmé Wingfield-Stratford, *The Victorian Sunset* (London, 1932), *The Victorian Aftermath* (New York, 1934); Harry H. Johnston, *The Story of My Life* (Indianapolis, 1923).

INDEX OF NAMES